NORTH VIETNAM TODAY

PROFILE OF A COMMUNIST SATELLITE

Edited by

P. J. HONEY

FREDERICK A. PRAEGER, *Publisher*

New York

BOOKS THAT MATTER

Published in the United States of America in 1962
by Frederick A. Praeger, Inc., Publisher
64 University Place, New York 3, N.Y.

Most of the material in this book was first published
in Great Britain in 1962 in *The China Quarterly*.

© *The China Quarterly* 1962
Library of Congress Catalog Card Number: 62-21093

This book is Number 117 in the series of
Praeger Publications in Russian History and World Communism

Manufactured in the United States of America

NORTH
VIETNAM
TODAY

Foreword

THE youngest of all the Communist bloc states at the present time is the Democratic Republic of Vietnam—Cuba can hardly qualify, since the full machinery of Communism has not yet been installed there— but it is also the Communist country about which least is known in the outside world. This state of affairs has not come about by accident, but it is rather the result of stringent security measures enforced by the North Vietnamese leadership. The bamboo curtain is, in practice, even more concealing than the iron curtain surrounding Eastern Europe and the Soviet Union. Only one foreign press correspondent not sympathetic to Communism was admitted to the Democratic Republic of Vietnam between 1959 and the middle of 1962, and he was specially invited so that he might be the channel through which some political statements by President Ho Chi Minh could be conveyed to the Free World. Once he had attended the interview, the correspondent was quickly ushered out of the country again.[1]

Like all Communist countries, the Democratic Republic of Vietnam devotes huge sums of money to propaganda, but the standard of its propagandists is abysmally low. The claims made are, in many cases, so extravagant that they cannot be taken seriously, and numbers of them are self-contradictory. During a showing of Vietnamese films at a specially hired cinema in London, even the humourless audience of Communist Party members and sympathisers was moved to laughter by some of the commentaries. In consequence, documentation emanating from the North Vietnamese authorities is invariably consigned to the

---

[1] The bamboo curtain works both ways and renders the Vietnamese Communists remarkably ignorant about the state of the outside world. On this occasion, Ho Chi Minh selected the popular, mass-circulation newspaper Daily Express (London) as the vehicle for his views, and he could hardly have made a worse choice. The foreign news editor did not publish the interview because he rightly judged that it was of too little interest to his readership. On March 27th, 1962, the Vietnam News Agency released the text of the interview, but it passed almost unnoticed.

However, since then Bernard B. Fall has also been admitted to the DRV and has had an interview with Ho Chi Minh.

wastepaper basket by reputable journalists who, unable to enter the country and to see for themselves what is going on, simply ignore North Vietnam altogether.

Nevertheless, it is vitally important that the Free World should be well informed about what is happening there, for this country is the Communist bridgehead in South East Asia, the spot from which Communism is striving to extend its domination over that important and populous part of the globe. United States policy in the region is directed towards the containment of Communism within its present frontiers, and to this end, America has poured money, goods, arms, technicians, and lately soldiers, into South Vietnam. She is already heavily committed, and her commitment grows daily greater, as is shown by her sending of marines to neighbouring Thailand. She may one day have to go to war in defence of South Vietnam; yet the American public remains almost totally ignorant of the enemy against whom all these resources are deployed. The publication of the present volume is an attempt to dispel some of that ignorance. It contains articles written by a group of specialists on Vietnamese affairs and covers a number of facets of life at the present time in North Vietnam. The opinions expressed by these specialists are not always identical, and in one or two cases even conflict, but it has been thought best not to change any of these articles, since they express the considered views of their authors. It is left to the reader to form his own judgements on the basis of the evidence presented.

Because so little is generally known about the background of the Democratic Republic of Vietnam or about the events which have led to the present situation in Vietnam, it has been considered advisable to include an introductory chapter setting these out briefly. Thus, the reader will be enabled to place the other articles in their correct context and to derive more information from them than he might otherwise have done.

P. J. Honey

Contents

Introduction

By P. J. HONEY

HISTORICAL

In 111 B.C., the ancestors of the present Vietnamese, who inhabited Tonking and part of what is today southern China, were conquered by the Han and commenced a thousand years of Chinese domination. During that time, they absorbed much of China's superior civilisation, but kept alive a strong spirit of nationalism, which enabled them to drive out their foreign masters in 939 A.D. From then until the middle of the nineteenth century they preserved their national independence, with the exception of a short occupation of the country by the Ming between 1406 and 1427.

Thrusting steadily southwards, the Vietnamese extended their frontiers until they reached the Gulf of Siam. The kingdom of Champa was destroyed in the course of this advance, and Cambodia lost much of her territory, but internal dissensions split Vietnam into two separate and mutually hostile states at the beginning of the seventeenth century. It is interesting to note that the dividing line between them was close to the present division between North and South Vietnam at the 17th Parallel. Not until the beginning of the nineteenth century were the two halves reunited, and then the country entered an era of isolationism and xenophobia, rebuffing American and European attempts to open trade relations and engaging in increasing persecution of Christianity. Such policies by a weak and backward state in the nineteenth century could lead to only one result and, in 1858, France attacked and captured the port of Tourane.

French control extended progressively, Cochin China becoming a French colony in 1867, and Tonking and Annam being made French protectorates in 1884. Effective government of the country remained in French hands until 1940, the date of the Japanese occupation.

The end of the Second World War marked the beginning of an independence struggle in which France tried to regain her lost possession, while Vietnamese Nationalists and Communists fought to secure the leadership of an independent Vietnam. Hostilities were ended by the Geneva Conference of 1954, which divided the country at the 17th

1

Parallel and placed the northern half under Communist rule and the southern half under Nationalist control. Free national elections to re-unify Vietnam had been envisaged for 1956, but these did not take place, because President Ngo Dinh Diem of South Vietnam did not consider that any elections held under Communist auspices could possibly be free. Since 1959, Communist North Vietnam has conducted a full-scale guerrilla war in the South, with the aim of overthrowing the government and gaining control of the state.

AMERICAN VIEWS

The United States government's attitude towards Vietnam has undergone some dramatic changes since the end of the Second World War. When travelling to the Yalta Conference in 1945, President Franklin D. Roosevelt held a press conference at which he spoke of Vietnam, or rather of French Indo-China. He said, "I suggested . . . that Indo-China be set up under a trusteeship—have a Frenchman, one or two Indo-Chinese, and a Chinese and a Russian, and maybe a Filipino and an American to educate them for self-government. . . . Stalin liked the idea. China liked the idea. The British didn't like it." Later in the same year, the U.S. mission in North Vietnam left no doubts of its sympathy for the Communist-led Viet Minh.

Throughout the early years of the fighting in Vietnam, the United States did not conceal its disapproval of French actions and condemned the war as colonialist. Not until China had fallen to the Communists and war had broken out in Korea did President Truman revise earlier American views enough to send help to the French and Vietnamese Nationalists. By that time, the Vietnamese Communists were in full control of the resistance movement and were already receiving military aid from China. United States economic and military assistance increased enormously between 1951 and 1954, but it was not able to avert the great Communist victory at Dien Bien Phu. At that time, there was talk in the United States of direct American intervention to save Vietnam from Communism, one of the leading protagonists of intervention being Admiral Radford. An American fleet was moved into the Gulf of Tonking, but it was finally decided not to intervene.

The International Conference on Indo-China, which met at Geneva during the spring and early summer of 1954, ended the fighting and divided Vietnam in two, but its agreements were not signed by the United States or by the Nationalist government of Vietnam, led by Ngo Dinh Diem. Both undertook, however, not to contravene the agreements. Fully aware by that time of the threat to the rest of Asia posed by Communist China and North Vietnam, President Eisenhower decided that Communism could not be allowed to advance beyond its existing frontiers. Into South Vietnam, which was then torn by internal dissensions, devastated by the long war and almost defenceless, the United States poured men and money.

Immediate results were little short of miraculous. Nearly a million penniless refugees from the Communist North were cared for and resettled in the South. Internal disputes were resolved and, by the beginning of 1956, Ngo Dinh Diem's government had established its control over the whole country. For the first time in many years, peace returned to the Vietnamese countryside. Although part of the American aid was wasted through Vietnamese inefficiency and part found its way into the pockets of Vietnamese officials—corruption has long been endemic in the Vietnamese public service—enough remained to accomplish a considerable measure of economic progress. Damage was repaired, new undertakings sprang up, and South Vietnam grew stronger.

When large-scale terrorism and guerrilla warfare commenced during 1959, the United States reacted by increasing military aid and by sending more military advisors. It was the new Democratic Administration under President Kennedy, however, which grasped the nettle of Vietnam firmly. Supplies of money, arms, equipment and military personnel were all increased, until today members of the U.S. Armed Forces pilot helicopters on combat missions and accompany detachments of the South Vietnamese Army in their clashes with the Vietnamese Communist guerrillas. It appears today that the United States is inescapably committed to the defence of South Vietnam against Communism, by direct military participation in a war there, if this should prove necessary.

THE DEMOCRATIC REPUBLIC OF VIETNAM

VIETNAMESE COMMUNISM

The story of Vietnamese Communism is largely the story of one man, Nguyen Van Thanh, alias Nguyen Tat Thanh, alias Nguyen Ai Quoc, alias a number of other names, but known to the world today as Ho Chi Minh. A founding member of the French Communist Party in 1920, he first visited Moscow in 1922, and later studied there at the University of Toilers of the East. From that time onwards, he devoted his whole life to serving the cause of Communism, accepting a Russian passport and working wherever he was sent by his Soviet masters.

From Russia he went to China on the staff of Borodin, Comintern agent with the Chinese revolutionary government in Canton, and there organised the Vietnamese Revolutionary Youth League, from whose ranks the founders of the Indo-Chinese Communist Party later emerged. Ho Chi Minh's betrayal to the French of the celebrated Vietnamese Nationalist leader Phan Boi Chau, who was living as an exile in China at the time, illustrates the true character of the man. He subsequently justified this action to his Communist colleagues by reciting the three reasons which motivated his behaviour. They were:

(1) Phan Boi Chau was a Nationalist, not a Communist, and would prove to be a rival to the Communists in their plan to take control of the Vietnamese anti-French resistance movement. In betraying him he had disposed of a future rival.

(2) The reward money which he had received from the French could be put to excellent use in forwarding the Vietnamese Communist movement.

(3) The execution of Phan Boi Chau would create the required atmosphere of shock and resentment inside Vietnam.

Such reasoning leaves little doubt of Ho's fanaticism, his calculating mind, and his ruthlessness. Today he affects the simple clothing of a peasant, is repeatedly photographed fondling young children, and is renowned for the moderate tone of his public utterances, but this disarming, almost saintly exterior conceals one of the most dedicated, callous, and intelligent Communists the world has yet seen.

Forced to flee from China by Chiang's break with the Communists in 1927, Ho returned to Moscow and left his Vietnamese Communists to fend for themselves, but they proved themselves incapable of doing so. By the end of 1929, they had quarrelled and split into no less than three rival Communist parties. He was called from his Comintern business in Thailand to resolve their differences and, after reconstituting a single party, he again departed. Once more the Vietnamese Communists proved their incapacity by attempting to establish Soviets in Nghe-an province in 1930 and, on this occasion most of the leaders were imprisoned.

Ho was himself imprisoned by the British authorities at Hong Kong in 1931, but following his release in 1933, he swiftly disappeared to continue his clandestine activities. All the imprisoned Vietnamese Communists were released from prison by the French Popular Front Government of 1936 and continued their anti-French activities in comparative freedom until the outbreak of the Second World War, when most fled to China. They were joined there by Ho Chi Minh, who wasted no time in forming the Viet Minh, in theory a broad coalition of all Vietnamese anti-French movements, but in fact a body rigidly controlled by the Communists. The vast majority of the non-Communist Nationalists did not participate and either joined the rival Nationalist coalition or worked independently.

Finding the Viet Minh the most effective organ for providing intelligence of Japanese-occupied Vietnam, the Allies helped it materially and eventually enabled it to establish a military force inside Vietnam. The United States supplied this force with arms and equipment for use against the Japanese, but all the evidence shows that these were stored for later employment against the French. Thus, after Japan's surrender in 1945, the Viet Minh alone was able to enter Hanoi with a show of force. On September 2, 1945, Ho Chi Minh proclaimed the independence of Vietnam and the establishment of the Democratic Republic of Vietnam. The French inhabitants were still in prison at the time, the Japanese had not yet been disarmed, and the Chinese Nationalist force deputed by the Allies to occupy North Vietnam had not yet arrived. Without any authority or popular mandate, opposed by the Nationalists, controlling only a tiny part of North Vietnam, lacking all the ordinary attributes of a government and having no administrative machinery, Ho proclaimed the Democratic Republic. It was a bold, almost rash action, but it proved successful.

THE INDO-CHINESE WAR

The story of how Ho Chi Minh overcame the countless difficulties which beset him and his Communists during the years 1945 and 1946 is too long and complex to recount here. Suffice it to say that he maintained both his own position as leader and the ascendancy of the Communists. In addition, he contrived to secure the liquidation of all his most dangerous Nationalist rivals, sometimes using his own supporters to assassinate them but more frequently arranging matters so that they were killed by the French. Vietnamese Nationalists were frequently blamed during the war for the incapacity of their chiefs, but virtually all the most able leaders of a generation of Vietnamese Nationalists had been killed during the two years in question. Very few survived to oppose Ho.

When the war proper broke out on December 19, 1946, most patriotic Vietnamese followed Ho into the countryside, for the fight was against their common enemy, the French. For over two years, this resistance movement survived against the French Army, largely because of two factors. Firstly, the French lacked the men and the supplies necessary for a quick victory, and these could not be sent from a war-devastated France, even if the shipping had been available. In the second place, the whole Vietnamese people assisted the resistance movement with information, food, and other supplies. As Nhu Phong's article on the Vietnamese intellectuals tells, the morale of the resistance movement was good, and little attempt was made to impose rigid Communist control. This situation changed abruptly after the victory of Mao Tse-tung in China, for the Vietnamese Communists then disposed of the support necessary for them to impose their doctrine upon the whole movement.

Although the Vietnamese resistance movement at no time during the war possessed any aircraft, the help provided by other Communist countries rendered its armed forces better equipped in many respects than the French or Nationalist Armies. Weapons of the most modern type captured from the United Nations troops in Korea were supplied to the Viet Minh, who used them against an enemy supplied by America with older, or even outdated weapons. Russia supplied Molotova trucks, better suited to the local conditions than the trucks supplied by the United States. Indeed, so confident of victory were the Viet Minh that they even commenced Chinese-style agrarian reforms in the areas under their control well before the war had ended.

GENEVA AND PARTITION

The Vietnamese Communists laboured under no delusions about the possibility of holding national elections as envisaged by the Geneva agreements, but they did not expect the government of South Vietnam to be able to establish its authority over the territory because of the indescribable chaos which existed there in 1954. Since the politico-religious sects were prepared for open armed revolt against the government, their own Communist stay-behind agents were ready to carry out widespread sabotage, and the loyalty of the Nationalist Army was open to grave doubts, the Communists can hardly be blamed for feeling optimistic. Moreover, the roads and bridges of the South had been destroyed by war, the railway lines had been torn up for their metal, and the absent Head of State, Bao Dai, could be relied upon to undermine Ngo Dinh Diem's authority. If the departure of over 800,000 refugees from Communist rule shocked and surprised them, forcing them to act promptly to prevent many times this number from fleeing, they could draw comfort from the thought that the refugees would cause further disruption in the South and hasten its collapse.

When things did not happen as they had foreseen, and when, on the contrary, South Vietnam overcame her immediate difficulties and began to progress economically, politically, and socially, the Communist leadership of the Democratic Republic grew more than a little perturbed. North Vietnam herself encountered difficulties of all kinds, but the most serious was undoubtedly the shortage of food. A solution had to be found to the problem of feeding the people of North Vietnam if the state were not to risk total collapse. The Communists' faith in the doctrinal solution of collectivisation of agriculture was soon shattered when they discovered that it tended to lower rather than increase production. In spite of the undoubtedly great efforts expended on increasing agricultural production and the placing of new land under cultivation, it has become apparent that North Vietnam cannot produce sufficient rice to feed her people. Hoang Van Chi has provided an original and convincing explanation of why collectivisation of agriculture has produced most disappointing results throughout the whole Communist world, but particularly in the case of rice-producing countries. The high birth rate in North Vietnam complicates the situation still further. Nguyen Ngoc Bich is undoubtedly correct when he sees the war in South Vietnam as primarily a battle for rice.

During the period of French domination in Vietnam, annual statistics were provided for the first time. These show conclusively that North Vietnam has long been a rice deficit area, and French authorities were obliged to transfer part of South Vietnam's rice surplus to the North each year, to make good the deficit. Since the division of Vietnam into two zones, all traffic across the frontier has ceased, which means that North Vietnam no longer receives any rice from the South. Consequently, she has been subjected to chronic and growing food shortages. In practice, she has smuggled quantities of rice northwards by sea, or through Cambodia and Laos, but the amount she has secured in this way has proved insufficient to bridge the gap between her own production and her consumption.

The basic economic plan for the Democratic Republic of Vietnam looks to industry rather than to agriculture to solve the country's difficulties. Since North Vietnam is a rice deficit area, it was argued that the way to economic self-sufficiency lies through rapid industrialisation. Once the new factories are producing goods, these can be sold abroad for foreign currency, which will then be used for the purchase of food. With an attitude of mind reminiscent of the Chinese Communists' "great leap forward" mentality, the North Vietnamese leaders appear to have believed that industry could be created almost overnight, but they have learned from bitter experience that industrialisation is a slow, long-term process. Exports are still very small and are likely to remain so for many years. Moreover, China's agricultural failures have led to famine conditions in that country, so that North Vietnam cannot hope to obtain supplies of rice from the Chinese. During the summer of 1961, the somewhat embittered joke which was going the rounds in Hanoi went as follows:

Q. The Party has at last found the only long-term solution for our food problem. Do you know what it is?

A. Capture South Vietnam.

CONDITIONS IN THE DEMOCRATIC REPUBLIC OF VIETNAM SINCE 1955

In 1955, as the whole of North Vietnam passed under the control of the Vietnamese Communists, the frontier between the two halves of the country closed, and all Vietnamese watched with interest the experiment of a Communist state in Vietnam. The period following the victory of Dien Bien Phu had been one of excitement, of military parades, of speeches congratulating every section of the community for the part it had played in winning national independence. Foreign observers were still present in North Vietnam, and efforts had to be made to persuade experienced administrators and technicians to remain at their posts, so the Communist leadership tended to be at its most reasonable and benevolent, promising all benefits to all people. Once the frontier had closed, however, and escape was no longer possible, Communism came into its own. The need for window-dressing had passed because the blind had been drawn down permanently.

In those parts of the country which had been under Communist control during the war, the agrarian reform campaign had already begun, and this was now extended to the whole country. While Party Secretary-General Truong Chinh boasted endlessly about the achievements of this campaign, identifying himself as its inspiration and its leader, special cadres were trained to carry it out and despatched to the countryside. People were classified, and the hundreds of thousands unfortunate enough to be placed in the landlord class were dragged before the people's courts for condemnation and execution. The atmosphere of terror spread throughout the land and nobody felt safe, for classification as a landlord often had little to do with whether one possessed any land or not. This campaign had three principal objectives. Firstly, to dispose of people liable to oppose Communism; secondly, to impress the whole people with the irresistible might of the Communist authorities; and thirdly, to confiscate land and place it in the hands of new people who would depend entirely upon the Communist authorities for their ownership of it. In addition, by forcing the whole population to participate in the atrocities of the people's courts, the authorities made everybody share in the blame for the criminal actions of these courts. By doing so, they sought to bind the whole population to the Communist regime by means of a shared guilt, for any other regime might seek to punish them for their actions.

The atrocities and the terror were pushed too far, with the result that spontaneous popular revolts broke out in a number of areas and the whole regime, but particularly the Communist Party, was in danger. Truong Chinh was made to resign his Party office—he could not be dismissed entirely because of the powerful backing he enjoyed from the Chinese Communists—and a rectification of errors campaign was carried out.

In the towns and cities, massive taxes quickly forced most of the privately owned shops and businesses to close down, leaving their owners unemployed and penniless. Money became very scarce, and the few goods still available for sale reached staggeringly high prices. The artisans, too, were forced out of work because there was not enough money in circulation to permit people to buy their goods. Unemployment reached gigantic proportions, and even the hard, poorly paid manual jobs such as road building were eagerly sought.

The census authorities, ostensibly gathering statistics for the compilation of a new census of population, in reality acted as a sort of security police force. Cadres would watch families for days on end, entering their houses and reading all their papers or documents. Fear and terror accompanied their operations.

The Hundred Flowers Campaign, inspired by Mao Tse-tung, took place during the fall and winter of 1956, and provided the more courageous of the intellectuals with an opportunity to describe the situation in which they lived, as well as to complain about government and Party abuses. The article written by Nhu Phong describes the actions of these men and the sufferings which they were subsequently forced to endure, but, if they achieved nothing more, they provided the outside world with a first-hand glimpse of what life was like inside the Democratic Republic of Vietnam.

Opposition to the Regime

Despite all the efforts made to dispose of opposition to the regime and to discourage would-be opponents by terror, the Communist regime has encountered determined resistance from certain quarters. The Roman Catholics, whose numbers are estimated at more than half a million, have proved to be the Communists' most persistent and uncompromising opponents. As in China, a "patriotic" Catholic Church was formed which owed allegiance not to Rome, but to the Communist regime. A very small number of Vietnamese clergy, either through fear or in the hope of personal advancement, transferred their allegiance to the new "church," but the overwhelming majority of the Catholic laity and clergy rejected it with contempt. Despite all the regime's efforts—

the Vietnamese Catholics have been threatened, obstructed, maltreated, and even cajoled—it has failed to win over the Catholics.

Cadres from South Vietnam who fought in the ranks of the resistance throughout the Indo-Chinese war, and who elected to go to the North after the 1954 armistice, very quickly became disenchanted with life in Communist North Vietnam. It fell very far short of the paradise they had been led to expect, and the thought was always with them that, of their own free will, they had left their homes and families to go and live there. Reunification, they had been told, would take place in 1956, when they could return home in triumph to receive the just acclaim they had earned by their long fight for Vietnamese independence. 1956 came and went without any immediate prospect of reunification, and even today their chances of being able to return to the South are as remote as ever. The resistance of these Southerners has grown rather than diminished over the years. Yet the Communist authorities are reluctant to suppress it by force, for this would proclaim to the whole world the true state of affairs in North Vietnam and alienate South Vietnamese sympathies. Southern cadres have been accorded special privileges, shorter working hours, higher pay, and much else besides, but their discontent continues to mount and to express itself occasionally in outbreaks of violence.

In the extensive highland regions of North Vietnam, the tribal peoples—Thais, Meos, Mans, etc.—have never relaxed their hostility towards the Vietnamese Communists. Before the arrival of Communism, these tribes had continued to pursue their own primitive pattern of life with the minimum of interference from the French authorities. Their contacts with the Vietnamese, a lowland people, were few and were restricted to the barter of goods. Although the Hanoi government has set up the grandiose-sounding Thai-Meo Autonomous Region, every tribesman is well aware that he enjoys no autonomy but is subject to the orders of the Vietnamese Communists in all matters. Since 1955, there have been almost continual revolts against the central government, with bloody counter-measures being taken by the Vietnamese People's Army. News of these is rarely published in the Vietnamese press, but a steady trickle of refugees from North Vietnamese highlands has kept the outside world informed of the determined and unyielding resistance of the tribal people.

Not least of the groups opposing the Communist regime—it is certainly the most numerous of all and its actions produce the greatest effect—is the Vietnamese peasantry. The peasant farmers suffered most from the agrarian reforms. They had been given their own land for a short time, but had it taken away again and were forced into agricultural collectives. It was the peasant who, by increasing his output and paying enormous taxes to the government, was expected to meet the cost of industrialisation; yet the Communists directed all their praise and consideration towards the industrial workers. His produce taken from him by government cadres in the name of taxation, the peasant found himself with insufficient rice to feed his family and without any money for the replacement of worn-out implements or clothing. In some rural areas, even the women have been obliged by the shortage of cloth to leave the upper parts of the body unclad, and the exposure of the breast is as shameful and shocking to Vietnamese women as it would be to their sisters in America or Europe.

Oppressed in this manner, the peasants reacted in the only way they could. They hid their produce and kept it for their own use, refusing to sell the allotted quotas to the government, and thus dealt a major blow to the economy. They ceased to devote their former care to the rice fields, for these no longer belonged to them, but to the collectives, and this resulted in a dramatic decline in food production. Hoang Van Chi has described very clearly in his article the reasons for this. But even if they contrived to conceal enough rice to feed their own families, the peasants were still desperately short of tools, of clothing, and of the money to buy these. Consequently, they sought to acquire money by selling some of their produce clandestinely, and from this practice grew the black market in food, which reached its peak during the terrible food shortages of 1961.

As the rations were reduced in the course of that year, some foods became quite unobtainable, meat and fats in particular. Peasants were not slow to exploit the opportunities opened to them by this situation. The lines of jog-trotting figures advancing from the countryside into the towns, each carrying two baskets slung from a shoulder pole, grew daily longer. They sold the scarce foodstuffs along the curbsides to the hungry town-dwellers for several times the government-controlled prices. Animals were secretly slaughtered by night, cut up, and brought in for sale until the numbers of draught animals had been seriously reduced. As the black market grew, more and more peasants left the collectives and resumed their old life as traders. At first, the authorities hesitated to act, and policemen shut their eyes to this blatant defiance of the law, but eventually the situation deteriorated to the point at which action had to be taken if the economy was not to founder. Some peasants were forced back into the collectives and, although the black market in food is still widespread, it is now conducted less openly than last year.

Embarrassed by the shortages of buffaloes to pull the ploughs in the ricefields, the government sought to reduce the meat-trading by publishing in its newspapers accounts of a serious and contagious disease which had killed large numbers of buffaloes and pigs. Alleging that the meat offered for sale came from diseased animals, the authorities tried to dissuade people from buying it, by saying that it was dangerous to health. Again, it blamed the shortage of buffaloes in certain regions upon peasants who had failed to look after them properly and had let them die of cold. Instructions were published in the press advising peasants who were without buffaloes to dig the ricefields with spades rather than attempt to pull the ploughs themselves.

From this very brief account it will be seen how gravely the Vietnamese peasants' resistance to government policy and their efforts to provide for themselves and their families has interfered with official planning. Food production has slumped very badly, as it has in China, and the peasants have shown unmistakably that they have no love for collectivisation. There is no doubt that if they were offered the opportunity to return to the old system of private ownership and capitalist marketing methods, the overwhelming majority would do so immediately.

Last of the important groups opposed to the Communist regime in North Vietnam is the intellectual class. Intellectual is a vague word of indeterminate meaning, but it is not difficult to define its application in the Vietnamese context. In that country, all who have completed a course of secondary education are considered to be intellectuals, a term which sets them apart from the mass of illiterates and people whose academic attainments are restricted to reading, writing and making simple arithmetical calculations. Vietnamese intellectuals, then, comprise teachers, civil servants, journalists, writers, professional men, and university students. It is these people more than all others who today find the rigid controls and restraints of the Communist regime quite intolerable. The articles of Nhu Phong and Gerard Tongas deal at length with the experiences of this class during the time of the resistance war and after, so that there is little point in discussing them again here. As a class, the intellectuals find few, if any, channels still left open to them for publicly voicing their disapproval of the regime, but they cannot be dismissed as ineffective for this reason. They are regarded with traditionally great respect by all Vietnamese and their influence upon the formation of Vietnamese opinion is out of all proportion to their relatively restricted numbers. It cannot be doubted that their disapproval of the present regime, disseminated in the course of ordinary social intercourse, private conversations, and even in their daily work, produces a considerable effect upon the attitudes of others.

The author met two Hanoi university students, who had escaped from the Democratic Republic of Vietnam and travelled southwards through Laos, upon their arrival in Saigon. When he asked them about the attitude of university students in Hanoi towards the regime, they explained the situation there. Some teachers and students had been placed in the university by the Communist Party for the purpose of spying on their colleagues and, for this reason, all had to be most guarded in their remarks. Nevertheless, in spite of this enforced reticence, it was perfectly clear to everyone in the university that the overwhelming majority of staff and students were disillusioned, dissatisfied and unreservedly opposed to the Communist regime. From time to time, students or members of the teaching staff disappeared and did not return. These disappearances were never discussed openly, but all knew that the missing persons had either escaped to the South or else been arrested by the security police. The two escaped students opined that, if the Communist authorities had not taken precautions to make escape to the South extremely difficult and hazardous, some 95 per cent of those now studying or teaching in the university at Hanoi would attempt to reach South Vietnam.

The political situation inside the Democratic Republic of Vietnam is very different from the propaganda picture presented to the outside world by the North Vietnamese foreign-language publications. A Communist regime is sustained there by force and the threat of further force, but it is resented by very large sections of the population. The Vietnamese People's Army, which receives specially favoured treatment and is constantly reminded of its proud record in the war against the French, has proved itself capable of suppressing such revolts as have broken out against the regime so far. It is not, however, principally the Army which has maintained order, but the ever present threat of massive Chinese intervention. The position in North Vietnam is not unlike that of Hungary in 1956, the lesson of which has not been wasted on the Vietnamese. The Army is truly a People's Army, the great majority of the soldiers being the children of peasants, so that its loyalty to the regime in the event of a massive popular uprising is very doubtful. If such an uprising were to come about, it would certainly be crushed by large-scale military intervention and would result in a Chinese-controlled regime even more oppressive than the present one. This is the true reason for the continuing rule of the Vietnamese Communists. If Communism is ever overthrown in China, the Vietnamese Communist regime would not survive for more than a few days.

THE PRESENT COMMUNIST REGIME

It will be apparent from later articles that the reins of power in the Democratic Republic of Vietnam are held firmly by the Lao Dong or Communist Party. The Party alone makes all the major decisions and most of the minor ones as well. This is not immediately apparent from the terms of the constitution, and the governmental apparatus is, to some extent, designed to suggest popular participation in ruling North Vietnam. When the 1960 constitution was being drafted, the public was asked to submit suggestions and was later thanked for doing so. Although no information was released about the number of such suggestions or their content, and despite the fact that the final constitution was little different from the draft published for public discussion, the impression was created that the people themselves played a part in writing the constitution. Again, elections for the National Assembly are held even though all candidates are hand-picked and most voters are given no choice, so that the democratic procedure of voting is carried out. However, even a short study of the practical, day-to-day running of the Democratic Republic of Vietnam reveals perfectly clearly that the Lao Dong party controls all and confirms Dr. Nguyen Ngoc Bich's statement that Ho Chi Minh is the source of all authority, and always has been.

In the early years of independence, when the Communist bloc was undivided, all difficulties were faced by a united Party which spoke with a single voice. True, there were personal differences between the leaders and even rival factions, but nobody doubted the ability of Ho Chi Minh to resolve these conflicts privately and to ensure that there was only a single Party policy laid down for each individual matter. But the growing divergence of views between the Soviet Union and China, which developed into an open dispute, placed a greater strain upon the Lao Dong Party than upon any other Communist party. Most of the senior Vietnamese Communists had been attracted to this political creed by the example of Russia, and all of them were aware of Communism's debt to Russia. On the other hand, it was in China that the majority of them had received their political training and their first experience of Communism. The Viet Minh itself had come into being on Chinese soil, and the victory over the French was due, in very large measure, to Chinese military aid. Thus, the loyalties of the Vietnamese Communists were divided, which led to a sharpening of differences between factions and strong pressures to side either with Russia or with China in the dispute.

Ho Chi Minh, a consummate politician, has held the ring up to the time of writing. This has been far from easy, and some of the difficulties are described in the author's later article. The Vietnamese Communists have, in the past, always prospered under Ho's leadership, but the Party foundered whenever he was absent. It is doubtful whether any other Vietnamese Communist could have overcome the difficulties which have beset the Lao Dong Party since the beginning of the Sino-Soviet dispute, but Ho has done better than this. Not only has he held together the pro-Russian and the pro-Chinese factions, but he has exploited the individual sympathies of his divided subordinates to the advantage of Vietnam.

The only potential military threat to North Vietnam at the present time, as well as in the foreseeable future, comes from China. Thailand and Laos are far too weak ever to consider aggression against the Democratic Republic of Vietnam, and the frontier with South Vietnam is policed by an International Control Commission. Even if the South Vietnamese government wished to attack the North, its armed forces would be unequal to the task and are too dependent upon American aid. United States approval for such a step would not be given, and without it no attack could take place. This leaves only China, and, under certain circumstances—North Vietnam's full support for Russia in the Sino-Soviet dispute, for example—a Chinese attack on North Vietnam must remain a possibility.

In this situation it would not be to the advantage of the North Vietnamese government to rely upon a military commander favorably disposed towards China for the defence of its territory. Vo Nguyen Giap, the Deputy Premier, Minister of Defence, and Commander in Chief is, and has long been, outspokenly hostile towards China, but there were pro-Chinese officials holding senior posts in the armed forces. These men have been removed by Ho Chi Minh, the most important of them being the former General Nguyen Chi Thanh, so that the armed forces are now under the undisputed control of Vo Nguyen Giap. Consequently, it is reasonable to suppose that, if Giap is an efficient Commander-in-Chief and Minister of Defence—his past achievements suggest that he is most efficient—detailed plans now exist in the Ministry of Defence for combating a Chinese attack on North Vietnam. Moreover, since it is most important that these plans be kept up to date, it is virtually certain that Giap's agents are actively engaged in gathering military intelligence inside China.

It is possible to cite other examples of Ho Chi Minh's exploitation of the present political difficulties and the differences within the Lao Dong Party, but that of Vo Nguyen Giap and the North Vietnamese Army will suffice here.

Russian pressures on the DRV at the beginning of 1962 were strong and were directed towards a negotiated settlement of the reunification problem, with an interim period of neutralism in South Vietnam, if this should prove necessary. Equally strong Chinese pressure called for an increase in the military campaign in South Vietnam and the forcible overthrow of Ngo Dinh Diem's government, at the risk of war, if necessary. In addition, terrible food shortages made the seizure of South Vietnam's rice imperative. A lesser political leader might have felt obliged to abandon his uncommitted attitude and to accede to the demands of one side or another, but Ho Chi Minh has contrived to find a way out of this seeming impasse. In January, 1962, he announced the formation of the People's Revolutionary Party in South Vietnam, a new Vietnamese Communist Party ostensibly independent of the Lao Dong Party, which was to play the leading role in the revolutionary movement of South Vietnam.

Ho Chi Minh now claims that the policy of peaceful reunification of Vietnam has been, and remains today, the policy guiding North Vietnam's attitude and behaviour towards South Vietnam. He takes pains to point out that the people of South Vietnam have the right, and indeed, the duty, to conduct their own revolution against the "corrupt, reactionary Ngo Dinh Diem clique and the American imperialist interventionists," and makes no secret of his sympathy and moral support for the Communist insurgents in the South. Ho still maintains publicly that the Viet Cong in South Vietnam is an entirely indigenous movement which receives no aid, material support, or reinforcement from the North.

Whilst visiting Bulgaria in May, 1962, Mr. Khrushchev claimed that the Soviet Union was opposed to the liberation of any country by outside intervention, but added that it gave its blessing to all wars of national liberation. "We are for peace between states," he said, "but we also stand for the class struggle and wars of national liberation." The similarity between recent utterances on this subject by Khrushchev and Ho Chi Minh is too great to be accidental and these seem to represent a compromise attitude accepted by member countries of the Communist bloc, on the view to be expressed in public about the war in South Vietnam. Meanwhile, the Democratic Republic of Vietnam continues to pour guerrilla fighters and military supplies into South Vietnam, but does so secretly. In this way, Ho Chi Minh would appear to be satisfying Russia by his public statements and China by his covert actions.

LIVING CONDITIONS IN THE
DEMOCRATIC REPUBLIC OF VIETNAM TODAY

Since 1955, life in the Democratic Republic of Vietnam has been an unremitting struggle for survival in the face of terrible shortages of almost every commodity, massive unemployment, desperately low wages and the absence of any prospect of amelioration. During the early months of Communist rule, morale was sustained by the heady exhilaration of having defeated the French and won independence, by the departure of foreign officials and their replacement with Vietnamese, and by the brave slogans which adorned every wall. The feeling was soon dispelled by terror of the agrarian reforms and the census, but people still clung to the belief that Communism possessed the secret of material progress and would, in the near future, provide a better and easier life for all who accepted it.

Years of disillusion followed, during which it became apparent to all that Communism was much the same as any other political· creed except that it was less tolerant, more demanding, and infinitely more dangerous for those who did not accept it. Factories were built and, in time, some home-produced industrial products entered the market, but their quality was so low as to render them virtually unusable, and a feeling of hopelessness pervaded the whole country.

Peasant farmers, who comprise the overwhelming majority of the population, were among the hardest hit, for they were forced against their wishes into agricultural collectives and lost their precious ricefields. Government demands for rice were so great that they left the peasant producers with barely enough to feed themselves and with no money to spend. Apathy replaced their earlier enthusiasm and rice production slumped, leaving the food crisis more acute than ever.

Seven years of Communist rule have enabled the Vietnamese people to learn more about the new regime, its weaknesses as well as its strengths, so that some of the awe for this seemingly irresistible new force, which was universal during the initial period, has been dissipated. Traditional Vietnamese resourcefulness is once again beginning to assert itself, and the typical traits of Vietnamese character, which some alleged had been permanently erased by Communism, are reappearing. Material conditions are extremely hard, and shortages of every description are the rule, but the North Vietnamese people have come to know the new regime better and have begun to exploit it to improve their own individual situations. The Communists, they have found, are as fallible as all other human beings, and they are turning this knowledge to their own advantage.

Peasants have, for some time, contrived to conceal part of the rice crop from the government collectors and to use it both for feeding their own families and for selling on the black market. During the great food shortages of 1961, large numbers of peasants killed farm animals, which they sold, together with vegetables grown on their own private plots of land or stolen from the collectives, in the hungry towns and cities. Private trading quickly assumed very large proportions and many thousands of peasants abandoned farming altogether to become traders, which produced detrimental effects on the country's agriculture. In an unusually outspoken article, the Party newspaper admitted in January, 1962,[2] that North Vietnam would never overcome its rice shortage. "We will be able to achieve," it stated, "seven million tons of paddy in the last year of the five year plan. But with this amount of paddy, we shall still be unable to provide sufficient food for the 19 million people we shall have at that time."

Under such conditions of scarcity, survival becomes an individual problem for each Vietnamese. That many resorted to un-Communist methods to solve this problem is hardly surprising, but their activities perturbed the Communist authorities. The Party newspaper[3] condemned "private enterprise traders who generally obtain their goods illegally and sell them as inflated prices." It went on to state that this private trading had achieved such proportions as to impede state efforts to control prices and allocate goods according to plan. Traders were inducing relatives or friends to queue up at state shops so as to obtain scarce goods, which were then hoarded and later sold for double the price. They were also buying materials from workers who stole them from state property. "A large part of this free market merchandise consists of materials stolen from building sites, state shops and other state organs, as well as smuggled goods."

Even the morale of the Party cadres, the main supporters of the Communist regime, seems to have cracked under the weight of the hardships and shortages in spite of the fact that these cadres form a privileged class in North Vietnam and enjoy material advantages not available to the ordinary people. Writing in the Party newspaper,[4] the DRV Deputy-Minister of Finance, Nguyen Son, complained that Party cadres had embezzled public funds and property. He accused them of forging official documents, of juggling figures in the account books, and of taking advantage of their position to steal money from public or cooperative funds.

Some of the instances of dishonesty cited by the Minister indicate that the scale of the cadres' speculations is far from negligible. In one province, for example, he has calculated that the amount of money which was lost in 1960 and the first half of 1961 almost equalled the total amount of money invested in that province during 1960. In the

[2] *Nhan Dan,* January 8, 1962.
[3] *Nhan Dan,* January 29, 1962.
[4] *Nhan Dan,* February 8, 1962.

case of a new factory being built, he admitted that the total of the money "misappropriated at the construction site" constituted 50 per cent of all the funds invested in that undertaking. Such behaviour on the part of the cadres produced "a very bad influence in the political field." No less culpable, according to Nguyen Son, are the cadres who tolerate this dishonesty and "fail to get angry."

It is difficult for readers in the West to visualise the actual day-to-day conditions under which the ordinary Vietnamese live, so this introductory article concludes with a few facts and figures about life in Hanoi during the early part of 1962. Food is the most important of all commodities and, owing to shortages, it is rationed. Vietnamese people live almost entirely upon rice, supplemented by meat, fish and vegetables. It is the staple diet and is eaten at every meal, but the monthly ration is only 12 kilogrammes. In most months, part of the ration is made up of old rice which has been stored in state granaries, but storage conditions are so bad that this rice is often inedible. Nevertheless, the people of Hanoi are fortunate in the matter of food, chiefly because of the presence of foreigners in that city who can observe what is happening. Hanoi citizens receive the full monthly ration of rice, but the less fortunate country dwellers, rarely seen by foreigners, have long received only 8 kilogrammes of rice and 4 kilogrammes of maize.

Meat and fats are included in the same ration, which at present stands at 30 grammes, approximately equal to one ounce, per adult per week. Not infrequently, however, this tiny ration cannot be bought because there are simply no stocks available to sell. Sugar, too, is very scarce, even though it is produced in Vietnam. The sugar ration is ½ kilogramme, or slightly more than one pound, per *family* per *month*. In order to live, people are forced to buy food in the black market, but not all have sufficient money to pay the high prices asked. Deaths from starvation in Hanoi are not registered as such, so that no exact figures can be given, but they are reliably reported to be high. The black marketeers, who operated in the main streets of the city during the summer and autumn of 1961, have since received some attention from the police and now deal more discreetly, in less conspicuous places.

Tet Nguyen Dan, the Chinese New Year, is the most important celebration of the year for Vietnamese people and it usually falls in February. Even the Communist authorities have felt constrained to make concessions to Vietnamese longing for the traditional feasting at this time of year and grant increased rations. These, although meagre by outside standards, at least offer a welcome break with customary austerity. In 1962, for example, a ration of ½ kilogramme of meat and fat per head was granted, 100 grammes (3½ ounces) of green beans, and

½ kilogramme of sticky rice. Other special rations were allocated on a family basis, each family being entitled to buy three packets of cigarettes (60 cigarettes), and ½ litre (1 pint) of a local alcoholic drink made from manioc. Large families were granted 200 grammes of tea and a kilogramme of marmalade, while small families received half these amounts. But even these special *Tet* rations demanded sacrifices. There was, for instance, no ration at all of meat or fats during the first three weeks of January, so that stocks might be built up to meet the larger *Tet* ration.

Contrary to many people's belief, the North Vietnamese winter is hard, with temperatures falling to about freezing point. The cold is more biting than the temperatures might suggest because of the all-pervading damp and mist, which saturates everything, and because heating arrangements, where they exist at all, are most primitive. Clothing, therefore, is a far more important consideration in North Vietnam than in any other South East Asian country, but cloth has long been scarce and has recently become almost unobtainable for the ordinary people. Severe shock was caused by the announcement of the government's cloth rationing programme for 1962. In January, 1962, all unused cloth coupons for 1961 were declared invalid, with the result that many Vietnamese who had been conserving these coupons until the issue of the 1962 coupons so that, with the two sets, they might buy a complete suit of clothing, found that they had forfeited the coupons they had saved. The 1962 ration of cloth is 3 metres (a little more than three yards) per adult, and only poor-grade, locally-produced cloth is available for the ration. As if this were not bad enough, the government has also decreed that a certificate of dire necessity, issued by the local "street committee," must be produced before cloth can be bought. This means that a Vietnamese with the necessary coupons and money still cannot buy any cloth unless he can persuade his street committee that he is in desperate need of it, and anyone who has lived in a small community will appreciate the petty spite and tyranny this measure creates.

Small quantities of superior cloth, poplin and khaki, are available, but may not be purchased by the ordinary people. They are reserved for the privileged class, the cadres. So that none shall find its way into the hands of the ordinary citizen, the better cloth is not sold in the shops but is supplied directly to the cadres by the particular institutions and organisations for which they work.

Extra rations are prescribed for certain special cases, and a new mother is entitled to 1 kilogramme of sugar, 1 kilogramme of meat, and one litre of fish sauce during the first month after the birth. The new-born baby receives ½ kilogramme of sugar and from 2 to 4 cans of condensed milk, but only if the mother cannot breast-feed it. She must submit herself to a strict examination before she can claim this ration. Extra cloth is granted for wrapping a corpse in the case of death and for dressing a bride and groom when they get married, but strong pressures are applied to prevent this cloth being bought and today most families "volunteer" to make do with the ordinary ration.

Transport is another of the major problems for the people of North Vietnam, because little is available apart from the few railway lines and Hanoi's tramway service. Motor vehicles have virtually disappeared from the roads with the exception of official, governmentally operated vehicles and the cars of high state officials or foreign diplomats. The ordinary worker often has to travel several miles daily between his home and place of work and, unless he happens to live close to Hanoi's tramways, finds himself without any means of public transport to carry him. Rickshaws and taxis no longer operate, and the very few bus services help him not at all. For this reason, the bicycle has assumed an unparalleled importance in North Vietnam and bicycle owners are everywhere envied by their less fortunate compatriots. The bicycles remaining in the country after the departure of the French have been grossly overworked and undermaintained, so that they are now at the end of their useful lives. A small number of bicycles has been imported from Eastern Europe for sale, and a few have been produced locally, but the former compare very unfavourably with the French machines, while the home-produced bicycles are almost useless. Nevertheless, so great is the demand for bicycles that, at the present rate of sale, it will never be satisfied. For the past year, an official permit has been required of anyone wishing to purchase a bicycle, but these permits have been delivered almost exclusively to cadres and state employees. The ordinary citizen has first to convince his street committee that he is in desperate need of a bicycle and, even if he is given the necessary permit, he must still compete with the cadres in order to buy one of these scarce but invaluable machines. In such competition, it is invariably the cadre who wins.

Special permits issued by local street committees have been found by the authorities to be an efficacious means of cutting down consumption. The committees are under the full control of the Lao Dong Party and are very sensitive to the lightest pressure of the Party, so that the merest hint by a Party official that it would be better if certain goods were not bought is sufficient to ensure that no permits will be issued. Alcohol and a number of consumer goods now require permits before they can be bought, and the number of items requiring permits grows steadily. News that lung cancer may be caused by cigarette smoking has been welcomed by the North Vietnamese authorities, who exploit it in order to justify the cigarette shortage. So solicitous are the authorities for the health of the people that cigarettes are now sold not in packets but in threes, and there is a widely believed report that the government is soon to introduce a scheme under which only confirmed habitual smokers with, of course, a certificate to prove it, will be allowed to buy cigarettes.

Emulation campaigns are another favourite way of cutting consumption. They are presently being exploited to reduce the already inadequate rations and the small salaries. The method works not at the individual but at the collective level. Collective farms boast that their members have "voluntarily" sold a certain number of kilogrammes of their own rice ration to the state, while the press devotes maximum publicity to each case. Factories claim that their workers have deposited so many piastres "voluntarily" in state savings accounts (from which it is all but impossible to withdraw money once it is in). A new variation on this theme is the claim that the money was saved by the workers' having voluntarily given up smoking. Such indirect pressures on the suffering people for still greater sacrifices—and there are large numbers of them—add greatly to the strain of daily life.

However great the strains and stresses of life in North Vietnam may be, the one thing no ordinary Vietnamese can afford to do is to fall sick. The almost complete absence of medicines of all kinds has obliged the government to bring in legislation under which prescriptions by private doctors, however highly these may be qualified, are invalid. No person in North Vietnam may purchase medicine on the strength of such a prescription. Only doctors in state hospitals are authorised to issue medical prescriptions valid for the purchase of drugs or medicine. So few and so small are the state hospitals in relation to North Vietnam's population that only a minute proportion of the population can possibly be admitted to such a hospital, and virtually all hospital space is taken by privileged persons such as cadres and state employees. However, private doctors are still permitted to make out prescriptions in the hope that the sick persons may somehow send them to relatives or friends in South Vietnam or abroad and thus have the necessary medicines despatched to them.

Privilege is a phenomenon everywhere present in North Vietnam at the present time. Senior Party and state officials are, of course, given everything they may require in the way of material comforts either free of charge or at a small nominal cost. Such persons receive a large house, servants, food, clothing, a car, and much else besides from the state.

Their cash salaries are small, a fact fully exploited by the propagandists, but there is little for them to spend these on since all they need is supplied. Numerically, this super-privileged class is small and its standard of living is so vastly above that of ordinary Vietnamese that the latter hardly bother to draw comparisons any longer. What rankles much more in the mind of the public is the privilege enjoyed by the more lowly members of the Communist "establishment," the cadres and state employees.

Housing is both scarce and bad in the cities and towns of North Vietnam. For the ordinary citizen it is frequently a source of worry. Even those people fortunate enough to have found accommodation reasonably suitable for their needs are obliged to pay dearly for it. The average monthly rent paid by a North Vietnamese worker is about 10 or 11 dongs. Cadres, however, are entitled to free housing from the organisation for which they work. Normally, these organisations control sufficient houses for their staffs but, in cases where they do not, they rent houses. State organisations do not pay the same rents as ordinary citizens when they take over houses for their cadres, but only two or three dongs monthly.

Cadres receive free medical care, hospital treatment, and medicine from the state but, what is more important, they are able to gain admission to the state hospitals. Their organisations have the influence and connections necessary to accomplish this, whereas the unprivileged citizen has neither. In practice, the cadres occupy all the available hospital beds while the ordinary Vietnamese manages as best he can without hospitalisation or medicine. This is why even a fairly mild illness is greatly feared and why, without treatment, it so often proves fatal.

Travel in North Vietnam is so difficult that it is almost beyond the reach of the ordinary Vietnamese. Even if he should obtain all the necessary permits, stamps, and signatures—almost an impossibility without special "pull"—he still has to overcome the difficulty of finding a place in a train, ship, or plane, and of paying for it. Holidays have, therefore, become a thing of the past for the Vietnamese. But let us suppose that, by some miracle, a Vietnamese worker had overcome all these hurdles between him and a trip to the seaside. He still has to solve the problem of how to live without any pay during the one or two weeks of his holiday, and of finding a job when he returns—so great is the unemployment that his own place will surely be filled. Cadres, on the other hand, receive an annual holiday of 10 days with full pay and all expenses of travel, etc., paid for them. This may seem a small privilege to a Western reader, but it does not seem so when viewed through the eyes of an ordinary Vietnamese worker.

State-controlled goods in the Democratic Republic of Vietnam frequently require a permit from the intending purchaser, especially those in great demand such as bicycles, cloth, certain foods, etc. For the cadre, such permits present little problem because he can obtain them from his organisation, but they are extremely difficult for the ordinary citizen. Consequently, the lion's share of such goods goes to the cadres and the public goes without. In the case of other goods, usually the imported goods, higher quality cloth, consumer goods, they rarely appear in the shops at all but are sold to the cadre directly through his organisation, and at a cheap rate. Where these goods have been sold in the shops, the prices have been up to 20 per cent dearer than those at which the cadres can buy the same goods.

Entertainment is scarce, and even the most propagandist film or theatrical performance helps to break the monotony of daily life, but tickets are usually distributed to cadres through their organisations before they are put on sale to the general public. Consequently, ordinary people have no chance of seeing the more popular entertainments but only the ones the cadres have disdained. When a Russian circus visited North Vietnam early in 1962, offering a rare opportunity for Vietnamese to see a show full of real entertainment, no tickets were sold to the public at all. Every ticket for every performance was distributed directly to the cadres.

Such is life in the Democratic Republic of Vietnam in the year 1962. It would be possible to go on for page after page with information about compulsory military service, the annual compulsory labour service, educational opportunities, work in factories, the armed forces, and a thousand and one other facets of life in this small state, but there is neither the time nor the space. It is hoped that this short introduction will supply at least the bare minimum of information about North Vietnam necessary for the full understanding of the articles which follow, and that this book will leave the reader with a greater knowledge and understanding of this new Communist state, its problems, its politics, its resources and its people.

The Struggle for the Unification of Vietnam

By PHILIPPE DEVILLERS

FOR many years, many thousands of Vietnamese patriots have sacrificed themselves for a double objective—the unity and independence of Vietnam—and it was in pursuit of these aims immediately after the Second World War that, first the Viet-Minh,[1] then the anti-Communist nationalists, brought into operation all the means at their disposal, both military and diplomatic. The Geneva Agreements of July 1954 confirmed the independence of Vietnam at international level. Yet, at the same time the country's unity, which for several years had no longer constituted a problem, was destroyed.

In fact, by splitting the country along the 17th Parallel, the Geneva Agreements made geographic a cleavage which had formerly been in evidence over the whole national territory, since it was by nature ideological and not racial or regional.

A military arrangement, the Geneva Agreement put an end to an armed conflict, and was solely concerned with fixing the limits of zones of regroupment for the two opposing forces after the cease-fire. The demarcation line was to be purely provisional; the principle of Vietnamese unity was not questioned, and the idea of partition was officially rejected with indignation by both sides. When military forces were regrouped and administrative divisions laid down, national political unity would be restored by free general elections—the only well-tested instrument for measuring public opinion. The Final Declaration at Geneva had provided for elections to be held at the latest by July 1956, and for authorities from the two zones to make contact in order to organise them before July 1955.

During the conference, French diplomatic strategy with reference to this problem had been wholly inspired by the idea that if the elections took place quickly, while the effects of what appeared to be a great success for the Viet-Minh were still apparent, Ho Chi Minh and his

---

[1] The term Viet-Minh is used in this article to designate not only this organisation which lasted ten years (1941–51), but also those which took over after it (the Lien-Viet, 1951–55, and the Patriotic Front). Viet-Minh is a useful and well-known term, even when it is not strictly accurate.

followers would emerge triumphant. On the other hand, given a reasonable delay, the prestige of the Resistance would have waned, the people, given time to recover, would be more aware of their best interests, more conscious of ideological affinities and an atmosphere of freedom, thus providing an opportunity for the non-Marxist parties (liberals, democrats, etc.), to step in.

THE PROSPECTS IN 1954

The majority of Western observers had undoubtedly few illusions about the non-Marxists' chances of " recovery." The political cliques which had formerly existed in nationalist Vietnam merely represented scattered bourgeois elements, whose political ideology was of the vaguest, or groups of civil servants, all of whom had practically no contact with the people. It was most probable, therefore, that they would all be carried away in the powerful stream of the wind blowing from the Viet-Minh. There were still, of course, the more coherent groups, such as the politico-religious sects in the South, the Catholics in the North, and the national army. But would they be able to remain standing, supposing the masses in the countryside and the towns were stirred up and worked upon by the Viet-Minh?

The disproportion between the monolithic power of the Viet-Minh, armed, and with the halo of victory, and the almost derisory weakness of the so-called nationalist Vietnam was such that, in the summer of 1954, almost no one thought that the two years' delay won by M. Mendès France at Geneva could be anything but a respite in which to salvage as much as possible from the wreck. At the end of the period, unity would certainly be restored, this time to the benefit of the Viet-Minh, the basic hypothesis then acknowledged by all being that the Geneva Agreements would definitely be implemented.

In actual fact—though this was ignored at the time—the peak hour had passed, and a more balanced state of affairs was beginning to take shape. The DRV (Democratic Republic of [North] Vietnam), exhausted, but still very strong, had been forced by its allies to agree to a less advantageous compromise than the one it might have hoped for (to go any further would doubtless have involved it in open war with the United States). The result was that for the moment it could no longer exercise force south of latitude 17°, but it was relying on the prestige of its leaders, its own political dynamism, and well-tried methods of warfare, to bring about the desired outcome within the period laid down.

Its chances of victory were, however, linked to two factors:

(a) the implementation of the Geneva Agreements;
(b) the possibility of preventing the consolidation of the South by

preserving the initial unequal situation, and maintaining the crushing political progress which it had been making at the time of the Geneva Conference.

Nevertheless, the Hanoi government was to realise very quickly that in both respects the situation was evolving in a way disturbing to it, without it being able to exercise any influence whatsoever on the process.

(a) As far as the legal aspect was concerned, who could guarantee that the Agreements would be respected and implemented? South Vietnam which was not a signatory, was already declaring that it was not bound by them. The United States had stated that it would not oppose the carrying out of the agreements, either by force or by the threat of force, but it had not identified itself with them. Where did France stand? The Geneva Agreements (on military regroupment and a cease-fire) had linked the commands of the Popular Army and the forces of the French Union, but the latter had not entered into any *political* agreement, certainly not in the name of a country like Vietnam whose full and complete sovereignty and independence France had just recognised. Thus, neither South Vietnam, nor its two allies, France and the United States, upon whom depended the implementation of the agreements, appeared to be really committed by them.

(b) The consolidation of the South was to take shape fairly rapidly. In the first place, American support contributed to stemming the wave of discouragement which followed the disaster, and reminded South Vietnam that it was neither alone nor abandoned.

For months the United States had been anxious to establish a line of resistance to Communism in South-East Asia. For Washington, the Geneva Agreements represented a cutting of losses—the amputation of the gangrenous part of Vietnam. It was now necessary to save the healthy part at any price, and transform it into a " bastion of the free world." The setting up of S.E.A.T.O. and the Treaty of Manila (September 1954) gave the states of Indo-China a guarantee on the part of the Western Powers against external aggression and even subversion. This was a pointer that the United States would not sit by quietly if faced with the prospect that South Vietnam might go Communist, even perhaps as a result of free elections. The threat of a Viet-Minh victory (brought about by pre-electoral manoeuvres) was offset for the time being by this American guarantee.

As early as September 1954 it became clear that the Americans' desire to hold on to the 17th Parallel at all costs, would constitute a serious obstacle to the reunification of Vietnam. The latter was in danger of being sacrificed to the demands of Pentagon world strategy. The DRV did not fail to realise this. It protested immediately, naturally without eliciting any response. It was open to query whether this American resolution would continue to hold if international tension were relaxed. For the moment, under the shelter of the American umbrella, South Vietnam had time to recover.

The second element acting in a way detrimental to the interests of the North, was the progressive coagulation of the still fluid mass of the South around a hard core.

THE RISE OF NGÔ DINH DIEM

M. Diem, the anti-Communists' last card which they played at the eleventh hour and in the worst conditions, had found himself, just after the armistice, practically without means of action and isolated in the midst of the hangers-on of the French administration (the politicians, sects, army, police, etc.). His personal prestige could not, on its own, make up for the absence of a faithful party and political cadres.

The Americans, having decided to place their stakes, had already reached the conclusion that South Vietnam could not reasonably be held and preserved without the help of anti-Communist nationalism as proclaimed by Diem and his family. As early as October 1954, a letter from President Eisenhower assured M. Diem of the unconditional support of the United States. On their side, the nationalists, who suspected the French either of gambling on a *rapprochement* with Hanoi, or of seeking to prolong the colonial régime by putting their friends in power, considered that, for themselves, the only hope of resistance was to stake everything on the American alliance.

The North, at this time, underestimated the importance of the fact that for the first time it was not confronted by people linked in one way or another to discredited colonial authorities, but by a man whose past testified to his patriotism and integrity, and whose uncompromising anti-Communism did not stem from calculated self-interest, but from deep religious convictions.

Furthermore—and to the detriment of the North again—military regroupment was accompanied by an important political " regroupment." Hundreds of thousands of people from all walks of life escaped southwards from the victorious Viet-Minh—and by their exodus showed that a great many Vietnamese (like the people of East Germany) preferred to risk everything rather than to live under Communist law.

The South was thus increased in numbers, reinforced, and revitalised by a flood of refugees, the majority of whom were Catholic—people who had not fled from the North to risk finding themselves two years later under the Communist rod of iron, or obliged to flee elsewhere yet again. These people would inevitably be hostile to reunification so long as it would seem that the Viet-Minh would profit by it. Knowledge of their experiences contributed greatly to reinforcing the potential moral resistance of the South, and spread amongst the people a lasting repulsion towards a régime so often based on the arbitrary authority of brutal, narrow-minded, and sectarian *can-bo* (cadres). It was among these refugees from the North that M. Diem recruited his guards and the cadres faithful to his régime.

It was now that Diem began to assert himself, to overcome the veiled resistance of the generals, and to ensure that the army over which he exercised control should be primarily devoted to the nationalist ideal. At the beginning of 1955, Diem, strong this time in American support (the French had just agreed to this shift of responsibilities), tackled the sects. South Vietnam was emerging from chaos. The Southern nebula was solidifying.

But the North still held a master trump: fear—based on the conviction of the majority of people in the South that the elections of 1956 would result in a victory for the Viet-Minh—a fear which encouraged each one not to compromise himself. It was Hanoi's interests to prevent fear being dispelled.

NORTH VIETNAMESE POLICY

It was not long before the DRV revealed its hand. As from February 4, 1955, it proposed the restoration of normal relations (for posts, roads, railways, air- and sea-traffic, etc.), between the two zones, and declared itself ready to carry this out immediately.

This was the first volley fired in a diplomatic shooting-match, which has practically never stopped for seven years, over the two questions on which the R.D.V.N. has chosen to concentrate: (a) the restoration of normal relations between the two zones, (b) the implementation of the Geneva " decisions " concerning pre-electoral consultations and general elections.

As far as the first question is concerned, the proposal of February 4, 1955, was to be repeated many times, in particular on March 7, 1958, and October 4, 1960, each time with no more success than previously, with the result that in 1962 the frontier of the 17th Parallel is one of the most closely sealed in the world. There is still no regular communication through any medium at all between North and South Vietnam. As for postal exchanges, these were and still are restricted simply to interzonal letters.

The Diem régime, to justify its refusal, has never ceased to assert that the North, in proposing this resumption of " normal relations " had no other aim than to infiltrate agents or propaganda into the Southern zone. It cannot be denied that there is a grain of truth in this, but it is possible to wonder whether the anti-Communists' lowering of this iron curtain (revealing a singular inferiority complex on their part) has not ultimately caused much injury to the Vietnamese nation, and has not made the ordeal of the whole people more difficult.

The intransigence of the South has, in fact, destroyed any hopes which the North might have had of putting its reconstruction policy and its economic development upon a " pan-Vietnamese " footing, and has forced it to seek the aid necessary to it exclusively in the Communist *bloc.* Instead of relying on the South to make good its food deficits, the North has had to intensify agricultural production at a costly price and in difficult conditions. The South's decision has probably contributed towards pushing the North into the arms of China, has been a justification for the pre-eminence of pro-Chinese elements in the inner councils of the Lao Dong Party (the Communists), and has certainly made it more difficult for the DRV to turn towards South-East Asia, as certain elements would have liked it to do. Has not the South, by its refusal, condemned itself to an ever-increasing state of dependence in relation to its great protectors?

Nor were the Geneva " decisions " implemented, and the strong position which the DRV believed itself to be in, was ultimately of no use to it.

The first date-line fixed by Geneva—for July 1955—passed without incident. The South, urged by Hanoi to take part in the consultative conference provided for, gave a negative reply (August 9, 1955), invoking the totalitarian nature of the Northern régime, the absence of guarantees, and the multiple violations of the agreement of which it had been guilty. It also requested that those held in the North against their will should be allowed to leave. Hanoi could only protest to the co-presidents of the Geneva Conference, and ask them to intervene.

To make an impression on the South, and, doubtless, to " attenuate " the totalitarian nature of the régime, the DRV employed time-honoured methods of deception: a new party was formed in September at Hanoi—the Patriotic Front which absorbed the Lien Viet. The aim was to unite in one immense organisation (which would be manipulated by the Lao Dong Party) all those who were working only for the independence and the unity of the country.

But the appeals made by the North fell on deaf ears in the South, where Diem, having secured army support, compelled the sects to go into hiding and forced the liberal and democratic politicians into exile, was now launching an attack upon corruption and the last vestige of the *ancien régime* in the person of Bao Dai himself. Following a hastily organised referendum, in October 1955, Diem replaced Bao Dai at the head of the Vietnamese state, and proclaimed the " Republic of Vietnam " of which he became President. Once again Hanoi could only protest against this " separatist " action.

The constitution of the South, which was largely inspired by American models, contained, certainly, a reference to the unity of Vietnam. But what it did in fact was to sanction the division of this unfortunate country and turn it into another Korea, another Germany. Saigon had fallen into line with Seoul, Taipeh and Bonn. In the same way as Hanoi, the Saigon régime (the only one recognised by the West as " free " and " untainted ") felt itself called upon to bring about (to its own advantage, of course), the unification of the country.

It would seem that for a long time the DRV relied upon the powers that had signed the Geneva agreements to make the authorities in the South respect the provisions made. Here again the Hanoi government was to travel a long road of rebuffs and disappointments.

THE FRENCH WITHDRAWAL

It was on France that Hanoi was relying most heavily. This was emphasised by M. Pham Van Dong when he declared on January 1, 1955: "It was with you, the French, that we signed the Geneva agreements, and it is up to you to see that they are respected." France was, in fact, the only great power which was both bound by the agreements and at the same time capable of action in South Vietnam, thanks to the important effectives still at her disposal there. Hanoi built certain hopes on the pressure which the " democratic " forces might be able to exert in Paris in a direction favourable to her. The presence and the attitude of the Sainteny mission in Hanoi had, for a certain time, encouraged Ho Chi Minh and his followers to hope that France, disappointed or exasperated by the affronts offered them by the followers of Diem, might change partners, and gamble on unification (in agreement with the North) in order to maintain her presence in Vietnam.

This was the same grave misunderstanding of the " balance of strength " as had been shown in 1946. For one thing, the so-called " democratic elements " were no longer in a position in France to impose any policy whatsoever, and certainly not on the question of Indo-China, concerning which there was a growing and widespread desire for disengagement, at a time when the events in North Africa were increasingly claiming attention. In addition to this, Hanoi was over-estimating the amount of influence wielded by those French who supported the idea of a change of policy, for in political circles in Paris they were of small importance compared with the adherents of a policy of loyalty towards the "free world " (the U.S.A.) and towards their former Vietnamese comrades-in-arms. Moreover, in a somewhat tragic reappraisal of her foreign policy,

France was, in fact, in the process of abandoning her political responsibilities in Asia to the Americans.

But what Hanoi had not foreseen was that France would disengage her forces so quickly. In withdrawing the Expeditionary Force at the end of April 1956, that is, three months before the deadline fixed for the elections, France was undoubtedly fulfilling her engagements towards Vietnam (*i.e.*, to respect the independence of the country and the promises made) but at the same time she was placing herself in the situation predicted by M. Pineau, where, as a guarantor of the Geneva Agreements, she no longer had the means of seeing that they were carried out.

This somewhat premature withdrawal of the French forces, on the eve of the date fixed for the elections, brought about a timid intervention on the part of the Powers. The occasion was a lesson to the DRV on the importance which the great powers attached to the problems of their small allies.

The government of the South having reasserted that it did not consider itself bound by the Geneva Agreements, and that it would refuse not only to assume in the mixed commissions the responsibilities formerly held by the French, but also to take part in pre-electoral consultations or in general elections, the great powers began to fear a rapid renewal of tension along the 17th parallel. It was to guard against this danger, and for that purpose alone, that they took action, and it was brought home to the DRV on this occasion how feeble was the support given to it by its great allies during this period of *détente* based on the *status quo*. China had asked that a new conference should meet in Geneva. The co-Presidents of the first conference (English and Russian) agreed simply to extend *sine die* the functions of the International Control Commission beyond the term initially fixed (July 20, 1956). Concerning the elections, which it was recognised would not be held within the stipulated period, the two parties were merely enjoined to advise the co-Presidents when they had agreed on a date to begin consultations and to hold the elections.

BURIAL OF THE GENEVA AGREEMENTS

This was, in fact, the occasion for the great powers to bury the Vietnamese problem. With the consent of the other signatories to the Agreements, unification by elections was to all intents and purposes postponed *sine die*, at least until Saigon, without which they could not be organised, had modified its attitude. If the United States had exerted pressure on M. Diem, it was not so much in order to soften his intransigence over the basic issue, as to persuade him to present his views in a more intelligent manner: henceforward, M. Diem would no longer question the very principle of elections, he would simply refuse to consider the problem as long as the Northern zone remained under Communist control or at least did not give way to a free multiple-party system.

Repeatedly, in May and June 1956, in July 1957, in March 1958, and in July 1959 and 1960, the DRV returned to the charge, suggesting to Diem that the pre-electoral consultative conference should be held, and offering to negotiate on the basis of " free general elections by secret ballot." Each time it met with scornful silences or stinging replies. Each time Soviet and Chinese support was restricted to kind words, warm gestures of solidarity, and a few propaganda campaigns.

There was a similar lack of support for the DRV among the nations of the Bandung group; neither India, Burma, nor Indonesia made any effective gesture—not even one merely intended to facilitate what Nehru and Ho Chi Minh's joint communiqué of February 1958 called " understanding between the two zones of Viet-Nam," and one may suppose that none of these powers, even today, is particularly anxious to see the red flag with the yellow star floating over Saigon.

By taking up the Communist challenge, by coldly refusing to lend himself to the electoral game provided for at Geneva, Diem had clearly freed the Southern populace from the fear complex which had been Hanoi's master card. The dangerous cape of the summer of 1956 was weathered calmly, without incident, to the astonishment of almost everyone. Diem's position was further consolidated the following autumn by the public revelation of the terror reigning in the North, by Giap's own recognition of the " errors " committed in the course of agrarian reform, and of the cruelties which had accompanied it. Coming immediately after the events in Budapest, the small peasant revolt of Nghe An, crushed in November 1956, was highly exploited by Diem's propaganda machine. The whole South vibrated at this time to tales of the brutalities suffered by " our brothers of the North," and there was a further revulsion from Communism. The mistakes of the Lao Dong Party and the successes of M. Diem seemed to be slowly immunising the South against contagion from the North. Better still, Saigon, with growing assurance, now spoke of " liberating " the North.[2]

From this time onwards, it would seem that Hanoi became painfully resigned to the situation. It was recognised in the course of the sixth session of the National Assembly (January 1957) that " the struggle for

[2] A Saigon daily paper at this time said: " In the North, the fall of the illegitimate régime is near. . . . As soon as the people's hatred of the Communist dictatorship is sufficiently mature for it to succeed in overthrowing it, then general elections which are really free will take place in the whole of Vietnam, and will peacefully bring about the reunification of the country.
" If he refuses to have recourse to force in order to liberate the North, while yet realising the dearest aspirations of the people, the supreme head of the Republic of Vietnam does so solely in order to avoid bloodshed and undesirable fratricidal strife." (Cong Nhan quoted by Vietnam Press, the official agency, November 9, 1956.)

unity would be long and difficult," and that a prerequisite would be the
" consolidation " of the already-liberated North: to disguise the failure
of the campaign for unification, they fell back on the building of
"Socialism within one country." [3]

After this there were merely patently ineffectual attempts to keep
alive " the desire of the Southern compatriots to achieve unification,"
attempts to procrastinate and keep the case open, and, before long, to
canalise the grievances of the Southerners. The enemy was all the tougher
because he depended only on himself and the Americans, and not on
public opinion, so that there was no way of getting a grip on him. But
Hanoi could reasonably hope for good dividends from a propaganda
campaign which put the blame for the division of the country on the
Americans, and denounced Vietnamese allies of the Americans as
puppets and lackeys. This was a line which, at one and the same time,
gained the favour of the Communist *bloc* and created the psychological
conditions for a North-South *rapprochement*; anti-Americanism, that
latest of national binding-forces, would permit the question of Communism to be relegated to a less prominent position. From 1956 on,
American intervention in the South was constantly denounced as the
principal obstacle existing in the way of reunification. But such denunciations were for long of a purely negative character. International
détente, until 1959, operated entirely in favour of Ngô Dinh Diem.

Apart from the United States, from which South Vietnam had
obtained real protection and support, it seemed that nobody henceforward
had the slightest hope of securing any softening of the rigid position
which the Saigon oligarchy had taken up, fully realising what it was
doing. In these conditions, it seemed likely that the division of Vietnam
would last long. The North would have had little hope of setting the
wheels of reunification in motion if the South had been able to forge
itself into a real nation, that is to say, if the Saigon government had
succeeded with its internal policies, and had received the full support of
the people. But the wheel was soon to turn, and the North was to find
itself with trump cards in its hand, for M. Diem had begun to dig his
own grave.

MISTAKES OF THE DIEM GOVERNMENT

The best is often the enemy of the good. The " mistakes " of the
South, from 1957 onwards, were to furnish opportunities to Communism
and to the movement for reunification which operated under its aegis.

As if not satisfied with the re-establishment of calm and security,

[3] It is to be noted that at this time (the beginning of 1957) the U.S.S.R., showing small
regard for Vietnamese national sentiments, proposed at the United Nations the simul-
taneous admission of the two Vietnams.

the Diem régime, haunted by a strange desire to bring back into being the society of former days, when there were no sects and no Communists, and reckoning that it would itself be safe in the future, accentuated its authoritarian and repressive character. There are serious reasons for supposing that it was encouraged along this path by certain American activist *milieux* who were alarmed by the agreement reached over Laos (the entry of the Pathet Lao into the government) and by the continued existence in rural areas in the South of certain cells and centres of Communist allegiance. The *de facto* integration of South Vietnam within the American military defence structure implied that the region ought to be secure, and, hence, ought to be purged of anything which might, however remotely, serve the Red cause.

Men who fought for the Viet-Minh (insultingly termed Viet-Cong) have since this date been to all intents and purposes outlaws. The Diem government, profiting from the wave of emotion aroused by the putting-down of the Hungarian revolution, and the events at Nghe An, launched out in 1957 into what amounted to a series of man-hunts. The population were called upon to redouble their vigilance and to denounce all Communist activity. The organisation of the police, which was already elaborate, was yet further strengthened. Guided by informers, "mopping-up operations" became only too frequent, especially in the Centre, where the President's brother, Ngô Dinh Can, had recourse to the toughest of methods.

A considerable number of people were arrested in this way, and sent to concentration camps, or political re-education camps, as they were euphemistically called, under conditions which, to be sure, reflected no credit on a state which proclaimed itself to be a respecter of the human person.

This repression was in theory aimed at the Communists. In fact it affected all those, and they were many—democrats, socialists, liberals, adherents of the sects—who were bold enough to express their disagreement with the line of policy adopted by the ruling oligarchy, which was now relying for its support upon two parties, the *Cach Manh Quoc Gia* (National Revolutionary Movement) and the *Can Lao Nhan Vi*. Often too (in error!) people of no political affiliations found themselves subjected to the repression.

It soon became evident to many Western observers, and to the most clear-sighted and best-informed among the Vietnamese themselves, that this policy was playing into the hands of the Communists, and warnings were frequently announced to this effect.[4]

---

[4] At the beginning of 1958 the press of Saigon, and the National Assembly itself (in the sessions of January 3–4, 1958) gave voice to the serious popular unrest provoked by the way the police were acting; the brutal behaviour of the prison

In 1958 the situation grew worse. Round-ups of " dissidents " became more frequent and more brutal. The enemy (those suspected of Communist activities or of being affiliated to the sects) were difficult to apprehend. The areas where they took refuge—the Rachgia and Hatien regions in the West, and the Bien Hoa-Thu Dau Mot-Tay Ninh region in the East, with their marshes and forests, were not favourable for operations by government forces. Moreover, the way in which many of the operations were carried out very soon set the villagers against the régime. A certain sequence of events became almost classical: denunciation, encirclement of villages, searches and raids, arrest of suspects, plundering, interrogations enlivened sometimes by torture (even of innocent people [5]), deportation, and " regrouping " of populations suspected of intelligence with the rebels, etc.

Diem never succeeded in winning the peasants and tenant farmers over to his side. His policy of agrarian reform, an extremely timid one in the first place, became bogged down before very long, and, what is more, the tenant farmers were afraid that the benefits which had been conceded to them during the war would be called in question by the landlords. For so long as it did keep order the régime could get certain measures accepted, even when they were unpopular; but now disorder and insecurity were returning, and the villagers, exposed to the depredations of foraging parties sent out by both the Communists and the sects, suffered even more from the reprisals and operations organised by the police and the army.

RESISTANCE BY COMMUNISTS IN SOUTH VIETNAM

As early as 1958 the cycle of events, so well described by the Viet-Minh theoretician, Truong Chinh,[6] was set in motion in Cochin China. The Communists, finding themselves hunted down, began to fight back. Informers were sought out and shot in increasing numbers, and village chiefs who had presided over the denunciations, village notables, and

authorities was mentioned in forthright terms. The semi-governmental newspaper *Tu Do* wrote (March 4, 1958): " We must have done with arbitrary arrests and imprisonment. The citizens of a free and independent country have the right to be protected in accordance with the spirit of the Constitution." Some days earlier, on March 18, the National Democratic Movement of South Vietnam launched an appeal to the French and American peoples in which it stated, " We enjoy neither justice nor freedom of the press nor free speech nor freedom to travel and meet together. A revolt is simmering."

But the régime had prepared in advance weapons to deal with such a situation. Ordinance No. 6, dated January 11, 1956, authorised the arrest or imprisonment of " any person considered to be a danger to the defence of the state or to national interests," and their detention until order and security were fully restored. By Article 98 of the Constitution, the President was empowered provisionally to suspend all liberties in case of danger.

[5] *Cf.* the case of Ng. Xuan Hieu and Lam Van Nanh heard by the Saigon Court of Appeal in January 1961.

[6] *Cf.* Truong Chinh, *La Résistance Vaincra*, 1947, Chap. XV.

members of the militia who took part, were frequently treated in the same way. The people of the villages, thus intimidated, fell silent. Diem's police and army saw their sources of information drying up one after another. To make good the lack, they resorted to worse barbarity, hoping to inspire an even greater terror among the villagers than that inspired by the Communists. And in that fateful year of 1958 they overstepped all bounds. The peasants, disgusted to see Diem's men acting in this way, lent their assistance to the Communists, and even to the sects, going so far as to take up arms at their side. The opposition (and deserters) found it increasingly easier to find hide-outs, they were able to set up more and more supply-dumps and outposts, and even to fortify villages according to well-tried methods, transforming them into bases for their operations.

In December 1958, the death of some 20 Viet Cong detainees in the Phu Loi concentration camp served to fan the flames of anger of the guerrillas—and gave Hanoi an opportunity for propaganda—and to bring them to the point where they decided to answer force by force. In the course of that December and the following January armed bands sprang into being almost everywhere. The ground was well prepared; many villages fell under their control and were straight away transformed into bases. To mark the festival of *Têt* 1959, the Resistance put on a large-scale raid, and a group attacked the outpost of Trang Sup near Tay Ninh in strength.

Keenly alive to the danger, the Diem government tried to re-establish its administrative hold over the lost villages. It launched against dissident regions (in the Plaine des Joncs and Eastern Cochin China) what amounted to a series of full-scale military operations, bringing infantry, artillery, paratroops and aircraft to bear. But this time the forces of Diem met with resistance from the inhabitants themselves in many places. At the end of March 1959 M. Diem told the correspondent of *Figaro* that " at the present time Vietnam is a nation at war."

Under the pressure of the rising tide of terrorism and sabotage, the Saigon government passed the celebrated Law 10/59, which provided for the " repression of acts of sabotage, of infringements of national security and of attacks upon the life or property of citizens." Special military tribunals were convened which could only pass sentences of death or of hard labour for life, with no provisions for appeal against their decision. In an effort to wrest the population from the grip of the rebels, the Diem government made various attempts to set up villages on new sites in groupings at key points, imitating the policy the French had tried in Tonkin in 1953 (Hanoi-belt experiment, especially Hoa My), only to find that it had played into Viet-Minh hands.

And, indeed, in the course of 1959 the battle spread and became

more intense. From the stage of scattered guerrilla operations it passed
gradually into partisan warfare. Caught between two fires, and in a
state of terror, the population witnessed tragic man-hunts. The power
of the Diem government, in spite of American aid, was, it is true, on the
ebb, but no village could feel that it was yet safe from the danger of
" reprisal " operations.

REACTION OF DRV GOVERNMENT

What did the authorities of the Democratic Republic of [North] Vietnam do in the face of these sad circumstances? They protested in
diplomatic notes. The members of the Viet-Minh cadre in the south, who
had been promised by Hanoi that unification would be rapidly achieved,
had to listen to the bitter remarks that were made to them about the
inability of the North to do anything about the Diem dictatorship. The
overriding needs of the world-wide strategy of the Socialist camp meant
little or nothing to guerrilla fighters being hunted down in Nam-bô. It was
in such a climate of feeling that, in 1959, responsible elements of the
Communist Resistance in Indo-China came to the conclusion that they
had to act, whether Hanoi wanted them to or no. They could no longer
continue to stand by while their supporters were arrested, thrown into
prison and tortured, without attempting to do anything about it as an
organisation, without giving some lead to the people in the struggle in
which it was to be involved. Hanoi preferred diplomatic notes, but it
was to find that its hand had been forced.

In March 1960 the " Nam-bô Veterans of the Resistance Association "
published a long declaration. After describing the reign of terror to
which the country was submitted by the Diem régime, it declared that
the government had " driven the people of South Vietnam to take up
arms in self-defence." The Veterans of the Resistance thus called upon
the people to intensify their struggle to oblige the authorities to change
their policies: to put an end to the bloody rounding-up operations, to
repression, to the pillaging of crops, to the moving of villages. They
almost certainly did not believe that the régime could be reformed, for
they declared that, in all this, they were fighting " to put an end to the
Fascist dictatorship of the Ngo family " and to " set up a democratic
government of National Union in South Vietnam . . . in order to realise
national independence and democratic liberties and to guarantee a
decent life to the people." But they added (and it is here that one can
see the tip of the Devil's ear poking out) that this should be " in full
and energetic implementation of the terms of the Geneva agreement by
entering into talks with North Vietnam with a view to the peaceful
reunification of the Fatherland. This government shall base itself on the
principles of the Bandung Conference and institute a foreign policy of

Peace and Friendship." A little after the date of this manifesto,[7] a People's Liberation Army of South Vietnam appeared in Nam-bô. From this time forwards it carried on incessant guerrilla operations against Diem's forces.

It was thus by its *home* policy that the government of the South finally destroyed the confidence of the population, which it had won during the early years, and practically drove them into revolt and desperation. The non-Communist (and even the anti-Communist) opposition had long been aware of the turn events were taking. But at the beginning of 1960 very many elements, both civilian and military, in the Nationalist camp came to a clear realisation that things were moving from bad to worse, and that if nothing were done to put an end to the absolute power of Diem, then Communism would end up by gaining power with the aid, or at least with the consent, of the population. If they did not want to allow the Communists to make capital out of the revolt, then they would have to oppose Diem actively.

OPPOSITION TO DIEM

In a manifesto dated April 26, 1960, eighteen well-known personalities of varying political affiliations demanded that Diem should liberalise his régime. If not, they added, a revolution would follow. On August 1, the Block of Liberty and Progress launched a petition to the same effect. Neither of these approaches elicited any response from the government. But among the Nationalist opposition the tone grew more bitter month by month. At the beginning of November an influential Nationalist journal, after indicating that the government would have in all probability to deal with a popular insurrection, wrote : [8]

> This rising is justified: in a country where the most elementary rights of the people are ignored, where the legality of the actions of the government has become an empty expression, the will of the people can only make itself felt by means of force, that is to say, by means of a revolution and the taking over of the government. . . . We Nationalists, all of us, know that there is a race against the clock taking place between the Viet-Minh and ourselves.

Even in the Army, the mood of the staff officers became hostile to the régime. But the abortive military *coup d'état* of November 11, 1960, followed as it was by a large-scale purge, of which the principal victim was brave Dr. Phan Quang Dan, leader of the " legal " opposition, was to show that the ruling oligarchy had made up its mind to hang on to its power and privileges at all costs.

---

[7] Declaration of the Veterans of the Resistance on the current situation in South Vietnam, March 1960.

[8] *Pour le Viêt-Nam*, Paris, No. 2, November 1960.

After the spectacular failure of this first right-wing Nationalist plot, the initiative passed to the Communist Party and its allies once more. But it would be as well to analyse in a little more detail the background to this development.

When it decided to take up arms against the Diem régime, the Resistance movement in the South placed the leaders of Communism in Vietnam in an embarrassing situation. In the field of international relations the Democratic Republic of Vietnam had in all essentials kept to the Soviet line of peaceful co-existence, taking great care not to give, through the slightest provocation, any pretext to M. Diem or to the Americans. But could the Lao Dong Party stick to this policy of " peaceful co-existence " when its result was, in effect, to allow the Diem police to proceed with impunity to take their toll of the best elements in the Party?

Whereas the leading group of the Lao Dong Party seemed to be afraid that they would be dragged, behind the " adventurism " of members from the South, into a series of international complications likely to hinder the diplomacy of the Socialist camp, some " activist " elements came out in favour of a bolder policy of effective support for Southern comrades. This tendency had already appeared at the meeting of the Central Committee of the Lao Dong Party in May 1959, and had made itself felt in the field in the shape of the aid given at the beginning of 1960 to the *maquis* of the High Plateaux (Pleiku-Kontum region).

These hesitations, and the divergence between the two tendencies, had an international bearing. And in the light of what happened at the Twenty-second Party Congress at Moscow (the Russo-Albanian dispute) we can better understand what was at stake in Hanoi during the Third Congress of the Lao Dong Party held there in September 1960. The question of national reunification was then at the heart of the debate, along with the question of support to be given to compatriots in the South. We have every reason to think that Moscow counselled prudence. It is interesting to note that the chief Soviet delegate, Mr. Mukhitdinov, stressed on that occasion that " peaceful co-existence was the only line which was in complete accord with the ultimate aim of Communism," [9] while the chief Chinese delegate, Mr. Li Fu-ch'un, reminded the Congress of the importance of Lenin's teaching " when one is struggling against Imperialists," and went on to denounce those revisionists who set about blackening the name of those who gave firm support to the Marxist-Leninist standpoint.

[9] The Soviet-Vietnamese talks which followed after the Congress, according to the communiqué issued, served to bring out " the complete identity of the points of view " of the two governments as regards " the essential aspects " of the problems discussed (among which was the international situation).

The prudent (and pro-Soviet) tendency finally won the day, but the " activist" faction scored many points. Ho Chi Minh demanded that " greater efforts" should be made to achieve unification, and it was a former guerrilla leader in Nam-bô, Le Duan, who was elected Party Secretary. In this way closer liaison with the South was assured: the situation was deteriorating there, and the Lao Dong Party was afraid that the situation would slip from its control.

THE " NATIONAL LIBERATION FRONT "

It is against this background that we must estimate the importance of the setting up in December 1960 " somewhere in Cochin-China " of the National Liberation Front of South Vietnam (*Mat-Tran dan-toc giai-phong*). The weakening of Diem's régime which resulted from the *coup* of November 11 made it, straightaway, the principal political force in South Vietnam. How effective its armed struggle was, and how serious a threat to the Diem régime it represented are now facts known to the whole world.

In the space of two years the Liberation Front of the South gained control of the greater part of the countryside in Cochin-China and also of a large zone between the fourteenth and seventeenth parallels. It built up a strong organisation by setting up at the various administrative levels (provinces, *huyen* and villages) committees which have already assumed governmental powers over whole regions, and then provided itself with effective means of action by attacking government positions, by desertions,[10] through accomplices in Diem's army, by setting up factories to manufacture arms, and also through outside aid of by no means negligible extent which furnished arms, ammunition, medical supplies and money. Its propaganda is skilful, and hits its mark. The growing power of the Front is shown by its very ubiquitousness, and by the increasing tendency of the forces of Diem to fall back on the main lines of communications and on the principal centres of population.

If it maintains and extends its hold over the countryside, the Front will be in an increasingly stronger position, and able to determine the policy of South Vietnam. Already it constitutes there a factor which cannot be ignored.

To what extent have the successes of the Front and the weakening of the Diem régime increased the chances of unification coming about? The situation is complex. The point of view of most foreign governments, in the West especially, is that the fighting going on in South Vietnam is simply a subversive campaign directed from Hanoi. The DRV, unable to get the better of Diem by means of diplomacy, and not daring

---

10 At the beginning of 1961, for example, Diem forces discovered, near the Khmer frontier, a hide-out where *400* deserters had taken refuge.

to resort to direct action, has chosen to attempt to overthrow him from within, sapping tirelessly the foundations of the régime and spreading terror.

The hypothesis is certainly a plausible one [11] (and to formulate it serves the purposes of Communist propaganda); but it leaves out of account the fact that the insurrection existed before the Communists decided to take part, and that they were simply forced to join in. And even among the Communists, the initiative did not originate in Hanoi, but from the grass roots, where the people were literally driven by Diem to take up arms in self-defence.

We do not at the moment know the composition of the Liberation Front of the South, or its leading elements, but it seems likely that it reflects the chequer-board variety of the political forces within the opposition (even if the delegates are not all representative). Now, the majority of the opponents of M. Diem are still anti-Communist, and the inhabitants of the South feel as yet only a slight sympathy for Communism. It is for this reason that the Communists, even though they do play a preponderant part in the National Front, are in no position to comport themselves as if they were the dominant force, and indeed have to proceed with great caution.

For the people of the South unification is not an essential problem. Peace, security, freedom, their standard of living, the agrarian question— these are far more important questions to them. The strong hold of the sects over certain regions remains one of the factors of the situation, as is also, in a general fashion, the distrustful attitude of the Southerner towards the Northerner, who is suspected of a tendency to want to take charge of affairs.

The Communists, whatever the extent of their loyalty towards Hanoi, have had to take this national or regional sentiment of the South into account. This is evident from the programme of the Front,[12] which, by and large, transposes on the level of internal politics the manifesto of the Veterans of the Resistance. While it does call for the overthrow of the government and the setting up of a government of national and democratic union, nevertheless the points most stressed are those concerning the establishment of a democratic régime guaranteeing peace for all and a decent standard of living, the giving of land to the peasants and political autonomy to ethnic minorities. Efforts have been made to give a " Southern " slant to the movement. The flag chosen by the Front is not that of the Democratic Republic of Vietnam: it is not red but red and

---

[11] Leading articles like that of April 3, 1961, in the *Nhan Dan* of Hanoi make it seem very likely.

[12] Programme published in the *Echo du Viêt-Nam*, No. 4, Paris, May 1961.

blue. As for the Front's attitude towards reunification, it is defined as follows in its programme:

> The National Liberation Front of South Vietnam advocates the progressive reunification of the country by peaceful means on the basis of negotiations between the two zones with the object of finding by common agreement what measures and practical steps towards reunification can be taken in conformity with the interests of the people and of the Fatherland.
>
> In the period before the reunification of the country, the governments of the two zones will meet to negotiate, and will engage themselves not to undertake any propaganda activities likely to lead to division and war, and will also pledge themselves not to use military force against the other party, also to encourage economic and cultural exchanges between the two zones, and to allow the inhabitants of the two zones full liberty to travel, trade, and carry on correspondence between the two zones.

All this is prudent and restrained enough. A simple matter of tactics, one might object : the Viet-Minh is out to gain the confidence of the population and to get itself accepted in order to win key-positions, and to set up its private army which will later enable it to lay down its own law. When it is master, it will oust its rivals one by one. Indeed, one observes that, wherever it can, it eliminates those men of recognised competence or of wide political influence who might prove awkward : certain rural agitators won over to the Nationalist opposition, for example.

PROSPECTS FOR THE FUTURE

Yet the problem of reunification must be considered without overdramatising it. In the present international context the Government of Hanoi knows quite well that it is impossible to realise this policy of unification without risking open war with the United States. It will try nothing in that direction, for it follows the " Khrushchev line." The only solution envisageable by Hanoi is to take advantage of the mistakes committed by the Americans in order to gain acceptance for a " Laostype " solution : that is to say, within the framework of a given nation where American policy has provoked an open conflict between Right and Left, to obtain, through military pressure, the overthrow of a reactionary dictatorship and its replacement by a democratic and neutralist government benevolently disposed towards them.

We should be quite frank with ourselves : this is the solution towards which we are heading directly. Month by month the forces of Diem are losing their hold on the countryside : before long there will only be a few pockets and bridgeheads left, and these they will probably be able to hold on to indefinitely with American aid. One thinks of Hué-Tourane, Nhatrang, the region of Saigon, and of perhaps one or two scattered

" hedgehog-type " defensive positions. But what can be the outcome of this? Neither side can allow such an *impasse* to continue for long, and sooner or later it will be necessary to come to the point of negotiating a political settlement re-establishing for this country the unity of the cities and the country regions. It is when this inevitable meeting takes place that we will be able to estimate what chances there are of speedy reunification.

At that moment everything will depend, on the one hand, on the balance of forces existing between the Liberation Front and its enemies (amongst whom one must include the Americans), and, on the other hand, on the balance of forces within the Front itself, exactly as in Laos. It is obvious that the stronger the Communists are when the moment comes, the greater the chances will be of a speedy reunification taking place (and to the extent that Hanoi is able at that time to furnish proof that it is truly independent, it is not certain that fundamental obstacles would be met with on the international plane).

This is the prospect that faces us. As things are at the moment, one can hardly see how the Diem Government, discredited and detested as it is, could restore its authority in South Vietnam. Its enemies will, henceforward, be strong enough both to resist any plans it may undertake and also to deny it the exercise of power in the countryside. The Americans are themselves aware of this situation. In May 1961, the Secretary of State, Mr. Dean Rusk, emphasised that it was no longer possible to oppose Viet-Minh threats by purely military means. The recent Taylor-Rostow mission has confirmed this point of view. Profound reforms are necessary, and the first thing to make sure of is that the Saigon Government is capable of inspiring confidence, which, under the Ngô family, it is no longer able to do.

The problem of the nature of the régime is thus, at the present moment, underlying all others in South Vietnam. Whether the process of unification is speedy or slow depends on whether it is solved or not. The methods and the nature of M. Diem's régime are indeed such that with every month that goes by the grip of the Communists in Vietnam grows firmer over the forces of the Resistance. The process which, under the French régime between 1930 and 1954, operated in favour of the Communist Party, operates still today, for the fact is that the people of Vietnam have always been caught between Communism and a form of anti-Communism which they could not accept. In the days of the French, they had to choose between Communism and a hated colonial régime; today the Americans give them a choice between Communism and a dictatorship of a type which is at one and the same time Fascist and medieval. Everything leads one to think that " if they had at all costs to choose between Communism and reaction, the masses of Vietnam would opt for the former." [13]

The longer Diem's régime lasts, the more enemies it has, and the stronger Communist and anti-American influences become within the Resistance. This development could doubtless be stemmed and reversed, but to do so would require a way out to be found from the terrible choice "either Diem or the Viet-Minh." It would require the emergence of another pole of influence. A change of Government in Saigon, with the advent to power of a popular and democratic Nationalist régime resolved to have done, once and for all, with the use of terror as an instrument of government and to follow an advanced economic and social policy would in all probability help towards the relaxation of tension, and would bring about the progressive sterilisation of the ground which now acts as a seedbed for Communism and Communist sympathisers. In the same way, if such a government abandoned the purely negative attitude adopted by the Diem régime towards relations with the North, the *détente* which would result, both in the minds of the people and throughout South-East Asia, would destroy many of the most cherished debating points of Northern propaganda.

For the die is not irrevocably cast, and the situation remains fluid. That part of the Nationalist movement in Vietnam which is not identified with Marxism has still a few good cards up its sleeve, but, unfortunately, it has very little time left in which to play them. It would be possible for it to play them to some advantage, even maybe win back the sympathy of the population, and this without abandoning its ideological references, truly democratic attitude, or its Western friends and the support they bring. But even if it ought to preserve a healthy suspicion of reunification for so long as it seems likely to be achieved to the advantage of the Communists alone, one can see no reason why it should fear contact with the North. After all, there are not two peoples nor two nations in Vietnam, and if certain regional interests diverge, if families and individuals look upon themselves as being for or against such and such a social system, this does not mean that they all of them want to live as strangers and enemies to each other. When one represents freedom (which ought to be the *raison d'être* of the South) one can, if one wishes, work effectively towards the mutual understanding and coming-together of the two Vietnams, and to that end put forward confederal solutions which would serve both the interests of the present time and the opportunities of the future.

The Liberation Front of the South constitutes, on the other hand, an unknown factor. The bigger it grows, the more non-Communist adherents

---

[13] *Cf.* Nguyen Ngoc Huy, "Open letter to Mr. Kennedy," in *Pour le Viêt-Nam*, No. 6, March 1961.

it contains. If there were a *détente* in Saigon, could the Communists remain dominant or preponderant in it? [14]   The risk now for Hanoi is that the Front, which is essentially a Southern movement, should remain open to non-Marxist influences coming from powers which, for example, considering the victory of the Front as a virtual certainty, might wish in this way at least to make some provision for the future.

These are merely conjectures. But can what happened in South Korea happen again in South Vietnam? The blindness displayed over Laos by the Western Powers, and by the United States in particular, leads one to think that for Hanoi the risks of failure are not large this time either, and that, as Ho Chi Minh has said, " Reunification is now only a question of time." At this very moment a process of osmosis is taking place between the North and the country districts of the South through that open sieve, the Laotian border, and it is taking place to the advantage of the Communists alone. The situation is thus evolving towards the tragic ranging of city against countryside to which allusion has been made above. Who is still able, at the present time, to make a new deal?

[14] The creation in January 1962 of a " People's Revolutionary Party " (a " party of the working class ") within the framework of the Liberation Front is probably designed as an insurance against the risk that they could not. It would be interesting to know whether this new move was made on the advice of the Chinese that it was essential to have in the South an ideologically solid core to ensure that the Front maintained a correct line. It was certainly the Chinese who advocated a similar relationship between the Viet-Minh and the Lien Viet in 1951.

The Position of the DRV Leadership and the Succession to Ho Chi Minh

By P. J. HONEY

SOVIETOLOGISTS and Sinologists have found it extremely difficult to assess the position which the Democratic Republic of (North) Vietnam (DRV) occupies within the Communist *bloc*. Some have concluded that it is simply a satellite of Peking, basing their judgment upon its geographical position and the fact that the Vietnamese leaders closely followed the policies of the Chinese Communists, at least during the early years of the state's existence. Others have stated that the DRV is more closely bound to the Soviet Union than to China, and they quote extracts from the speeches of Vietnamese leaders to confirm this opinion. Still others maintain that the DRV enjoys a substantial measure of independence of both Russia and China and may, like Tito's Yugoslavia, break with the Communist *bloc* at some future date. They point out that the Vietnamese, like the Yugoslavs, won their own independence without the backing of the Russian or Chinese army. All of these conclusions are too facile and prove, if they prove anything at all, that their authors have not taken into account all the factors which have a bearing upon the events in the DRV. As in all Communist states, the formulation of policy is the responsibility of a few leaders, but these men, whatever their personal political inclinations, are restricted in their choice of policy by the circumstances in which they find themselves.

Most important of these limiting circumstances is the geographical position of the DRV, which shares a common frontier with southern China. In the course of her history, Vietnam has been a colony of China, has owned suzerainty to China, and has sent tribute to China. It would be strange if the Chinese Communists, who appear to find no incongruity in using the fact of former imperial domination of a foreign country as proof of their present right to rule that country, did not regard the DRV as at least a sphere of special Chinese interest. If this is the case—and it almost certainly is—then China is likely to resent the efforts by other states, even Communist states, to acquire a predominant influence or control over the affairs of the DRV. The fact that the DRV is geographically far removed from other Communist states renders the Chinese position very strong, and China could, in the last resort, send her troops into North Vietnam in order to maintain her influence there.

Against this, almost every Vietnamese is well aware of the past role of China in Vietnamese affairs and is justifiably apprehensive about future Chinese policy and actions in so far as these are likely to affect the DRV. Experience has convinced every Vietnamese that the Chinese are, by nature, imperialists and that whenever China is strong then Vietnam is threatened by Chinese imperialism. They also know that the Chinese are acquisitive and that whenever China has dominated Vietnam the Vietnamese have been mercilessly exploited to enrich the Chinese. If they had forgotten the lessons of history, the short Chinese occupation of north Vietnam after the Second World War, when the Chinese soldiers stripped the country of every item of value which could be moved into China—the houses were stripped of even their roof-tiles, their electrical wiring, and their doors—was sufficient to give a most unpleasant jolt to Vietnamese memories. Arguments that the Chinese character has undergone a change for the better with the advent of Communism carry no conviction among the Vietnamese, and a DRV propaganda campaign which festooned north Vietnam with slogans recalling the " historic friendship between the Vietnamese and Chinese peoples " [1] had to be called off abruptly before the gales of embittered Vietnamese laughter.

Under the French colonial régime Vietnamese suffered the indignity of being ruled by foreigners, saw their patriots imprisoned, and watched Frenchmen grow rich from their exploitation of Vietnam. But they also enjoyed the benefits of efficient government, experienced the rule of law, and saw their country endowed with modern cities, roads, railways, hospitals, factories, and the like. In French times large numbers of Vietnamese prospered, tasted the delights of Western education and culture, and developed a liking for Western consumer goods. Unless the Communist régime can convince the Vietnamese of the superiority of Communism by surpassing the French in the provision of material and intellectual benefits, then it is unlikely to win popular approval. But China is herself a backward country and incapable of supplying the factories, machinery, and technicians so badly needed to raise living standards in the DRV. This is why the Vietnamese Communists must look to Russia and her European satellites for the help they need in developing North Vietnam.

A further reason for seeking Russian interest and help stems from the Vietnamese apprehension of China already mentioned. With the support of Russia, the DRV may hope to preserve some degree of independence from Communist China. If, however, Russia should ever withdraw her current interest in Vietnam and agree with Mao that the

---

[1] This campaign was organised early in 1955, when the streets of cities, towns and villages were hung with slogans, while the press and radio were daily filled with reminders of this historic friendship.

country falls within the Chinese sphere of influence, then the DRV will very quickly be reduced to a mere satellite of China, little more than a Chinese province. All Vietnamese are acutely aware of this, and it is a factor which encourages them to court Russian favour assiduously.

The existence of a non-Communist government in South Vietnam poses a constant threat to the DRV. So long as there is an alternative Vietnamese government, the Communists in the north will be obliged to struggle for the loyalty of the whole Vietnamese people. While the present division persists, the DRV must act in a way calculated to win the approval of, or at least to avoid antagonising, opinion in south Vietnam. Up to the present time, this has entailed restricting Communist programmes, maintaining in high office non-Communists of such bourgeois background as to make nonsense of much of the Party teaching, and making propaganda boasts about progress and prosperity in the DRV which every citizen in that state knows to be false.[2]

In spite of numerous pledges given to the Vietnamese people that the resistance war would continue until the whole country had been liberated, the DRV signed the Geneva agreements which ended the war and placed only half the country under Communist control. South Vietnam steadfastly refused to countenance the division of the country and did not sign the agreements, so that the responsibility for the unpopular division rests squarely upon the shoulders of the DRV. Pham Van Dong signed these agreements under very strong pressure from the Soviet Union,[3] a fact which few Vietnamese were slow to notice, and then attempted to justify his action by proclaiming that the agreements envisaged the holding of national elections in 1956, so that Vietnam would be reunified at that date. Now the clause dealing with national elections was not embodied in the signed agreements but formed part of an unsigned " Declaration of Intent," the legal validity of which is extremely doubtful, and President Ngo Dinh Diem refused to agree to the elections. A further loss of face for the DRV was thus occasioned by their inability to insist on these elections, and it became imperative for the Communists to bring about national unity as quickly as possible. In consequence, a very important factor influencing the DRV preference for Chinese or Russian policies is the likelihood of these policies to bring

---

2 It is worth citing the remarks of Gerard Tongas on this subject: " Les statistiques de toutes sortes foisonnent et sont abondamment diffusées, car elles servent à alimenter la propagande. Or, precisement, comme elles ne servent qu'à cela, *elles n'ont absolument aucune valeur.*

" Les chiffres de production donnés ne sont pas simplement truqués, les pourcentages ne sont pas simplement augmentés, les uns et les autres sont la plupart du temps inventés de toutes pièces, et avec quelle ardeur !"

G. Tongas, *L'Enfer Communiste au Nord Viet-Nâm* (Paris: NÉD, 1961), p. 213.

3 *Cf.* Jean Wetz in *Le Monde*, July 13, 1954; Jacques Fauvet in *ibid.*, July 23, 1954; *Manchester Guardian*, July 23, 1954, and many others.

about national unity in Vietnam and to accept the inevitable risks of war inherent in the achievement of reunification.

These are but a few of the more important factors to be taken into account by anyone seeking to assess the position of the DRV within the Communist world. There are many more, but an examination of all of them is outside the scope of this article.

DRV AND THE SINO-SOVIET DISPUTE

Within the present DRV leadership exist factions which favour Chinese-style Communism and Russian-style Communism. The motives which impel leading Vietnamese Communists to support one or other of these two factions are varied. Personal rivalries have existed between some of the leaders for a very long time, and the adherence of one such person to a particular faction was sometimes sufficient to drive his rival into the opposite one. The most celebrated of these quarrels between individuals is that which has divided Vo Nguyen Giap and Truong Chinh for many years,[4] so that it is hardly surprising to find that when Giap, who has never concealed his distrust of China since his student days, became a leading protagonist of the Russian cause, Chinh gave his allegiance to that of China. Other leaders lend their support to one or other faction for reasons of self interest and the hope of preferment. Many of the second rank DRV leaders are bound to one or other of the first rank leaders, for they owe their present positions to the patronage of these latter, so they follow their patron into the faction of his choosing.

At first glance, the current dispute between Russia and China might appear to be advantageous to the DRV. North Vietnam is overpopulated and the mass of this large population is concentrated in the Red River delta, for most of the remaining land is mountainous and Vietnamese will not readily live in upland areas. The food situation is precarious. During the period of French occupation, rice always had to be sent from Cochin China to Tonking to feed the population. If the DRV is to achieve a reasonable standard of living for her people, then she must industralise and export the produce of her industries in order to purchase adequate supplies of food and clothing. Under these circumstances, it might seem to be to the advantage of the DRV to exploit the rivalry which exists between the two largest Communist countries in order to acquire from them the maximum quantities of aid, thus affording the DRV authorities some hope of solving their acute economic difficulties.

However, President Ho Chi Minh would seem to have reached the

---

[4] The quarrel became public knowledge early in 1950, when Truong Chinh accused Giap of insecurity in his choice of personnel. It was further aggravated towards the end of that year when Truong Chinh accumulated enough evidence to secure the execution of Tran Chi Chau, chief of Giap's military supply service.

conclusion that the disadvantages of the Sino-Soviet dispute outweigh the potential advantages so far as the DRV is concerned. If the differences now dividing China and Russia increase, and they have shown no signs of lessening up to the time of writing, then there is a very real danger of a complete rupture between these two countries. In the event of an open breach, the other Communist states would be obliged publicly to declare their allegiance to either Russia or China. Such a situation almost developed during the meeting of the world Communist Parties at Moscow in November 1960 for the Chinese at first appeared to be unwilling to sign the final declaration. It is interesting to note that Ho Chi Minh, more than any other Communist leader attending the Moscow meeting, worked tirelessly to bring the Russian and Chinese leaders together. To reconcile the differences which divided the two was impossible, for these were too great, so that Ho's objective could only have been to convince both sides of the necessity to conceal their quarrel from the non-Communist world. This meant that terms acceptable to both sides had to be worked out for the final declaration, and Ho arranged several meetings between them to this end.

In the event, Ho was successful and the Chinese did sign the final document. Had they refused to do so, then the DRV would have been faced with the choice between signing the document herself and refusing to sign it. Signature would have incurred the gravest displeasure on the part of China, and the consequences of this can only be guessed at, while a refusal to sign would have produced the same effect upon Russia. Thus, the principal requirement of the DRV during the Moscow meeting was the avoidance of a situation in which she was obliged to make this agonising decision. But even though the danger was averted at Moscow in 1960, a similar situation may arise at any time so long as the dispute continues. For this reason, the guiding policy of the DRV in all her dealings with the Communist *bloc* countries is to avoid at all costs an open rupture between Russia and China. A consequence of that policy is that the extent to which she can lend support to the rival views of Russia and China is severely limited. She simply cannot run the risk of coming out in full support of one side or another, whatever the personal inclinations of individual Vietnamese political leaders, but must follow a carefully chosen path between the two, veering towards one side or the other only within the limits of safety.

POSITION OF HO CHI MINH

Yet another factor which must be taken into account in any consideration of the DRV leadership is the advanced age of President Ho Chi Minh. Ho is now in his seventies and cannot be expected to shoulder the burdens of leadership for very much longer. His health has never been good since he contracted tuberculosis in the 1930s, and he has had to bear the most severe strains and anxieties since 1945. On more than one occasion during the past five years, the press has been forbidden to photograph him. It seems likely that such a ban was imposed when he was ailing so as to keep the evidence of his failing health from reaching the citizens of the DRV and the outside world. It would be surprising if he were not removed from office during the next few years by death or retirement. Under the terms of the constitution, if Ho were to die then the presidency would pass, in the first instance, to Vice-President Ton Duc Thang; but he is older than Ho and he, too, is not in good health.

Under these circumstances, the question of who is to succeed Ho as supreme leader of the DRV, both in name and in fact, becomes daily more immediate. Ho himself has long enjoyed a great ascendancy over all the other DRV leaders. As Nguyen Ai Quoc he became a legend in Vietnam through his anti-French and anti-colonialist writings during the period immediately following the First World War; he was the first Vietnamese to become a Communist, and the first to receive a thorough revolutionary and political training in Moscow; he worked with the Borodin mission in China and later directed the " South Seas " Communist Party; he formed the Vietnamese Revolutionary Youth League,[5] which selected and trained most of the present DRV leaders. So, no other leader can hope to rival the length of his service to Communism, his importance in the Communist world, his vast political experience, or his prestige among the ordinary people of Vietnam. For all these reasons, as well as for reasons of his own outstanding intelligence and personality, he has achieved an ascendancy over his colleagues quite as great as that of Stalin over the other Russian leaders, with the result that his succession seems likely to create difficulties as great as did Stalin's.

One of Ho's tactics for safeguarding his pre-eminence in the DRV has been to keep his own counsel and to disclose his intentions to nobody. His appointment of the aged, almost senile, Ton Duc Thang to the Vice-Presidency is an example of this. The constitution makes provision for a Vice-President, and this official will become acting President on the death of the President. Clearly, the appointment of one of the younger leaders to this office would be construed as a mark of special regard or favour, and it would place the man appointed in a very advantageous position by comparison with the other claimants. Admittedly he might

[5] Viet Nam Cach Menh Thanh Nien Dong Chi Hoi, founded by Ho Chi Minh at Canton in June 1925. For further information see Gouvernement générale de l'Indochine, Direction des affaires politiques et de la sureté générale; *Contribution à l'histoire des mouvements politiques de l'Indochine française*, Vol. 4 (Hanoi: 1933).

be removed, as was Malenkov, but this would be difficult to encompass. In order to avoid such a situation, Ho selected an old man who was no longer regarded as a serious contender for the highest office, and this had the effect of keeping the more likely contenders in a state of uncertainty. In their own interests, if for no other reason, they are obliged to support and obey Ho Chi Minh so as not to prejudice their chances of succeeding him at some future date.

THE SUCCESSION TO HO CHI MINH

Nevertheless, the question of who is to succeed Ho must be upper-most in the minds of DRV leaders, and some of these at least must be considering how best they can press their claims to become the overall leader. Who, then, are the leaders with a reasonable hope of being able to attain Ho's position? The number of Vietnamese occupying very senior posts in the most important institutions of the state is large, so that the list of candidates might seem likely to be long, but a sizeable number of these persons may be eliminated straight away, for they exert very little influence upon the running of the DRV now and are unlikely to do so in the future.

Throughout the resistance war in Indo-China it was essential for the Vietnamese Communists to disguise the true nature of the resistance movement. The Communists themselves were no more than a tiny minority, and the Vietnamese people had no interest in fighting for the establishment of a Communist state. Indeed, most Vietnamese would have been repelled by the idea because it implied subservience to Russia or, still worse, after Mao Tse-tung's victory in 1949, to China. Conse-quently, it became necessary for Ho Chi Minh to create the impression that the resistance movement was a broad alliance of patriotic Viet-namese fighting only for the defeat of France and for the full indepen-dence of Vietnam. To accomplish this, he was obliged to appoint known non-Communists to some of the highest positions in the DRV govern-ment, and even took the unprecedented step of dissolving the Communist Party. These steps had to be taken if the resistance movement were to attract all shades of Vietnamese nationalist opinion, and without this mass support the struggle would have been doomed to failure.

Since 1954, when the Geneva agreements were signed, the war ended, and Vietnam was divided into two states, Ho Chi Minh has established a Communist régime in the northern half of the country. However, non-Communist South Vietnam remains to be won, so that it is still necessary for Ho to secure support for his régime among southern Vietnamese. As part of his efforts to achieve this end, he has launched a full-scale propa-ganda campaign designed to reassure the apprehensive southerners about the nature of his régime. One feature of this campaign is the retention in the highest offices of non-Communists and the accordance of all the appropriate marks of respect to these men. Everyone in the DRV, and the less gullible southerners, is aware that they exercise no real power or influence in the state, but Ho still considers them worth keeping for their propaganda value. Their numbers include such people as Phan Anh, the Minister for Foreign Trade, Hoang Minh Giam, the Minister of Culture, Phan Ke Toai, once the Imperial Delegate to Tonking but now a deputy-Premier and Minister of the Interior, Nguyen Van Huyen, the Minister of Education, and many more besides. Indeed, all the non-Communists may be set aside, for they have no chance of providing a successor to Ho Chi Minh, and attention must focus upon the members of the Lao Dong Party.

Under the terms of the 1960 constitution, the most powerful body in the DRV is the National Assembly, but its members meet twice yearly and the sessions last for only a few days. During the long periods of recess, all its powers save that of amending the constitution are vested in the Standing Committee, which remains in permanent session. However, a detailed study of how the DRV is controlled in practice reveals that it is not this Standing Committee but the Politburo of the Lao Dong Party which makes all policy decisions. Once made, these decisions are then approved by the Standing Committee of the National Assembly. So that nothing may be left to chance, the Chairman and Vice-Chairman of the Standing Committee are also members of the Politburo. The Politburo of the Lao Dong Party is, therefore, the most powerful body in the DRV, so that it is more than probable that one of its members will eventually succeed Ho Chi Minh.

The DRV Politburo comprises eleven full members and two alternate members, who are responsible for state security and owe their membership to the posts which they occupy. Thus, if the names of Ho Chi Minh himself and of the two *ex-officio* members are set aside, there remain only ten candidates in the running for the succession. This number can be further reduced to eight since one member, Nguyen Chi Thanh, is a protégé of one of the other members, Truong Chinh, and there is reason for supposing that another, Pham Hung, was elected to membership at the insistence of Pham Van Dong in order to offset the influence of Truong Chinh in that body. These eight candidates are, by name, Le Duan, Truong Chinh, Pham Van Dong, Vo Nguyen Giap, Le Duc Tho, Nguyen Duy Trinh, Le Thanh Nghi, and Hoang Van Hoan. It seems very probable that one of these men will succeed Ho Chi Minh when the latter lays down his responsibilities.

FACTIONS WITHIN THE POLITBURO

It has already been stated that two of them, Vo Nguyen Giap and Truong Chinh, have long been political enemies, and this is not the only division which exists within the membership of the Politburo. Almost as well known is the quarrel between Le Duan and Le Duc Tho, which has lasted for a number of years.[6] However, there is not sufficient evidence available to permit the membership of the Politburo to be classified with any certainty into rival groupings. Some clues as to the probable alignments of these eight men after the departure of Ho Chi Minh may be perceived by studying their behaviour during times of crisis. Since the Communists assumed power in North Vietnam there have been three major crises.

The DRV agrarian reforms, with which Truong Chinh had publicly associated himself, proved in 1956 to have been a disastrous failure. The brutality, the murders, and the injustices so incensed the population that a halt had to be called and a " Rectification of Errors " campaign set in motion.[7] Truong Chinh, at that time Secretary-General of the Party, was obliged to resign this post and to make a public self-criticism. So precarious was the position of the Party that Ho Chi Minh himself found it necessary to bolster it with his personal prestige by assuming the post of Secretary-General, although the duties were, in fact, carried out by Le Duan.[8] The moment was a real test of Truong Chinh's importance, for he was the most hated man in North Vietnam and the Lao Dong Party could, by expelling him, have diverted some of the popular anger from itself. In the event, Truong Chinh was permitted to retain his membership of the Politburo, and his principal enemy, Vo Nguyen Giap, did not appear to derive any benefit from the incident. This suggests that Truong Chinh was considered too valuable a Party leader to be sacrificed to popular discontent and, conversely, that the importance of Vo Nguyen Giap was not great enough to permit him to exploit his enemy's disgrace to his own advantage.

A second crisis occurred in the autumn of 1957, and the happenings at that time have never been satisfactorily explained. The principal events, as seen from outside, were these. President Ho Chi Minh, who had only lately returned to the DRV after a long foreign tour, left Hanoi in October to attend the celebrations for the fortieth anniversary of the

---

6 In 1950 this quarrel led to a virtual split in the Communist leadership of South Vietnam. This was resolved in 1951 when Le Duan was recalled to North Vietnam and Le Duc Tho was left to manage South Vietnam.

7 See Ho Chi Minh's open letter of August 18, 1956, published by the DRV press and radio.

8 There were numerous indications between 1956 and 1960 that it was Le Duan, not Ho Chi Minh, who performed the duties of Secretary-General of the Party, and these would seem to have been confirmed by Le Duan's official appointment to the post of First Secretary in September 1960.

October Revolution in Moscow. He left in company with Le Duan, but without any of the customary ceremonial which, on all other occasions, has accompanied his departures. Moreover, he did not return home until late in December, long after the ending of the Moscow celebrations. From the time of his departure until his home-coming, Ho Chi Minh's name was not mentioned by the DRV press or radio, an omission so unusual that it gave rise to rumours of his death. Between early October and late December, Vo Nguyen Giap was neither seen in public nor mentioned by press or radio. This, too, gave rise to rumours about the fate of Giap, for it was known that he had not gone to Moscow. The celebration of the Russian anniversary in the DRV that year was on a much smaller scale than hitherto, being restricted to the showing of some Russian films, a bicycle race, and a public meeting. The platform at this meeting was unusual, Vice-President Ton Duc Thang occupying the first place, Truong Chinh the second, Nguyen Duy Trinh the third, and Pham Van Dong the fourth. In the DRV, as in other Communist states, great importance is attached to protocol, so that it was extraordinary for Truong Chinh and Nguyen Duy Trinh, who are Vice-Premiers, to take precedence over the Premier, Pham Van Dong. Furthermore, the principal speaker was Nguyen Duy Trinh, who, in spite of the fact that it was the occasion of a Russian anniversary and that a delegation from the Supreme Soviet was present, quoted extensively from the works of Mao Tse-tung.

On the face of it, the reduced scale of the celebrations, coupled with the content of Nguyen Duy Trinh's speech, suggested that the DRV was being deliberately insulting to Russia. This, in turn, suggests that a pro-Chinese faction of the DRV leadership had won an ascendancy over the rest and was, for the time being, running the government of North Vietnam. If this was the case, then Vo Nguyen Giap's absence can be explained, for he has not infrequently voiced sentiments uncomplimentary to China in the past, and would not be likely to collaborate with any group especially favourably disposed towards China, particularly when Truong Chinh was occupying so prominent a place in that group. Both Truong Chinh and Nguyen Duy Trinh are widely believed to advocate Chinese-type rather than Russian-type Communism, and Trinh later made an uncompromisingly pro-Chinese speech when he represented the DRV at the Albanian Party Congress in 1961. Ton Duc Thang is not important, for he is now very old and might well have conceived it his duty as Vice-President to occupy the first place on the platform in the absence of Ho Chi Minh.

The case of Ho Chi Minh, who has long held the view that the DRV must maintain relations with both Russia and China if she is to survive, may possibly be explained by his unwillingness to countenance a government of North Vietnam committed to the support of China alone. It may well be that he left Hanoi in haste after a dispute with the Truong Chinh faction—hence his unceremonious departure—and refused to return from abroad until the DRV leadership had agreed to accept his policy on relations with the Communist *bloc*. Le Duan is believed to favour the Russian side in the current dispute, and he might reasonably have been expected to remain abroad with Ho Chi Minh until the latter's terms for a return had been accepted. As Prime Minister, Pham Van Dong probably felt constrained to remain at home to ensure the continuance of the administration, but his lowly position on the platform suggests that he was far from being an enthusiastic supporter of a pro-Chinese faction.

Once again, in 1960, Vo Nguyen Giap made a prolonged disappearance from the public life, the press, and the radio of the DRV. On this occasion, he was not seen or heard of from May until August, the month preceding the DRV Party Congress. Again, his absence would seem to have coincided with a period of dispute within the Party. At the Congress itself, it very quickly became apparent that the DRV was looking with great favour upon Russia, but was far from being as kindly disposed towards China. In fact, she treated the visiting Chinese delegation in an insulting fashion.[9] Such behaviour indicated another change in the Party line, for, since the crisis of 1957, the DRV had followed a carefully plotted middle course between the two major Communist countries. It appeared, on this occasion, that the balance had swung in favour of the pro-Russian faction in the DRV and that the Truong Chinh group was on the defensive.

Two months later, during the meeting of the world Communist Parties in Moscow, Ho Chi Minh worked harder than anyone else present to avoid an open breach between Russia and China, thereby showing that his policy requirement mentioned earlier in this article was still valid in spite of internal factional rivalries in the DRV. Again, during the 22nd Congress of the Russian Party in October 1961, Ho refused to join in the general condemnation of Albania for the same reason. His action on the latter occasion was wrongly interpreted in much of the Western press as indicating support for China, which it was not.

CONCLUSIONS

In the light of what happened during the three DRV crises briefly mentioned, and of the background information available about the persons involved, it is possible to make a tentative assessment of the

---

[9] See " North Vietnam's Party Congress " by the present author in *The China Quarterly*, October-December, 1960.

eight candidates who may possibly succeed Ho Chi Minh as leader of the DRV. Truong Chinh and Nguyen Duy Trinh would seem to head a faction of the leadership which is more favourably disposed towards China than Russia, while Vo Nguyen Giap and Le Duan head a second, which tends to look towards Moscow. Le Duc Tho, because of his long-standing differences with Le Duan, may be expected to lend his support to Truong Chinh, while Pham Van Dong, who indicated that he was not an enthusiastic supporter of the pro-Chinese line and sought to reduce Truong Chinh's influence in the Politburo by sponsoring Pham Hung's membership, will probably emerge on the side of Vo Nguyen Giap. Le Thanh Nghi and Hoang Van Hoan do not seem to have played a decisive role in the formulation of DRV policy, to judge from their writings and speeches. Indeed, both appear to be specialists, Le Thanh Nghi in economic planning, and Hoang Van Hoan in foreign affairs and diplomacy. It is quite possible that both owe their membership of the Politburo to their special qualifications in these fields rather than to their importance as leading personalities. For these reasons, it is unlikely that either will have a decisive role to play in the eventual struggle for the succession to Ho Chi Minh. They will probably seek to be on the side of the faction which emerges victorious.

It is impossible to forecast which group will eventually provide the successor to Ho, for the outcome may well be decided by the timing and the circumstances of Ho's departure. Developments within the Communist *bloc*, which may be quite beyond the control of the DRV, could also change the present alignments, although they are hardly likely to resolve the personal differences which divide individual leaders. It can be said with a fair degree of accuracy that, so long as the Sino-Soviet dispute continues to exist in its present form, then the room for manoeuvre of a future DRV leader will be very restricted. He will be able to move closer to the Russian line or the Chinese line according to the demands of circumstances or his own judgment, but he will not be able to give full support to either side. Should the dispute between China and Russia develop into an open rupture, then probably the first casualty in the Communist *bloc* would be the DRV. If she sided with Russia, she would certainly be subjected to great pressures from China and might even be the victim of direct Chinese intervention, while if she sided with China, she could expect to be brought increasingly under Chinese influence until she became little more than another Chinese province. In any event, a Sino-Soviet rupture would strengthen the position of Truong Chinh.

The DRV leadership can thus be expected to continue to steer a middle course between China and Russia, but not to accord full support to either country so long as the dispute continues. Their principal foreign policy requirement will be to prevent this dispute developing to such an extent as to cause a public breach, and they may go to very great lengths to achieve this aim. Internal quarrels and rivalries may be expected to occur from time to time, but they will probably not be allowed to grow to such proportions that they risk affecting the all-important foreign policy.

Power and Pressure Groups in North Vietnam

By BERNARD B. FALL

As in many other Communist states (and quite a few non-Communist ones) there is in the DRV (Democratic Republic of [North] Vietnam) a sharp difference between the theoretical and the actual structure of governmental powers.

Article 4 of the DRV Constitution of January 1, 1960, adequately covers the subject of the theoretical source of power in North Vietnam: " All powers of the DRV belong to the people, who exercise them through the intermediary of the National Assembly and of People's Councils at every echelon, elected by it and responsible to it. . . ."

In actual fact, however, government power is in the hands of several distinct groups, some of which operate within the government structure while some others operate entirely or in part outside of it. Some of the power groups can be considered as forming part of the " traditional " Communist elite—old party leaders, trade union chiefs, and a sprinkling of military men—while others spring from the ranks of the " New Class " —the Party bureaucrats, the newly urbanised factory workers, and the new managerial class of the largely nationalised sectors of the industrial economy.

As in all Communist states, the actual changes of power are fairly subtle at first and must often be culled from a welter of minor administrative changes or from such seemingly innocuous details as the line-up of political, party, or military leaders at a formal function. It is still a matter of some debate as to whether too much is not often read into such pictures by the " Kremlinologists " who, like the priests of certain older cults, try to forecast the future from such tenuous signs. The fact remains, however, that for the time being the Communists themselves have often chosen that means as a public symptom of a shift of power or of policies within their own camp, as the events in Moscow in October and November 1961 tend to show once more.

POWER GROUPS AND PRESSURE GROUPS

In order to avoid any misunderstanding in the use of the key terms in this study, a brief statement on definitions will be necessary. Within the frame of reference of this study, a " power group " is an informal body of operators exercising their influence upon the formal structure of government from *inside* that structure; while the " pressure group " may exercise similar influences in a far more inchoate way and from *outside* the formal structure.

In the precise case of the DRV, it is possible to distinguish *two* major policy alternatives subject to pressure or influence from such groups; and a total of *six* power and pressure groups. The two major policy alternatives are: alignment with Moscow or alignment with Peking, with subtle sub-gradations or compromises between the extremes.

The pressure and power groups can also be divided into two segments respectively:

1. Power Groups:
   (a) The Lao-Dong [*i.e.*, Communist] Party
   (b) The Vietnam People's Army
   (c) The Administrators and Managers
2. Pressure Groups:
   (a) The Intellectuals
   (b) The Urban Labour Force
   (c) The Peasantry

Little can be said about the two policy alternatives that is not already self-evident, and was not made even clearer during the memorable debates at the Twenty-second Congress of the Communist Party of the Soviet Union in October-November 1961 in Moscow: North Vietnam, historically indefensible against its northern neighbour, had to walk the tightrope between its ideological preferences and geopolitical and economic realities. This was best shown by Ho Chi Minh's own attitude at the Moscow Congress: while he could not avoid aligning himself on China's " hard " line, Ho nonetheless did not leave Russia when Chou En-lai did but went on a tour of the country instead.

Within North Vietnam's government and Lao-Dong Party structure, the two policy alternatives are represented within every organisation in differing degrees of concentration at various times, the exact degree depending very often upon the changing fortunes of the Cold War.

PEKING *v.* MOSCOW WINGS

The struggle between the two policy wings within the DRV may have gone on as early as the 1920s, when Ho came to Canton from Moscow and Paris, while such men as Dan Xuan Khu joined the Vietnamese Communist movement after training and working with the Chinese Communist Party. Dan Xuan Khu is better known under his present *nom de guerre* of Truong Chinh (" Long March "), fully indicative of his political sympathies.

During the years of war against the French, differences between the two wings were largely immaterial since Moscow was far away and not in a position to help directly in the war effort and, furthermore, was at least in the beginning not particularly interested in helping Ho Chi Minh's cause.[1] With the cease-fire of 1954, the problem immediately became more acute since Chinese Communist influence, hitherto largely limited to military assistance, now also became preponderant in the economic field in the form of huge grants, loans, deliveries of machinery and goods; and the presence of Chinese advisers in nearly every field of endeavour. From 1954 until 1956, the pro-Chinese wing held the field within the Lao-Dong Party and included many workers and managers, and even some intellectuals—with the Vietnam People's Army under Vo Nguyên Giap representing a stronghold of lukewarm feelings towards Peking.

The peasant rebellion of Nghe-An in November 1956 (of which, significantly, the Army political commissars had warned the Lao-Dong) gave Ho Chi Minh a good pretext to purge the most ardent pro-Peking elements, at least temporarily: Truong Chinh was replaced as Secretary-General of the Lao-Dong by Ho himself, and other minor luminaries of the "Chinese wing" disappeared temporarily from view. But it was obvious that the very presence of China next door did not permit the total elimination of the Chinese wing. Soon Truong Chinh and his friends began their slow climb to new power.

The collapse of the Summit Conference of May 1960 (which, like any other peaceable contact between Moscow and the West, had not exactly been looked upon favourably by Peking) brought a return in force of the Peking clan which now claimed that the C.P.R. had been " clairvoyant " all along in its thesis that one could not negotiate with the " imperialists."

The year 1960 brought about three events which were to influence even further the struggle between the two policy wings: in January a new constitution was promulgated which brought about a far more stringent political control of the government machinery; followed on May 8 (the sixth anniversary of the French defeat at Dien Bien Phu) by the first legislative elections since 1946 [2]; and in September of the same year by the third National Congress of the Lao-Dong.[3]

---

[1] It is an often-forgotten fact that until the collapse of the 1947 Foreign Ministers' Conference, there was solid hope that France would turn Communist on short notice, along with all her colonies. Thus, Moscow (while lambasting British and American " colonialism " in India, the Philippines and Malaya) carefully abstained from even mentioning French operations in Indo-China in its propaganda; and at home, the French Communist Party did not break cabinet solidarity when the Blum government submitted credit requests (including $7 million for purchases of weapons in the U.S.A.) for the prosecution of the first year of the Indo-China war. Cf. B. Fall, "Tribulations of a Party Line: The French Communist Party and the Indochina War," in *Foreign Affairs*, New York, April 1955.

[2] Fall, B., *Le Viet-Minh*, Paris, 1960: Armand Colin; also *ibid.*, " North Viet-Nam's New Constitution and Government," *Pacific Affairs*, September 1960.

[3] Dang Lao-Dong, *Third National Congress of the Viet-Nam Workers' Party* (Hanoi: Foreign Languages Publishing House, 1960). Four vols.

The creation, within the structure of the DRV government, of an
"Organ of People's Control" introduced a new element of political
surveillance into the administrative machinery; and the reshuffles within
the government after the legislative elections of May 1960 clearly showed
that the process seemed to favour the pro-Chinese elements: Truong
Chinh became Chairman of the Permanent Committee of the National
Assembly; while two other pro-Peking stalwarts, Hoang Quoc Viet (head
of the Vietnam Confederation of Labour) and Pham Van Bach (the
southern guerrilla leader) found themselves in control of the court system
and of the "People's Control Organ," respectively.

In fact, the ascendant of the pro-Peking group seemed so strong that
at the Party Congress of September 1960 the long-time Prime Minister
of the DRV, Pham Van Dong, a scion of the mandarin class and one
of Ho Chi Minh's earliest and most faithful followers, stood in danger of
losing his post, had not Ho Chi Minh thrown his personal prestige in
the balance in order to save his companion.

The hardening of Moscow's relations with the West brought about a
closer alignment of the position of the two policy camps in Vietnam and
some personnel changes to substantiate the view that the pro-Moscow
group was regaining some of its earlier strength. In February 1961, Ung
Van Khiêm, the former chief of the Executive Committee for the
Nam-Bô [South Vietnam] and Vice-Minister of Foreign Affairs, stepped
into the post of Minister of Foreign Affairs; while in March 1961, three
People's Army Generals: Lt.-Gen. Van Tien Dung, Maj.-Gen. Hoang
Van Thai, Maj.-Gen. Dong Hao, well known for their devotion to
General Giap and their lack of enthusiasm for Red China, were appointed
Vice-Ministers of Defence. On the other hand, Brig.-Gen. Nguyên Chi
Thanh, a Party fanatic who, as Chief of the Political Department of the
People's Army [*i.e.*, Political Commissar-in-Chief] had been known for
his unswerving devotion to the Peking line, found himself side-tracked in
the unenviable job as Minister of Agricultural Co-operatives at a time
when North Vietnam faced some fairly grim food crises.

The relinquishment in September 1961 of the top political post of
Lao-Dong Secretary-General by Ho Chi Minh in favour of Lê Duan,
generally considered as at least partly favourable to Peking (or at least
not objectionable to it) may be considered both as a renewed sign of
weakness on the part of the pro-Moscow wing, or as merely an outward
concession without deeper meaning. After all, Ho Chi Minh had once
before snatched the job away from a pro-Peking man when he felt that
circumstances demanded such a change. It remains to be seen whether
the more stringent measures taken against "anti-Party" elements in
Moscow will have an echo in Hanoi. Much will depend on Peking's
reaction to them.

THE POWER GROUPS

As of late 1960, the Vietnam *Dang Lao-Dong* (Workers' Party) counted half a million members throughout the country.[4] This figure compares with a 1946 level of 20,000 and a 1948 figure of 168,000.

The Communist Party thus represents the largest single organisation in the country, encompassing all activities and reaching from the highest councils of government and army to the lowest village in the rice fields. But the Party's ubiquity and numerical strength does not truly express its position of influence within the DRV. That influence is far better evident in the fact that several of the key members of the North Vietnamese régime are at the same time members of the Central Committee (*Tong-Bô*) of the Lao-Dong.

It is in that position that they have succeeded in imposing their imprint upon the whole country: harsh co-operativisation measures, trials of landlords; ideological control of all communication media, etc.

Yet, the Party itself, as has been shown previously, is not a monolith. Not only is it split along the Moscow-Peking axis, but it is also split along age-group lines: there are the "old Bolsheviks" of the calibre of Ho Chi Minh and Ton Duc Thang, in their seventies and dying out fast. Their education is generally broader, for they have not only fought the French but lived with them; to them the West is not merely a Frankenstein myth. That group, small as it was, is being rapidly overtaken by the Party bureaucrats—those whom this writer has called elsewhere the "civil servants, but not the combatants, of the Revolution." These bureaucrats —Lê Duan is fairly typical of them—are those who can be trusted with the reading of morose and long-winded speeches about the new general line; of droning on with interminable production statistics and even higher future economic goals; and of carrying out those tasks with an efficiency untouched by feelings of compassion.

For the time being, like the Soviet Communist Party two decades ago, the Lao-Dong leadership still suffers from the fact that, although pretending to lead a proletarian movement, it still has deep roots in the bourgeoisie. While more recent statistics on the subject have not been published, a 1953 self-critical study of the Party showed that out of 1,855 senior Party positions no less than 1,365 were held by intellectuals or bourgeois, as against 351 positions held by members of rural origin and 139 held by workers.[5] Considering the fact that Vietnam as a whole is 90 per cent. agricultural and certainly less than 1 per cent. "intellectual" (*i.e.*, composed of persons pursuing a liberal profession), it is very obvious that the Lao-Dong, as a power group, cannot claim to have deep

---

4 *Ibid.*, p. 11.
5 *Le Viet-Minh, op. cit.*, p. 173.

roots within the population—even assuming that all 500,000 Party members (out of a population of 30 million in both zones) were fully enthusiastic about the present leadership and political line.

The peasant rebellion of 1956 clearly showed up the weakness of the Party base in the rural areas and in 1957 the Lao-Dong officially changed its aim towards an increase of its urban and intellectual base, apparently considering the peasantry as a whole as " too reactionary."

> For a certain time [according to the Vietnam News Agency on April 19, 1957], the Party shall above all increase its strength in the cities and industrial centres, with the aim of recruiting best sons and daughters of the working class. At the same time, attention shall be paid to the development of the Party among the revolutionary intellectuals working at present in various branches of the public services.

It was probably through the massive recruitment drive of that period that the figure of 500,000 Party members was reached. As subsequent events were to prove, that increase in size did not solve the Party's problems of " rapport " with the people at large. It merely multiplied its cadre problem.

THE ARMY

The Vietnam People's Army is a power group perhaps second in size to the Lao-Dong, but surely ahead of it and of any other North Vietnamese organisation in effective power. Recruited largely from among the peasantry but also including units from the cities (such as the 308th Division, recruited in Hanoi) or even from the upland minorities (such as the 316th Division, or the 324th), it can truly claim to have deep roots within the country.

The recruitment of its senior officers also shows a far wider spread than that of the Lao-Dong. While such men as General Vo Nguyên Giap (with his Ph.D. from Hanoi University) can be described as " intellectuals," many other officers were trained in the hard school of the jungle itself, or rose from the lower and other ranks of the French Colonial Army. One of the senior commanders, Maj.-Gen. Chu Van Tan, was a former chief of pirates from the Thô minority and is now President of the Viet-Bac Autonomous Zone—one of the two areas comprising the major part of the mountaineer minority populations. Several other senior officers, such as the now-dead General Nguyen-Son, were trained in China and, like their Party counterparts, tend to espouse the views of their erstwhile teachers.

Thus, the V.P.A. is both more " people-based " than the Lao-Dong and at the same time harsher in the execution of unpopular policies because it perhaps feels more secure in its position in the country than the Lao-Dong does. During the peasant rebellion of 1956, the 325th Division crushed the unarmed farmers with the same iron discipline with which

Khrushchev's armour liquidated at precisely the same moment the Hungarian freedom fighters in Budapest. While farm co-operativisation encountered many difficulties among the peasants, the V.P.A. proceeded to man the first true collective farms (or, rather, state farms along the Sovkhoz model) in North Vietnam with farmer-soldiers culled from among the regulars.

It was also the political commissars of the V.P.A., who, meeting in a congress at Hanoi, warned the Lao-Dong of the possibility of a peasant uprising and criticised the Party functionaries for their ignorance of "real conditions" in the country. In fact, like many other professional armies, the V.P.A. had sufficiently shown its contempt for the intellectuals to warrant an open warning from the Lao-Dong's official newspaper *Nhan-Dan*:

> ... there seems to be an excess of prudence [in the V.P.A.] when it comes to entrusting intellectuals with posts or mission in accordance with their abilities. This shows a certain narrowness of mind which operates against the intellectuals. ...

From the V.P.A.'s viewpoint, developments in North Vietnam have not taken too favourable a turn. To be sure, the People's Army is the *enfant chéri* of the régime, receiving the best food in a period of severe shortages and having first call for equipment, clothing and housing. Its drab wartime and combat uniforms have been replaced by Soviet-patterned issue whose multi-coloured insignia and badges (not to speak of gold-braided shoulder boards not exactly suited to the tropical climate) is almost second to none in the Soviet *bloc*. A multiplicity of specialised military schools assures the V.P.A. of suitable cadre replacements—but still, there seems to be some discontent in the ranks, for in fact, the "civilians" (*e.g.*, the Party and government) had deprived the Army of the rightful fruits of its military victories in 1954 when they agreed to the splitting of Vietnam at the 17th parallel *not* out of military necessity but in obedience to Soviet pressures.[6]

With the prospect of more anti-DRV revolts in the offing (see below) and renewed tension between the pro-Moscow and the pro-Peking factions, the attitude of the V.P.A. leadership may well become a decisive factor in any North Vietnamese power struggle.

THE MANAGERIAL ELITE

The managerial elite, in North Vietnam, is neither large nor proficient. Largely composed of Party faithfuls or discharged army officers, it deserves mention here only because of its many contacts with Soviet *bloc*

---

[6] *Cf.* Lacouture, J. and Devillers, P., *Fin d'une guerre—Genève 1954* (Paris: Editions du Seuil, 1960). The generally accepted assertion is that the USSR traded North Vietnamese territory against a hope of prying France loose from her Western alliances.

technicians which give it a singularly important role in shaping North Vietnamese views of the outside world.

Many are the complaints on both sides, with the Eastern European experts privately (and even openly) asserting that the North Vietnamese are " unteachable " and unwilling to accept sound advice; and the Vietnamese (their professional as well as their national pride stung) are not loth to reply that the technicians from the " fraternal countries " are more aloof than even the colonialists of yesteryear and their machinery often less well adapted to local conditions than some of the old French machinery which, though on its last legs, at least has the advantage of being familiar.[7]

The hard fact is that North Vietnam, for years to come, simply lacks the engineering manpower to go with its industrial ambitions and that its Soviet *bloc* supporters are equally loth to loan out personnel whose skills are in short supply at home. For example, as recently as two years ago, the cotton mills of Nam Dinh, which employed forty-seven French engineers and foremen for 12,000 workers, had not one single qualified engineer; while the Quang-Yen—Hongay coal fields which, under French management, had employed more than 150 engineers and foremen, now had to make do with two " technicians " for their 11,000 miners.

For the time being, therefore, the North Vietnamese managerial class can be considered as a " power group " in the negative sense only, *i.e.*, by what it cannot do rather than by what it can do. In many cases it has been made the scapegoat (for, by virtue of its low quality, it is always easy to find some shortcomings in its activities) for all the errors in economic planning made by the régime and the present deteriorating economic situation has resulted in placing a heavy burden of responsibility on its shoulders.

THE PRESSURE GROUPS

In any totalitarian state, pressure without power is a fragile reed indeed. North Vietnam is no exception to the rule, and those groups among its population which have attempted to influence the course of events outside the accepted channels of the régime, have had to pay dearly for their daring. Of the three major groups in that category, two so far have made the attempt: the intellectuals and the peasantry. The third, the industrial labour force, for the time being enjoys the same privileged position as the Vietnam People's Army.

The intellectuals, at first, had been the most faithful supporters of the North Vietnamese régime: its firm anti-colonialist stand, its erstwhile

---

7 To quote but one precise example, a French " Peugeot " bicycle, although at least eight years old by now, fetches a second-hand price that is twice as high as that of a brand-new Czechoslovak bicycle.

lack of corruption, its seeming classlessness, all these contained powerful appeals which the competing southern régime lacks to this day. On the other hand, the harsh police state methods (whose imitation in the South is far more lax), and compulsion to total uniformity in the arts (almost totally absent in the South), form a yoke whose weight, in the long run, is unbearable. The result, in North Vietnam, was a gradual estrangement of the intellectuals from the régime. In disaccord with the Party, distrusted by the Army, many of them soon became guilty of " internal emigration," of *attentisme*.

When the " Hundred Flowers " movement drifted from China to North Vietnam in 1957, a veritable explosion took place in various art forms, which the régime found itself unable to control short of full-fledged measures of repression. By the time the intellectuals had returned to full conformism, many of them had found their way to labour camps along the Bac-Hung-Hai irrigation canal where they were able, according to the North Vietnamese press,

> . . . to see for themselves the vast work potential and creativity of the masses . . . [and where the intellectuals] finally understood that culture, literature and the arts spring from the masses and are destined to serve them, for it is the masses who are the most able to assimilate them and judge them. . . .

The peasant, representing 90 per cent. of the country's population and its economic backbone in the truest sense of the term, is both more vulnerable and more powerful than the intellectual pressure group. He is more vulnerable because a government decree, backed up by the ever-obedient People's Army, may deprive him of his livelihood or send him to a working party along the roads and canals of Vietnam. On the other hand, deliberate sabotage of the crops—an act that is as effective as it is suicidal—or the withholding of cattle from deliveries to the cities, can literally bring the country to the brink of ruin.

That is precisely what has happened in North Vietnam in 1961. According to *Nhan-Dan* of June 8, 1961, cattle deliveries had dropped to less than one-half the prescribed rate. Faced with rumours of impending complete collectivisation, peasant riots broke out in several areas and in Haiduong and Cao-Bang, large rice granaries were stormed and burned by the irate populace in April 1961. Coming at a time when natural calamities had reduced the rice crop to almost starvation levels, the DRV government found it more expedient to compromise than meet its peasantry head-on. Promises were made that more of the crop would be left in the hands of the peasants to sell at free market rates and that they would receive priority treatment in the attribution of essential consumer goods. It is unlikely that such concessions are more than a temporary " tactical retreat " in North Vietnam's struggle with its peasantry, but they are nonetheless an interesting sign of the strength of the DRV's peasantry as an informal pressure group.

Some Conclusions

While it is certain that the DRV, like all the other régimes of the Soviet orbit and many other non-Communist dictatorships, has at its command several levers of government which permit it to ride out some severe crises without immediate fear of a major explosion, it has, at the same time, to face the hard fact that is far less monolithic than it would like to be.

The fact that the People's Army is to a large extent loyal to the régime as presently constituted, gives the régime an inner strength which should not be lightly dismissed. On the other hand, that Army, like those of all the other Communist states, is but a tool in the hands of the political leadership. " Zhukovism," in Communist terminology, is a heresy only second to that of Titoism—and neither China nor Russia are likely to be willing to let North Vietnam become another Albania.

The tug-of-war between the Muscovite and Chinese wings of the Lao-Dong Party could, under certain circumstances, assume serious proportions, particularly if the succession to Ho Chi Minh's post were to open up in earnest. For the time being, in any case, neither of the two groups is likely to upset the precarious balance.

This leaves the peasantry of North Vietnam, endowed with a long tradition of endurance of hardships and hopeless rebellion, as the chink in the armour. A succession of bad crops could very well bring it into a state of open revolt with almost bare hands against one of the best armies in Asia, in which case the ultimate result may well be along the lines of Budapest in 1956—unless the West is willing to do something in Vietnam that it has carefully refrained from doing elsewhere.

And that is highly unlikely.

Intellectuals, Writers and Artists

By NHU PHONG

OF all intellectuals, the most highly respected and appreciated by Vietnamese society are the doctors. Indeed, it is hardly surprising that they should enjoy the esteem of a society the great majority of whose members are uneducated, impoverished, and beset by chronic disease and sickness. However, the reasons are twofold; medical degrees are academically superior to all others, and medicine, of all the professions, is the most useful on the purely practical plane. The doctors themselves are accorded the honorific title of " Thay," and the medical profession is popularly referred to by the descriptive phrase " savers of people and helpers of life." This is why, on the thirtieth anniversary of the Indo-Chinese Communist Party and the fifteenth anniversary of the Government of the Democratic Republic of (North) Vietnam, the " Doctor of Doctors," Ho Dac Di, who is Chairman of the North Vietnamese Medical Association as well as Director of the University and Specialist Colleges,[1] was invited to make a speech. Here is what Dr. Ho Dac Di said on that occasion:

> The future of the intellectuals is a glorious one, because their activities bind them closely to the proletarian masses who are the masters of the world, the masters of their own country, the masters of their history, and masters of themselves. . . . On this, the thirtieth anniversary of the foundation of the Party, all those classes who work with their brains, and the scientists in particular, sincerely own their debt of gratitude to the Party and proclaim their complete confidence in the enlightened leadership of the Party, as well as in the glorious future of the fatherland. They give their firm promise that they, together with the other classes of the people, will protect the great achievements of the revolution.[2]

Sixteen months later, on May 2, 1961, this elderly doctor, in his capacity as President of the North Vietnamese Medical Association, was obliged to sign the resolution to strike off the medical register one of his own former students, Dr. Le Van Long. This young doctor, trained in the North Vietnamese University of Socialist Medicine, had been condemned by the Hanoi People's Court to a suspended sentence of six months' imprisonment " for conduct calculated to deceive the sick, and for contravening the professional regulations laid down by the national

---

[1] This post is roughly the equivalent of that of Vice-Chancellor at a British University.
[2] *Tin-tuc Hoat-dong Khoa-hoc* (*News of Scientific Activities*), the information bulletin of the State Scientific Committee, January 1960.

authorities." At 6 p.m. on February 25, 1961, Dr. Le Van Long was caught red-handed by the People's Police in his own surgery at Tran Quoc Toan Street, Hanoi, when he was injecting a patient with two drugs, as he alleged, but was found to be using an empty hypodermic syringe. He had told the patient that he was injecting streptomycine and vitamin B.1, and he was making a charge of five *hao*[3] for the treatment.[4]

Dr. Ho Dac Di's complete capitulation to the Communist Party in the 1930s, when he was a graduate of the Faculty of Medicine in Paris and a member of the aristocracy of the former Imperial Court of Hue, was described by the Communists as a " positive facet of the intellectual class," while the stupid deceit of a doctor of the 1960s for the sake of a ridiculously small sum of money, the act of one of those " intellectuals with a glorious future," was described as a " negative facet." Do these two facets, " the positive and the negative," permit us to diagnose a state of " destruction of the soul ".[5] among the intellectuals as a class inside North Vietnam after fifteen years of life under the red flag ?

THE SPOILT CHILDREN OF THE ANTI-FRENCH RESISTANCE

One year after the Indo-Chinese Communist Party, the " seed of the Viet Minh leadership," had seized power, had founded the Democratic Republic of Vietnam, and had assumed control over half the territory of Vietnam, the Secretary-General of the Party, Truong Chinh, regretted that one of the four weak points of the August 1945 " revolution " was that the Communist Party had " failed to suppress the counter-revolutionaries." In August 1946 in the newspaper *Su That*, the organ of the Association for Marxist Studies,[6] he wrote :

> Because we failed to carry out a thorough suppression of our own reactionaries, the French reactionaries and the international reactionaries have been able to create difficulties for the revolutionary authorities and to divide the ranks of our people. We must ask ourselves: " Why, when it was first established, did the Cochin-Chinese Executive Committee not imprison immediately the traitorous pro-French clique of Nguyen Van Thinh, the most dangerous and cunning of the pro-Japanese traitors, and those specialists in subversion, the Trotskyists, but allowed them to prepare the way for the return of the French by their provocations before and during Independence Day [September 2, 1945]?" We must ask ourselves " Why were so many Vietnamese traitors, the treacherous pro-Japanese and the lackeys of

---

[3] 5 *hao* is roughly equal in value to sixpence (7 cents).
[4] *Nhan Dan* (*The People*), the Vietnamese Communists' daily newspaper, March 30, 1961.
[5] French dictum " Science sans conscience n'est que ruine de l'âme."
[6] After the meeting of the Central Association at Hanoi on November 8, 9, and 10, 1945, the Vietnamese Communist Party voluntarily dissolved itself. From then until 1951, the Vietnamese Communists operated under the pseudonym of the Association for Marxist Studies.

foreigners, permitted to remain at large once the People's Government had been established in the capital ? " [7]

The majority of the counter-revolutionary elements to whom the Secretary-General of the Indo-Chinese Communist Party referred were Vietnamese intellectuals, writers, journalists, scientists, technicians and teachers, who led the other anti-French nationalist parties and who fought against the Communist authorities in a civil war which lasted from August 1945 until July 1946 in Tonking.

A small minority of the Vietnamese intellectuals, on the other hand, those who had formerly served the French or the Japanese, wasted no time in making their submission to a new master, the Communists, as soon as the red flag was hoisted over Hanoi. The Imperial Delegate, Phan Ke Toai, who had been appointed by the Japanese Army to direct, on behalf of the Imperial Court at Hue, the French administration left behind in North Vietnam, invited the Communists into his official palace and voluntarily surrendered his authority to them. During that same period, well-known journalists who shaped public opinion in South Vietnam, men such as Phan Van Hum and Ta Thu Thau, were condemned to death by special Viet Minh courts because they were found to be "reactionary Trotskyist elements."

During its early years of power in North Vietnam the Communist Party was unable to execute one clear-cut policy towards the intellectuals in general. Developments followed one another so rapidly that it had no time to apply the tactics which Lenin and Stalin had applied to the Russian intellectuals. In the event, throughout the first year of the Government of the Democratic Republic of Vietnam, the Communists were fully occupied with the intellectuals. They were engaged in a desperate struggle to win the sympathies of those intellectuals who maintained a neutral attitude in the civil war being fought in Tonking and, at the same time, they were striving to counteract all the artifices—such as bribery and flattery—employed by the French to win over the intellectuals of Cochin China to the French side. At the beginning of the second year, when they had only just repulsed the armed forces of the rival nationalist parties and driven these across the Chinese frontier, but before they had been able to mop up all the bases which these forces had left behind, the Communists had to face the rapidly increasing pressure of the French Expeditionary Corps, to which they themselves had conceded the right to establish military bases at a number of places in Tonking. But the real Indo-Chinese war did not break out until December 19, 1946.

At that moment, with the exception of a very small number of intellectuals whose hostility was too well known to the Communists and who

7 Truong Chinh, *The Vietnamese August Revolution* (Hanoi: Su-That Publishing House [reprint], 1954), p. 35.

knew they had no chance of survival if they left the cities, virtually all the Vietnamese intellectuals felt that they had no choice but to go to the countryside to avoid any form of collaboration with the French Expeditionary Corps. They would have regarded that as a betrayal of their country. Their natural patriotism spurred them into joining the resistance at once and offering any talents and abilities they possessed in order to halt the advance of the invading French soldiers. Most of these men had not forgotten the Communist nature of the resistance government, but were encouraged by the hope that they might use the resistance organisation to assemble nationalist elements and to create a force which would actually tilt the balance of the scales against the Communists within the ranks of the resistance.

The Communist leaders of the resistance government for their part, to avoid surrender to the French Expeditionary Corps, had no alternative but to encourage and welcome all assistance volunteered to them, and the intellectuals were in the van of the volunteers. The Secretary-General of the Indo-Chinese Communist Party understood only too well that, if he exploited the circumstances of the resistance in order to correct the shortcoming of "failing to suppress completely the counter-revolutionaries," the only result he could hope to achieve would be to drive the intellectuals into an agreement with the French to establish a Vietnam " independent within the Indo-Chinese Union and the French Union."

The murder of Khai-Hung, former editor of the newspaper *Viet Nam*, the central organ of the anti-Communist nationalist forces during the civil war in Tonking, was the only case of eliminating intellectuals to be established beyond doubt during the opening months of the resistance war. His murder took place in the countryside of Nam-dinh province, and the two contributory causes seem to have been the excessive zeal of the local Communists and the resolute anti-Communism of the victim himself. There is no evidence to suggest that this murder was premeditated or carried out on the orders of the Central Committee of the Communist Party.

A colleague and very close friend of the writer Khai-Hung was Dang Thai Mai, a man who followed the Communists simply because his daughter was the wife of Vo Nguyen Giap, had the following to say about the attitude of the Vietnamese writers during the early stages of the resistance war:

> From the very beginning, they (the writers) applied themselves with enthusiasm and energy to whatever activity their country demanded of them in time of war. They fought alongside ordinary coolies, resisted their country's enemies side by side with the peasants. They shared with

these men the terrible privations of life in the jungle and, like them, they lived and worked in an atmosphere of the most fervent patriotism.[8]

This is an accurate assessment, though it is the *only* judgment which is correct in the whole article on Vietnamese literature, by the Chairman of the North Vietnamese Arts and Letters Association, from which it is quoted. He goes on to recall how the engineer, Ho Dac Vi [9] rolled leaves up in newspaper and smoked them instead of cigarettes while he was working with a team of engineers constructing an iron foundry at Thanh-hoa; how Dr. Pham Huu Chuong,[10] dressed in peasant clothes, would journey backwards and forwards close to the battlefields between Chi-ne and Phu-nho-quan supervising the mobile clinics which treated the wounded soldiers and, at the same time, training his students; how the writer Phan Khoi,[11] already well beyond sixty, would follow the units of soldiers as they moved about in the jungle-clad mountains of Viet Bac, leaning on a stick as he hobbled along. . . . But this atmosphere of concord and peace between the intellectuals and the Communists quickly vanished after Mao Tse-tung had made himself master of mainland China.

Early in 1950, in addition to the arms, the munitions, the military and political advisers sent by the Chinese Communist Party across the border to help the Vietnamese Communists, who had by then been driven back by the French into the wild, mountainous and jungle-covered areas, there was a plentiful supply of Communist instruction books suitable for use with people of every intellectual level. Vietnamese intellectuals with a knowledge of Chinese were mobilised to work in shifts all around the clock translating into Vietnamese the basic documents on Marxism-Leninism-Maoism, Mao's utterances before the Central Committee of the Party, texts on the Chinese revolution, articles by Liu Shao-ch'i on thought reform, and countless others of the same kind. All had to be translated so that the Vietnamese leaders might study them and try to find Chinese methods applicable in Vietnam.

It required only one training course, given by the Secretary-General himself to specially selected cadres brought together from a large number of places, in which Truong Chinh explained the ideas which he had just gleaned from his study of Chinese documents, to set in motion a great wave of intellectuals returning to the French-controlled zone. The

---

8 Dang Thai Mai, "Vietnamese Literature," *Europe*, No. 387–388, July-August 1961, Special Number on Vietnamese Literature, p. 91.

9 The younger brother of Ho Dac Di, mentioned at the beginning of this article. He is now working as a specialist in the Ministry of Agriculture, Republic of (South) Vietnam.

10 Now President of the Medical Board, Republic of (South) Vietnam.

11 The editor of the paper *Nhan Van* published in Hanoi towards the end of 1956. He was one of the leaders of the group struggling for democratic freedom in North Vietnam during the 1956–57 period.

Vietnamese even invented the slang phrase " *dinh te ve te* " [12] to describe the act of returning to the French. The more the principles learned from the Chinese Communists were applied, the longer became the lines of disillusioned intellectuals abandoning the ranks of the resistance movement. Doctors, engineers, professors, lawyers, writers, and journalists, together with tens of thousands of others, abandoned their posts as inspectors, directors, committee members, headmasters, and the like, to make the long journey past hundreds of checkpoints manned by the people's guerrillas, resistance soldiers, and the people's security police, back to the cities of North and Central Vietnam. Five years earlier, when they had left these same cities, they had sworn never to return before every trace of the French soldiers had been obliterated. Only those who were too far away from any of the zones controlled by the French soldiers and the Bao Dai Government, and those who had already penetrated too deeply into the Communist organisations, resigned themselves to the disgrace of remaining to work side by side with the Communists.

Not a single intellectual harboured any more illusions about the nationalist character of the resistance government any longer. At the beginning of 1951, the Indo-Chinese Communist Party convened its second National Party Congress and officially changed its name to the Vietnamese Lao Dong (Workers') Party, the change of name to date from February 11. This was done so as to remind itself of its twin duties—to advance the proletarian revolution and to provide leadership for the resistance struggle throughout the whole country.

BREAKING WITH THE PAST

After the Indo-Chinese Communist Party had been re-established and given a new name, almost all the intellectuals still remaining in the resistance zone were invited to become members of the party. They were threatened that, if they refused membership, they would be denounced as reactionaries, and, at the same time, were tempted to join by promises of special privileges. By means of this twofold persuasion, the Central Party Organisation engineered a great increase in Party membership, and it did not insist that the new members should have acquired all the qualifications laid down as necessary in the Party regulations.

The artists and writers were objects of very special attention in the sudden expansion of the Party because their talents and abilities were badly needed by the Party for the purpose of producing its propaganda. The first course of " thought reform " to be given to a group of young artists and writers who had newly joined the Party was hastily organised

---

[12] A closer translation is " To return to the zone in which order has been restored by the French."

at Viet Bac in 1951. The sole object of this thought reform course was not so much to instil into the students a basic knowledge of Communism, but simply to provide them with a vocabulary which would pass for a Communist one. As soon as they had completed the course, these young men were immediately promoted in rank and distributed among the many resistance organisations, particularly among units of the armed forces, their duties being to conduct propaganda and, by this means, to increase the reputation and influence of the Party.

At the end of their first year in this work, the Party selected from among the new cadres those whom it considered to be endowed with exceptional abilities. The cadres hand-picked in this way, who were destined eventually to become Special Communist Cultural cadres, were sent to China for further training. There they were instructed by their " elder brothers on the other side of the frontier " in the " Chinese system of arts and letters " and were then sent back home to apply inside Vietnam what they had learned. One young poet from the resistance forces in Son-la Province, Tran Dan, was declared a bright new star in the cultural firmament of Viet Bac simply because he had studied the Chinese system of arts and letters.

Thanks to the enormous aid which the Chinese supplied in every sphere, the Vietnamese Communist Party achieved a very great measure of success during the first two years of its existence. The soldiers of the French Expeditionary Corps had been defeated in several large battles along the Sino-Vietnamese border and, most important, in Hoa-binh, the gateway which led from the upland jungle regions into the rice granary of the Red River Delta. Hoa-binh was also the bridge which linked the fourth and fifth interzones of Central Vietnam with the central organs of the Party in the Viet Bac interzone. Although they had scarcely raised the level of their understanding of Marx-Lenin-Engels-Stalin-Mao-ism at all, the Vietnamese Communists had certainly contrived to generate a new spirit by their military victories.

In the spring of 1953, while the military might of the Vietnamese Communists was being hurled into the attack on the Red River Delta, the fourth assembly of the Party's Central Committee decided to proceed with agrarian reforms conducted along exactly the same lines as those laid down by the Chinese Communists. The *Principles of Land Ownership* which were approved by this assembly stated unequivocally :

> The system of land ownership in force in Vietnam under the rule of the French colonialists must be destroyed completely, and the feudal system of ownership of ricefields by landlords must be abolished. A system of land ownership by the agricultural workers must be established, so that the land belongs to the man who works it.

The resistance intellectuals, who had collaborated for so long with the Party, were filled with dread by the new principles because, if the principles were fully applied, then every Vietnamese intellectual would be found to have been born in a class which the Party called " the feudal landlord class," " the enemies of the proletariat." However, because it was eager to " isolate and disperse the landlord class, and to limit the area of land owner," the Political Office of the Party Headquarters temporarily assigned the intellectuals to the ranks of the resistance.

For the very first time, the class of people known as intellectuals was defined in *The List of Social Classes Determined by the Government*.[12a] The definition runs as follows :

> *Intellectuals*: Intellectuals do not form a distinct class of their own. The class to which intellectuals belong will be determined by the class to which the families from which they originated belong. Those intellectuals who have earned their livelihood by working at a trade or profession for periods of one year or more, and who are not dependent on their families, will be classified on the basis of the work which they have performed.

The profession of the intellectual is referred to in clearer terms in the section devoted to " Persons working in the liberal professions " :

> These are persons working independently at their own professions and not exploiting others, such as lawyers, doctors, physicians, writers, journalists, comic actors, tragic actors, etc. When such people employ others as assistants, they cannot be regarded as exploiting these. If such persons work for an industry, for a private organisation, or for the state, they will be known as officials.

However, the two passages cited above were not sufficient to enable the great majority of intellectuals to escape from the charge of being " exploiting landlords." The reason for this is that the overwhelming majority of the resistance intellectuals were

> persons owning agricultural land, but not working that land themselves, or working only part of it, the principal source of whose livelihood was the exorbitant rent from the land.

For this reason, yet another section of persons was created, that consisting of " Progressive Personalities." This was defined as

> individuals of the landlord class who participated positively in the resistance war against the imperialist interventionists, against the traitorous Vietnamese puppets, and who have enthusiastically supported the popular democratic authorities, wholeheartedly executing the agricultural and all other democratic policies of the Government.

In order to be regarded as " Progressive Personalities," those intellectuals who owned land were obliged to " voluntarily present all the land

---

[12a] *The List of Social Classes Determined by the Government (Temporary List)*, No. 239–B/TTg was promulgated by the Prime Minister of the Democratic Republic of Vietnam in March 1953.

they possessed to the people" in good time, that is to say, before the date of the promulgation of the Land Reform Law. They had, at the same time, to undergo a course of re-education so that, with the help of the Party, they might break completely with their old way of life.

Generally speaking, the thought reform courses for the intellectuals proceeded quietly enough, but those attended by the writers and poets were accorded the maximum of noisy propaganda. The names of the poets, the authors, and the journalists were far better known among the ordinary people than those of the doctors, the professors, or the teachers. For this reason, the best-known writers were invited to produce written confessions in which they admitted to more serious crimes than any of the others. The poets The Lu, Xuan Dieu, Huy Can, Luu Trong Lu, Che Lan Vien, and Tu Mo, all people whose names had been well known to the Vietnamese people for ten or even twenty years, were more enthusiastic than any one else, once their thought control course had been completed, in denouncing all the works they had produced before the date of their entry into the Party. All these poets noisily proclaimed that the poems which everyone had acclaimed in the old days were, in truth, no more than the products of a decadent culture. They avowed that all those people who had encouraged them and led them to follow the career of writers were, in fact, Vietnamese traitors acting upon French orders and simply trying to push them along the path of decadence themselves.

Tens of thousands of copies of the confessions and self-criticisms produced by the writers on completing their thought reform courses in 1953 were published by the Party and distributed to cadres of all grades in every branch of activity, with special attention being paid to military units. They were used as documents for study so that they might cleanse the decadent thoughts which had been introduced into the brains of these cadres and soldiers by the earlier writers of Vietnamese literature.

THE MOVEMENT TO WIN DEMOCRATIC FREEDOM IN TIME OF PEACE

The preliminary thought reform courses for the intellectuals, which were directly connected with the agrarian reforms, had scarcely ended when the Indo-Chinese war entered its final stage. As a consequence of the desperate and ferocious battles fought on the bloodstained plains of north Vietnam, and in particular, of the gigantic slaughterhouse of Dien Bien Phu, both the French and Communist troops were completely exhausted in July 1954. The Geneva Conference brought the Indo-Chinese war to an end.

But those clauses of the Geneva agreements which imposed a temporary barrier across Vietnam at the 17th parallel, dividing the country into a northern and southern zone, as well as those granting a period of

300 days in which the people of both zones were free to choose the place where they wished to reside, in the event, brought no advantage to the intellectuals and writers who had collaborated with the Communists during the resistance. The confused, almost chaotic situation in south Vietnam, allied with the continuing presence of French Expeditionary Corps soldiers, made this zone appear to these intellectuals to fall very far short of the promised land for which they sought. Moreover, a fierce pride filled the ragged skeletons to which eight years of merciless war had reduced their bodies, so that they regarded their old friends, whom they saw leaving the north, as spiritless lackeys abandoning their responsibilities as Vietnamese and following the enemy southwards in the hope of being rewarded with a little butter or a tin of condensed milk. The news that the South Vietnamese Government was receiving every sort of aid from the United States and from the other Western democracies had been hopelessly distorted by the time it reached their ears.

Again, the ill-defined attitude of the South Vietnamese Government towards the intellectuals and writers of north Vietnam impelled a number of Tonkinese, even though they were in no way favourably disposed towards Communism and had not fought in the resistance movement for a single day, to remain in the north. These were men such as Dr. Pham Khac Quang, an intellectual who in 1943 had been tracked down by the French intelligence service for his crime of organising subscriptions of money for the anti-French movement headed by Tran Trong Kim and Ngo Dinh Diem; such as Ton That Hoat, regarded as the envoy of the northern intellectuals going south to investigate conditions on the spot, who left the north with all his worldly possessions, but who returned once more to Hanoi; such as the hundreds of other writers, journalists, and professors whose political attitudes were too clearly defined or who had held important posts under the Bao Dai or French régimes.

For its part, the Communist government was obliged to devote all its attention and energies to the takeover of the administration of north Vietnam from the French and to transforming, in a very short space of time, the existing military apparatus into an apparatus capable of governing in time of peace. It is true that its efforts to accomplish these two tasks were directed by large numbers of Chinese and Russian advisers, but it would never have succeeded without the co-operation of all the intellectuals in north Vietnam. This fact was recognised very early on by the Communists, which is why the Ho Chi Minh government sent out, well before it was entitled to enter Hanoi in September 1954, very large numbers of cadres to approach the intellectuals in the city and to terrorise or to coax them into remaining in north Vietnam. The writers in the ranks of the resistance displayed tremendous energy and enthusiasm in their propaganda campaign against the wave of refugees moving southwards. They met with little success among the masses of city workers or peasants, but in some cases they were able to persuade numbers of their former colleagues from going to the south.

Throughout the whole of the 300 days which had been granted to allow both sides adequate time to assemble and regroup their armed forces, the Communist Government of North Vietnam maintained a most liberal attitude towards such of the writers, the intellectuals, and the specialists of the former régime as agreed to remain behind and work for the new one. These men were paid the same salary each month as they had received from their former employers, while their colleagues working alongside them, the resistance intellectuals, received only the monetary equivalent of 100 kilos of rice per month. To compensate these latter, the Communists accorded them plenty of honours and praise. This is the explanation for all the orders of meritorious service in the revolutionary resistance which became widespread in so short a space of time. The only Communist poet in Vietnam, To Huu, who is a member of the Secretariat of the Party Central Committee, has recalled the whispered comment on the lips of all the intellectuals with meritorious service to the resistance orders in 1955: " The Party can supply expert leadership in fighting the enemy, but now is the period for constructive work. The Party can no longer lead, but should give way to the intellectuals." [13]

As far as the artists and writers themselves were concerned, their slogans were doubly strong: " Politics cannot control literature or the arts." Leading this group were the artists and writers of the People's Army. In the year 1955, the poet Hoang-Cam, in his capacity as Battalion Commander in charge of the Military Arts and Letters Bureau, Tran Dan, who represented literature, Tu Phac, who represented music, and almost thirty other artists and writers drafted a resolution to the Party Central Committee " demanding the abolition of the General Political Bureau's leadership over arts and letters in the army." [14]

Accompany this resolution was an " Outline Policy for Arts and Letters," in which the artists and writers in the army made three principal demands :

(1) Hand over the leadership of arts and letters to the artists and writers. (2) Establish an arts and letters association within the structure of army organisation. (3) Abolish the existing military régime insofar as it affects the artists and writers serving in the armed forces.[15]

To demonstrate its contempt for this movement, the Central Political Bureau resorted to direct action. It arrested the soldier poet Tran Dan,

13 *Van Nghe (Arts and Letters)*, No. 13, June 1958, p. 17.
14 *Van Nghe*, No. 11, April 1958, p. 106.
15 *Ibid.*, p. 79.

whom it regarded as the principal advocate of this opposition to the Party. While in prison, Tran Dan severed his jugular vein, but he survived this attempted suicide and was nursed back to health, and, after he had been " investigated," was temporarily released.

A year after this, as a result of developments both inside North Vietnam and abroad, the resistance movement of the writers and intellectuals was able to seize democratic freedom and again went into action, this time overtly and twice as strongly as before. While Khrushchev was destroying the image of Stalin in Russia at the 20th Party Congress of the Soviet Union, the agrarian reforms in North Vietnam had entered their most decisive phase. Exactly in accord with the instructions given to it by the Chinese Communist Party, the Vietnamese Lao Dong Party " unleashed the might of the masses to destroy the landlord class." From village to village the landlords and their families were all punished by the special " Land Reform Courts," and after them the rich peasants and the middle peasants whom the " masses' representatives " considered to be landlords. Scenes of the most horrifying kind were witnessed in every village and hamlet. Battalion commanders in the People's Army were recalled from their military camps to their native villages, where they were stripped of their Party offices, stripped of their military rank, stripped of their decorations for bravery, and then beaten and sentenced to prison for their crime of " being the children of landlords." " Young children of six " [16] were forced to fend for themselves and to beg for food because their parents had had to " pay their debt of blood," or, in plainer language, had been executed.

The first to rise in indignation against these terrible happenings were the intellectuals who had been classified among the revolutionary and resistance personalities, and in the van were the writers, the poets, the journalists, the lawyers, and the university professors with their students. One month after Mr. Khrushchev made his political denunciation before the 20th Congress of the Soviet Communist Party, those same artists and writers of the North Vietnamese People's Army who had drafted the resolution refusing the leadership of the Party over arts and letters a year before, on their own initiative published a journal which proclaimed publicly to the masses their opposition to the Party. The name of the journal was *Giai Pham Mua Xuan* (*Literary Masterpieces of the Spring*), and it was published in March 1956. The opening of the " Hundred Flowers " campaign by the Chinese Communist Party in May 1956, followed soon after by the revolt of the Polish workers in Poznan, rekindled in the hearts of the Vietnamese, who had suffered so much

[16] The title of a poem published by Hoang Cam, *Giai Pham Mua Thu*, September 1956.

pain and hardship during the eight years of war against the French, the desire for liberty and democracy.

The confusion of the Lao Dong Party before the conditions of extreme disorder, poverty, and hunger brought about by the agrarian reforms, afforded an opportunity for the North Vietnamese intellectuals to advance still further. August saw the publication of the first number of *Giai Pham Mua Thu* (*Literary Masterpieces of the Autumn*), and this issue was published with the support of far larger numbers of writers, artists, and intellectuals. Moreover, its articles attacked the Party in less veiled fashion than hitherto. In September, to forestall the outbreak of a rebellion aimed at " overthrowing the Democratic Republican régime and the leadership of the Party," the Central Committee of the Lao Dong Party admitted that " a number of grave errors had been committed during the execution of the land reforms." In addition to promising that these errors would be corrected, the communique of the 10th plenum of the Party's Central Committee also announced that the Party would " extend democracy, safeguard democratic liberties and enlarge the system of democratic legality." At the same time, it announced that it would " improve the conditions of life of the workers, the soldiers, the cadres, and the officials."

Exactly copying the policy of Mao Tse-tung, when he launched his " Hundred Flowers " movement, the Vietnamese Lao Dong Party allowed the " different tendencies the freedom to discuss and argue " for a limited period of time. On September 15, permission to publish the journal *Nhan Van* (*Humanities*) was granted and its first number appeared. The editor was Phan Khoi, a very old journalist who had devoted the whole of his life to opposing with his pen the French colonial régime in Indo-China and who had followed the soldiers during the resistance war, hobbling along with the aid of a stick, to encourage them in their fight against the French. In addition, *Giai Pham Mua Thu* published a second and a third number, and then changed its title to *Giai Pham Mua Dong* (*Literary Masterpieces of the Winter*). One development which took the Lao Dong Party by surprise was the fact that all the journalists who were most outstanding in their professional work and in political theory published pieces in the journal *Nhan Van*.

Every shade of political and non-political opinion attacked the Party. There were the nationalists who believed simply in the final victory of a free Vietnam, the national Communists, even the Communist revisionists, and all were represented by distinguished spokesmen. They were the " trumpets of the August 1945 revolution, the drums of the anti-French resistance," in the words of the musician Van Cao, the writer of the Vietnamese national anthem, which is still used to this day. There were writers whose works were compared with the " glorious victory of

Dien Bien Phu " like Tran Dan, the author of the novel *Nguoi Nguoi Lop Lop*, which the writers of north Vietnam regard as the only literary work of permanent value to emerge during the whole eight years of resistance war. There were men who had believed unswervingly in Marxism for decades, like Tran Duc Thao the philosopher who, in 1951, had abandoned his post of professor at the Sorbonne to return to Vietnam and play his part in the resistance war, like the journalist Nguyen Huu Dang, the Vice-Minister of Youth in Ho Chi Minh's first government. There were men who, until then, had always striven to avoid allegiance to any political doctrine, men like the artist Tran Duy, the poet Nguyen Binh, the professor of history Dao Duy Anh, and the professor of law Nguyen Manh Tuong. There were outstanding writers from the ranks of the resistance movement in south Vietnam like Hoang Hue. Copying the example of the older intellectuals, artists and writers, the students of the universities in Hanoi published their own journal, *Dat Moi* (*New Land*), in which they too attacked the Party.

Within the space of three months, however, this movement was smashed. In mid-December 1956 the journal *Nhan Van* was closed down, while all copies of *Giai Pham Mua Dong* and *Dat Moi* were confiscated, their circulation forbidden, and their very existence hushed up. The artists, writers, and intellectuals who had led this movement against the Party were accused of " plotting to incite the masses to carry out counter-revolutionary demonstrations in order to overthrow the popular democratic régime and the leadership of the Party." It was too late for them to follow the example of the Hungarian people. The leaders of the movement against the Party shared the same fate as their Chinese colleagues, Ting Ling, Feng Hsüeh-feng and the rest.

TOWARDS A POLICY OF REFORMING THE INTELLECTUALS, WRITERS, AND ARTISTS

The storm had reduced the danger, and the Party was now well aware of the necessity for applying a harsh policy towards the intellectuals, artists, and writers, if it wished to avoid a new outburst of all the anti-Party tendencies. First a restricted meeting of senior Party officials responsible for the leadership of the intellectuals, artists and writers, was convened in the middle of December 1956. Its objects were " to unify Party views and thoughts on the subject of arts and letter, to reach a decision about the journal *Nhan Van*, and to point out the direction of future progress." [17]   Progress, in the form of applying the Party's new policy, was no more than the repetition of the old tactic " move back one pace in order to advance three paces." The pace backward took the form

[17] *Van Nghe*, No. 13, June 1957.

of a discussion meeting, arranged for January 1957, of 300 intellectuals, artists, and writers, both inside and outside the Party. In the course of the discussion meeting, both sides attacked and criticised one another before finally agreeing to convene a general meeting of the National Association of Arts and Letters on February 20, 1957.

While the non-Party artists and writers were busily preparing resolutions to put to the General Meeting which would secure the initiative for the liberal wing, their Party colleagues were furiously studying Party policy towards writers and artists. All the important Russian and Chinese documents dealing with methods of controlling intellectuals, artists and writers were translated into Vietnamese for use as models by the cadres responsible for providing leadership to the intellectuals. One of the basic documents to be circulated was the " Statement on the Question of the Intellectuals " by Chou En-lai.[18] Translations of documents like this had been made by the Central Training Section of the Party by the first week of November 1956. Four principles for reforming intellectuals which had been put forward by the Chinese Communists were adopted by the Lao Dong Party in their entirety. According to these principles, intellectuals, artists and writers must :

1. Change their old philosophy of life and develop a revolutionary philosophy.
2. Adopt the standpoint of the proletariat.
3. Study Marxism/Leninism and the thoughts of Mao Tse-tung.
4. Harden themselves by manual labour.

Nevertheless, in the course of the second National General Meeting of the Arts and Letters Association, the representatives of the Lao Dong Party made no reference to the question of reforming the intellectuals, writers, and artists. On the contrary, they strove to mislead the latter into thinking that the Party had agreed to abandon the policy of forcing them to tread the path of Communism. Truong Chinh, who had recently resigned from his post as Party Secretary-General, addressed the Meeting on February 24, 1957, and the title of his speech described the leadership of the Party as simply " Striving for a popular arts and letters (movement) under the flag of patriotism and socialism." [19] To Huu, the Deputy Minister of Culture and the man who had been most bitterly attacked by the anti-Party intellectuals during the preceding months, speaking on behalf of the President of the National Association, made the following affirmation on February 28 :

> In cultural and artistic activities, we can and should have different
> tendencies in our common standpoint, for this is of benefit to our

[18] Professor of the Trung-Nguyen University in China. The Vietnamese translation was published by the Su That Publishing House, March 7, 1957.
[19] *Van Nghe*, No. 162, March 1-7, 1957.

country and our people. All ideas and all artistic tendencies can and must result from discussion.[20]

As a result of this National General Meeting, the establishment of a new organisation, the Union of Arts and Letters, was announced, an organisation embracing all the existing associations of persons engaged in literature, art, architecture, music, the stage, the circus, and films. All the intellectuals who had so actively attacked the Party during the past year were appointed to the executive Committee of the new organisation. Van Cao, who had denounced Communist members at the top of his voice and had told them all to get out,[21] was elected Deputy First Secretary of the new Union.

The Association of Writers, as a member body of the newly formed Union of Letters and Arts, was authorised to publish a weekly journal called *Van (Literature).*

The first number of *Van* appeared on May 10, 1957, but the journal was published only up to No. 37, which appeared on January 17, 1958, when its authorisation was withdrawn. Although it had correctly observed the resolutions of the second National General Meeting of the Arts and Letters Association, *Van* was accused of continuing the anti-Party agitation. In spite of the fact that it simply used its " right to have different tendencies " and was only " striving for a popular arts and letters (movement) under the flag of patriotism and Socialism," the real crime committed by *Van* was to have published the work of artists and writers who had so strongly attacked the Party in 1956. The truth is that, at the beginning of 1958, the Lao Dong Party saw that the danger threatening it had passed and that the Party must now apply a strong policy in order to prepare North Vietnam for its journey along the " road to Socialist construction."

Before the weekly *Van* was closed down and the whole propaganda apparatus of the Party and Government was mobilised to unleash a mass movement and clear away all obstacles from the " thought front," a resolution of the Political Bureau dated January 6, 1958, decreed:

> By exploiting the weaknesses of the arts and letters front, and in particular the confused nature of the thinking of the majority of artists and writers, the saboteurs have contrived to continue their activities and to cause very serious damage. It is clear that the anti-Socialist and anti-Party elements have profited from our laxness to continue their attacks on us in the sphere of ideas and under the guise of arts and letters. The activities of these saboteurs among the artists and writers constitute a most dangerous threat and must be dealt with urgently.

For a period of six whole months without respite, between January and June 1958, at every level in every branch of every organisation

---

[20] *Ibid.*
[21] He published the poem " Have You Noticed?" in *Giai Pham Mua Xuan,* 1956.

throughout the whole of North Vietnam, the cadres and Party members were forced to take part in a " struggle against the saboteurs on the arts and letters front." Hundreds of newspaper articles all spoke with one voice, reviling seven writers and three intellectuals regarded as the representatives of the anti-Party tendency. Thousands of resolutions, bearing millions of signatures from cadres, soldiers, workers, and peasants, were collected by Party officials in all localities and forwarded to the Central Office of the Party and to the Government demanding that they should straightaway punish the " saboteurs, the agents of the enemy, now undermining us in the field of ideas and thoughts."

Two re-education courses were opened for nearly 500 writers and artists on January 26, 1958, while the Party's Thought Police carried out investigations to secure the arrest of elements spreading the spirit of the U.S./Diem lackeys who were hiding in the Art Associations, Theatrical Workers' Associations, and Musical Associations. They observed that these associations concealed exactly the same phenomena as had been discovered in the Writers' Association.

In the universities, places which the Party regarded as the " bastions of counter-revolution," especially the Teachers' Training College and the letters and history faculties, the teachers and the students studied " through struggle " so as to eradicate completely the " disciples and teachers of Trotskyism," the doctrine which Professors Tran Duc Thao and Truong Tuu had spread. Among the people, particularly in the cities and big towns, the Party also launched a campaign to denounce capitalist saboteurs who had assisted, either by encouragement or by more material means, the former Deputy Minister Nguyen Huu Dang and the former " Democratic Personality " Tran Thieu Bao, who directed the Minh-Duc publishing house, to produce the anti-Party periodicals and books in 1956.

A re-education course which lasted from March 3 until April 14, 1958, was given to 304 writers, artists, and intellectuals. During the course, every one of these was obliged to make a self-criticism which set out clearly the crimes or the errors which each had committed during the period when he was directing or participating in the anti-Party movement and struggling to win democratic freedom. Through this re-education course it become known that a group of musicians and poets led by Van Cao had decided to flee to South Vietnam, and that a group of artists, writers, and intellectuals who subscribed to the revisionist Communism advocated by Professors Tran Duc Thao and Truong Tuu had " decided to flee to a non-Communist country, perhaps even France." [22] On completion of the course, " all 304 artists, writers, and literary cadres " had signed a letter dated April 14, 1958, to the Headquarters

[22] Admitted by Le Dat, *Van Nghe*, No. 12, May 1958.

of the Lao Dong Party in which they voluntarily accepted the four principles for the reform of intellectuals laid down by the Party.[23]

Four days before the termination of the course, on April 10, 1958, the Hanoi police arrested and imprisoned the journalist Nguyen Huu Dang, the poetess Luu Thi Yen, who wrote under the pen name of Thuy An, and the publisher Tran Thieu Bao on the charge that " during the year 1956 this group had disguised itself in the trappings of literature and art in order to carry out anti-Government and anti-régime activities, and that since that time they had continued their sabotage operations." [24]

Twenty-one months later, this case was brought before the court for trial. However, in the Hanoi People's Court on January 19, 1960, the case had lost all its former character of a trial connected with arts and letters. The accused were charged with the crime of " acting as spies and as psychological warfare cadres for the U.S./Diem clique." Six people, among whom were a poetess, two journalists, a theatrical producer, and a publisher, received sentences ranging from five to fifteen years' imprisonment.[25] *Van Hoc*, the new organ of the Writers' Association, supplied the following additional information:

> Other elements who were involved in the plots and the activities of the Nguyen Huu Dang group, bore a lesser degree of guilt. These persons have not been charged before a court of law, but have been assisted by the Party and the Government. They have been sent to study in re-education camps so that they may become good and worthwhile citizens.[26]

The elderly writer Phan Khoi, the spiritual leader of the movement of the intellectuals, writers, and artists to struggle for democratic freedoms in 1956, died three days before he was due to face trial at the age of seventy-two. Seven months later, his only son, Phan Thao, the editor of the publication *Thong-Nhat (Unity)*, which is the organ of the Fatherland Front in Hanoi, also died.

RE-EDUCATING THE OLD AND TRAINING THE YOUNG

Since the middle of 1958, when it " smashed the hostile political thinking and the reactionary ideas of the artists and writers," the Lao Dong Party has wasted no time. It has exploited the ascendancy which it won by its harsh treatment of the offenders to push ahead immediately with the task of re-educating the existing intellectuals, artists and writers, and at the same time, with training the new men to be completely Socialist.

In June 1958, Ho Chi Minh appeared in person to open the ten-month political re-education course for senior personalities and intellectuals throughout the whole of North Vietnam. In July, while the Union of

---

23 *Van Nghe*, No. 12, May 1958.
24 *Nhan Dan*, April 19, 1958.
25 *Nhan Dan*, January 20, 1960.
26 *Van Hoc*, No. 80, February 5, 1960.

Arts and Letters was carrying out the directives of the Party Headquarters by organising the first course of " study through manual labour " for a group of fifty-eight artists and writers in mines, factories, and agricultural co-operatives, the Ministry of Education was opening a forty-five-day re-education course for all the secondary school teachers in North Vietnam, 3,175 people in all. In August, the second batch of 148 artists and writers, divided into thirty-two squads, was sent off to perform manual labour at various sites. In November, the Ministry of Education arranged political education courses for a total of more than a thousand professors and lecturers from the universities and technical colleges and for some 15,000 of their students. During the same month, all the teachers and students of the Medical school were assembled, divided into sixteen squads, and despatched to " perform productive labour and to organise higher standards of hygiene in the various regions . . ."

A member of the Central Committee of the Lao Dong Party who was responsible for supplying leadership to the intellectuals, Bui Cong Trung, spoke as follows when he addressed the second course of writers and artists going off to perform manual labour in 1958: " This is a reforming of the spirit which will create completely new men. This disciplining of the spirit will, not unnaturally, be hard and painful, and it will extirpate everything that still remains of the past." [27] These remnants of the past were called by the Lao Dong Party " capitalist ideas." Documents treating of the re-education of intellectuals from other countries in the Communist *bloc* were constantly being translated into Vietnamese and printed in the publications of the Party so as to provide the political commissars with extra arguments to confound the objections of the intellectuals on this course.

It was the members of the Hanoi Socialist Party who proved the hardest of all to re-educate. They accepted with much reluctance the leadership of the Lao Dong Party, but they refused to accept the " principle of working class leadership." Indeed, they were never really convinced of the ability of the Lao Dong Party to lead. In the course of working side by side with members of the Lao Dong Party in the various organisations to which they had been sent, the members of the Socialist Party regarded the political commissars of the Party as persons sent to keep a watch on them and never accepted their political guidance.[28] To forestall the reaction of the intellectuals, the political commissars frequently repeated the utterance of the Hungarian Communist Gyula Kallai: " At the present time, people frequently resort to the expression ' the atomic age ' in order to stress the leading role of the

---

[27] *To Quóc*, the organ of the Vietnamese Socialist Party, No. 114, November 1, 1958.
[28] *Ibid.*, No. 125, April 16, 1959 (Editorial).

intellectuals. However, we must understand clearly that the atomic age will not affect the historic development of Socialism at all." [29]

THE RESULTS OF THREE YEARS OF CULTURAL DEVELOPMENT

In 1958, the Lao Dong Party began to implement its " three-year plan for developing and reforming the economy, and developing culture ", designed to run from 1958 until 1960. As far as the development of culture was concerned, the aim of the plan was to

> mobilise all cultural, scientific, educational, and technical forces in order to educate the people in Socialist thought, to encourage everybody to exert all his strength in order to create Socialism in North Vietnam, to raise the cultural and technical level of the people, and to create intellectuals loyal to their fatherland and to Socialism.[30]

In order to accomplish the plan to create these intellectuals and specialists it was decided that, by the end of 1960, the universities would have 9,300 students, an increase of 81 per cent. over 1957. The total number of cadres to be trained inside North Vietnam or to return home after graduation at an overseas university during the period of the plan was to be 2,430. In the matter of other cultural activities, the plan laid down that " publishing, newspapers, broadcasting, literary studies, technology, and films would all raise their Socialist content." Because this Socialist content cannot be measured, the only visible cultural effect of this order was the increase in book publishing of 19 per cent. over the three years in question, and the increase of 40 per cent. in newspaper and magazine publishing.

In terms of the figures quoted above, it appears as though the three-year plan of cultural development has produced some results. At the beginning of the academic year 1961–62, the total number of students registered at the five universities and the three other colleges was 18,598 (this figure includes students attending evening classes and 3,000 students living outside the capital and taught by correspondence course). This means to say that the number of students has been increased by 36 per cent. over the number for the previous year, 1960–61.[31]

Official announcements have nowhere been precise about the number of books published, and different documents give quite different figures. The special issue of the magazine *Van Nghe* (*Arts and Letters*) produced in September 1960 to commemorate the fifteenth anniversary of the establishment of the Government of the Democratic Republic of Vietnam stated that, in the period extending from the beginning of 1955 until May

[29] " The Reform of the Hungarian Intellectuals," *To Quoc*, No. 125.
[30] Speech made by Nguyen Duy Trinh, Deputy Premier and Chairman of the State Planning Board, to the 9th session of the National Assembly (Hanoi: Su That Publishing House).
[31] *Thoi Moi*, September 15, 1961.

1960, 514 Vietnamese works and 153 translations of foreign works had been published. *Hoc-Tap*, the theoretical and political journal of the Lao Dong Party, informs readers that, during the year 1959 alone, 1,070 works had been published, and that the number of copies was 17,737,274. Of these, the majority were educational books, and the number of general books (including political, scientific, and cultural books) constituted more than one-third of the total. This same journal states that the number of books published in 1959 was 1,727 times greater than the number published in 1939.

The intellectual and cultural productivity indicated by the above figures would appear to be enormous if viewed simply in the context of North Vietnam during the past fifteen years. Unfortunately, intellectual and cultural values cannot be assessed simply by reference to a few carelessly produced statistics, particularly when the works produced are obliged to carry a " socialist content." However, a few observations worthy of attention have been made by the cadres responsible for leading arts and letters.

Since the middle of 1958, the Lao Dong Party has been anxious to remove all artists and writers who matured under the old social order and to replace them by new men who are young and possess a pure, unadulterated socialist consciousness. Following a series of literary examinations held successively in the different regions of North Vietnam and then in the capital, a conference of young writers was convened in April 1959. From a total of 300 such young writers who attended, the majority of whom were sprung from the families of workers, peasants, soldiers, or cadres, there was not a single one to whom literary circles or the readers of books paid any real attention. People did remember the names of a few of them, such as Nong Trung, because he was a Nhang tribesman and had come down from the mountain regions, or Hoang Minh Top and Hoang Thi Ru, because they were a worker and a peasant who wished to adopt the new career of writing but who had such outlandish names.[32]

Summing up the art and letters of North Vietnam during the past fifteen years, a cadre responsible for the leadership of the artists and writers, Hong Cuong, said:

> The number of published works written by the young writers have accounted for 66 per cent. of the total published output of the Van Hoc press, and they have also produced 90 per cent. of the articles published in the periodical *Van Nghe Quan Doi* (*Military Arts and Letters*) and of the books published by the Quan Doi Nhan Dan (People's Army) press.[33]

Nevertheless, in his article " Fifteen Years of Prose Writing," which

[32] *To Quoc*, No. 125, April 16, 1959.   [33] *Van Nghe*, August 1960.

was written as a preface to *An Anthology of Vietnamese Writing, 1945–1960*, the author To Hoai affirmed that, of all the many writers to appear during the eight years of resistance war, only a mere six could now be called to mind. These were Tran Dang, Thep Moi, Minh Loc, Nguyen Van Bong, Vo Huy Tam and Vu Tu Nam. Of all the thousands of young writers who had been helped to come forward during more recent years, To Hoai could bring himself to mention only three, Nguyen Ngoc, Nguyen Khai, and Bui Duc Ai.

If the number of publications worthy of notice is extremely limited, the number of books which have been directly copied, both in form and subject-matter, from works of other authors is far from small. In its issue of January 1961, the magazine *Van Nghe* remarks on this "evil phenomenon" in the sphere of poetry and suggests that a campaign of stringent critical examination be started. A much more important instance of literary plagiarism was denounced by *Van Nghe* in its April 1961 number. This was the play *Nguoi Con Gai Dat Do* (*The Girl from the South*), written by the Reformed South Vietnamese Theatrical Company and performed in Hanoi towards the end of 1960. The Hanoi Communist press was most enthusiastic in its acclaim for this play. However, in February 1961, when the Cantonese Theatrical Company performed in Hanoi, everybody discovered that the play was an almost exact copy of a Chinese Communist play, with only a few minor details altered.

In fact, it seems as though the leaders of arts and letters in North Vietnam are themselves perfectly aware of the low quality of the literary works selected for publication in the recent past. Indeed, even the magazine *Van Nghe* itself complained in its issue of March 1961 that the Party's publishing houses

> had translated and published far too many foreign books, most of which were very second rate. Even those foreign books which have nothing at all to offer have been publicised with expressions of high praise, while the publicity for books published inside North Vietnam has been restrained and hesitant.

This same magazine asks, in forthright terms, why "the great literary classics, which have been beloved by mankind for hundreds, or even thousands of years, have not yet been translated into Vietnamese," the Greek and Latin classics, the plays of Shakespeare, and so on.

EPILOGUE

There is, at the present moment, a heated controversy raging in North Vietnam between the intellectuals, the artists and writers, and the cadres who lead them, about a recent published literary work. It centres about a book entitled *Song Da*, written by the writer Nguyen Tuan and published by the Van Hoc publishing house in July 1960. The author is one of the " old capitalist writers " who has collaborated with the Communists throughout the past fifteen years. During the struggle to win democratic freedom in 1956 he maintained a neutral attitude towards the dispute, but he was nevertheless despatched by the Party to perform manual work in the Thai-Meo Autonomous Zone, and there he worked in a mountainous, jungle region on the borders of Vietnam and Laos from August 1958 until the middle of 1960. He wrote the book in question during this period of manual toil. It was accounted only " moderately good " by the critical cadres responsible for supplying political leadership. Several passages were said to be incompatible with Socialism, and these were cited as evidence that Nguyen Tuan himself had not been correctly re-educated. Criticisms of the work itself and of Nguyen Tuan were produced by a senior arts and letters cadre named Nam Moc in a critical article which ran to seventeen pages and was published in the May 1961 issue of the magazine *Nghien Cuu Van Hoc* (*Literary Research*). According to this senior cadre, public opinion about the book was divided, one section acclaiming *Song Da* and the other criticising it sharply. The section which approved of the book comprised a number of writers and some people who had retained their liking for Nguyen Tuan since the old days. The ranks of the book's critics were made up of young workers, peasants, and working class intellectuals, that is to say, precisely the young and completely Socialist people about whom Nguyen Tuan wrote in his book.

By way of reply to the criticism his book had caused, Nguyen Tuan did not seek to make a straightforward defence of what he had written. Instead, he expressed his own feelings by publishing an article about a Vietnamese writer who lived in the last century. " Thoi Va Tho Tu Xuong " (" The Times and Poetry of Tu Xuong "), as this article was called, appeared in the May 1961 edition of *Van Nghe* and introduced the work of a famous Vietnamese satirical poet who lived in the latter part of the nineteenth century and died early in the twentieth. Indeed, his life coincided with the period when the French were beginning to establish their colonial régime in Vietnam.

In writing about the times of Tu Xuong, Nguyen Tuan sought to draw a comparison between the period when the French came with armed might to set up a government and a machinery of exploitation, and the present time, when the Communists were building a régime which they called socialist in North Vietnam. Nguyen Tuan devoted much attention to one short poem in which the author expressed his longing for the old life of Vietnam, ousted by the changes, introduced by the French, of which Tu Xuong disapproved. The implications, one can be quite sure, have not been misunderstood by readers in the DRV.

Indoctrination Replaces Education

By GÉRARD TONGAS

THE cultural level of North Vietnam is undoubtedly one of the lowest imaginable. Eighty per cent. of the population is illiterate, ignorant to an incredible degree and subject to the most extraordinary superstitions.[1] Apart from the masses there remains the élite—and the hopes that one should be able to place in the youth. But here, also, we find the same deep division that was created in the population as a whole by the war—on the one hand the members of the Resistance and on the other those who remained outside it.

In addition, other significant distinctions must be drawn. Among those young people who did not take part in the Resistance there are vast numbers who have not studied at all, and whose fate is typical. Also, certain terms are interpreted by their leaders in a manner completely different from the sense they bear in our own terminology. For the Vietnamese Communists the words *culture, education* and *teaching* have only one meaning, namely *indoctrination*. In North Vietnam, a man of reasonable culture, education and learning, is one who has been continuously subjected to indoctrination in Marxist-Leninist ideology (or what passes for it), one who no longer thinks for himself but accepts in their entirety as Gospel truth, all the concepts systematically inculcated by carefully graded propaganda. From now on such indoctrination will be the lot of the élite and the youth. This is what passes for school and university education and the education of the mass of the population, and it is also the sole source of inspiration permissible to writers, thinkers and artists.

I shall not, therefore, in this article [2] refer to culture, education or instruction, but quite simply to what has usurped their place in the DRV —indoctrination.

Of this there are three kinds, the first being applied to the children of the cadres of the Comunist régime, the second to the children of those who did not join the Resistance but continued to live under the French, and the third to the population as a whole.

---

[1] I have given a detailed account of these facts in my book, *L'Enfer Communiste au Nord Viet-Nam* (Paris: Nouvelles Editions Debresse, 1961). Readers of this book will know of the privileges that I enjoyed as an official of the DRV—(I was professor of French at the Lycee Chu-Van-An in Hanoi, whilst my wife taught English there)—and of the many secrets that were entrusted to me, and the valuable documentation I was able to obtain there.

[2] Readers will find fuller details in my book.

THE INDOCTRINATION OF YOUNG CADRES AND THE
CHILDREN OF CADRES

The children of cadres lead a very specialised life, and are placed in schools reserved exclusively for them, and have practically no contacts with the remainder of the population. They spend their whole time solely and continually in one another's company, under the control of teachers who are all experienced cadres of the Resistance and are often members of the Communist Party. Their studies are not on a higher level than those of other children, but are much more strongly influenced by Party directives, as the primary aim of these schools is the formation of the inflexible cadres of the future. These children are docile and well disciplined, used to living in Spartan simplicity; having previously known no other life than that of danger and privation which they led during the war in the jungle, their standards are not very high and they take quite naturally to the intensive indoctrination to which they are subjected. Ignoring as they do the misfortunes and miseries—or at any rate the reasons for them—and also the discontent of their compatriots, they represent a genuine and powerful source of strength for the régime. Indoctrinated as they are in close confinement, they are completely segregated from that atmosphere of terror and suffering which constitutes the environment of the rest of the population. Finding their own existence perfectly satisfactory—as they know no other—they are not even aware of the disillusionment and the discouragement of their relations or their seniors, and retain intact the enthusiasm of a favoured section of the youth. These exalted and fanatical youngsters are both happy and proud to be the " pioneers " of the country which, they are told the whole day long, looks to them for its future prosperity, greatness, and happiness.

I cannot say the same of the children of those cadres who came from South Vietnam and were regrouped in the north as the result of the signing of the Geneva Agreements in July 1954. Both their fate and their outlook are of a different kind. These children from the south are placed in schools which are exclusively reserved for them, and all their teachers are *cân-bô* [3] who came with them from South Vietnam. The latter are fiercely hostile to the Communist régime, and one can easily understand the spirit in which they educate the children. The Party does not relax its vigilance over them and actively imposes its will upon them. Yet it must still proceed cautiously in the case of its South Vietnamese compatriots. If only in the interests of its propaganda prior to the unification of Vietnam, it is obliged to act gently towards them. This gives rise to a certain weakness of which the *cân-bô* from

3 Cadres.

South Vietnam know how to take advantage in a negative if not in a positive sense, by calculated inertia if not by increased hostility.

The most enthusiastic and zealous of all these children of the cadres will continue their studies either in the U.S.S.R., China, Eastern Germany or Czechoslovakia, some of them going abroad at the age of seven, but in any case for an uninterrupted term of ten years or so. The young cadres also leave in large numbers for periods lasting from five to ten years. Many of these *cân-bô*, their loyalty more or less shaken by the cruel disillusionments they have suffered during recent years, regain their illusions and their faith once they are far away from their country and its suffering. Made much of by their Soviet or Chinese instructors, they regain their hope in the future and soon become fanatics. As for the others, who had never lost it, they are only encouraged in their convictions or their opportunism by the period spent among their foreign " comrades."

THE INDOCTRINATION OF THE SCHOOL AND UNIVERSITY STUDENTS TAINTED BY THE FORMER RÉGIME [4]

The tutorial corps includes two categories of teachers—qualified teachers who were active before the imposition of DRV authority, in 1955, over the whole of North Vietnam, and the *cân-bô*. Nearly all the former had a sound pedagogical training and a certain amount of experience; many of them are graduates of the *Ecole de Pédagogie* of Hanoi or hold degrees from French universities. In general the teachers had obtained the French *Brevet Elémentaire*. With certain exceptions, the *cân-bô* are mostly unqualified teachers, for during the jungle Resistance it was necessary to provide some form of education, however elementary, and at that time those chosen to teach were not the most highly qualified but those considered to be most reliable. All of them are full of good intentions and do their utmost to carry out their duties conscientiously; most of them, however, lack the requisite knowledge and many of them know no more than they themselves have learned from the textbooks they use. Certain of them possess Soviet textbooks in French from which they may learn that it was the peasants and workers who made the French Revolution of 1789, or else that under the Third Republic the electors were obliged to pay " quit-rent " before being qualified to vote! Others have so little knowledge of Vietnamese that they are obliged to read *Nhan Dan*—the Party newspaper—aloud in order to be able to understand it. Many a time my wife and myself were obliged to leave the teachers' " common-room ", driven out by the disagreeable brayings that disturbed the few moments of tranquillity we had sought there.

---

[4] By the " former régime " I am referring to that which was in existence before the Geneva Agreements.

Children under seven are not allowed to go to school; there are neither kindergartens nor any elementary instruction. They go first to the primary schools and later to the sixth form of the *lycée*, finishing their secondary education in the eleventh form.

As well as the primary schools and the State *lycées* there are also a large number of private schools. In these the *cân-bô* are in charge of political instruction and are also responsible for supervising the other teachers. Overburdened by taxation, these schools merely vegetate until such time as they are ordered to close down; the régime is intensively training new teachers to cope with the students from such schools.

The entrance examination to the university is basically only concerned with the soundness of a candidate's political education; here, also, Marxist-Leninist indoctrination takes pride of place. The intellectual standard is extremely low. Most of the professors are completely incompetent; nearly all of them are *cân-bô*. The few who are properly qualified are rare exceptions.

At each stage—whether primary, secondary, or higher—there are, in addition to the courses to be followed, frequent political meetings which have to be attended by the entire staff and all the pupils in each establishment. As indoctrination is placed far above any scholastic instruction these political meetings are regarded as of very great importance. They invariably take place without previous warning. When one arrives at the school, whether it be at seven o'clock in the morning or at one-thirty in the afternoon, one finds the microphone already set up and the pupils gathered out-of-doors, in a semi-circle, some squatting on their heels, others standing, awaiting the first speaker. The following are examples of some of the subjects of such meetings : " Pham Van Dong addresses a call to Ngô Dinh Diem for the establishment of normal relations between North and South Vietnam "; " Algerian Day : moral support for the F.L.N."; " Decisions reached at the Moscow XXth Congress "; " Events in Hungary "; " Fortieth Anniversary of the October Revolution "; " The Launching of the Sputnik " and so on.

The head of the institution opens the proceedings by announcing the subject of the meeting, and is followed at the microphone by a teacher or a distinguished visitor, by pupils and sometimes, also, by the school janitor or an orderly.[5] The meeting may last for half an hour or two hours; how long is never known in advance, as the length will depend on the verbosity of the speakers. Sometimes it takes place after the recreation period or at the end of classes. As these meetings may interrupt the teaching schedule, the time-table is frequently changed at the very last moment.

---

[5] The latter also participate in the teachers' meetings for discussion of the pupils' work and they have plenty to say for themselves there!

I have given an account of the education provided for the children of the cadres and those belonging to bourgeois or other families living in the towns. There remain the immense numbers of young people who, both in the towns but especially in the villages where there are extremely few schools, receive no education higher than the elementary level. And there remain, as well, the enormous numbers of adolescents who, in the towns, are doomed to unemployment or unskilled labour or, in the villages, to obligatory labour service in the rice-fields, and the maintenance and reconstruction of the irrigation dykes and canals.

Thus, in North Vietnam, an overwhelming majority of children and adolescents receive no education, but wander around the streets of the cities or the dykes and roads of the countryside.

Fight Against Illiteracy: Indoctrination of the Masses

The façade of the " fight against illiteracy " is designed to enable the propagandists to claim alleged successes in overcoming " the obscurantism left behind by the colonialists and the feudalists."

In what has this fight in fact consisted, and what have been the results of it? During the first two years after the signing of the Geneva Agreements it seemed as if the entire population were participating wholeheartedly and with unlimited enthusiasm in this crusade. Evening classes were started almost everywhere in the towns and villages. Volunteers flocked to them, both to teach and to learn. The older pupils of the secondary schools and the university, as well as business men and other members of the bourgeoisie, volunteered to act as teachers. Old people and young children in large numbers sat side by side on the school benches, clumsily tracing the letters of the alphabet and also, very quickly, learning the slogans of the régime. For in truth the " fight against illiteracy "—in so far as it concerned the " elementary stage " at which the vast majority of the population was included—merely consisted in teaching the illiterate masses to recite twenty or so slogans and to copy them more or less legibly—" Long live President Ho!" " Long live the Vietnamese Workers' Party!" " Long live Peace!" " The Imperialism of the Americans and their lackeys will be defeated!" " Long live our Soviet Comrades!" etc. Such were these slogans. The illiterates [6] were to see them written thousands of times on walls, streamers, and in the newspapers; they would be able to recognise them, but never to read anything else!

Those who could already read and had acquired some slight vocabulary were enrolled in " complementary classes ". There they learnt what

---

[6] For there still remain illiterates, in spite of their official promotion to the ranks of the educated, in order to swell the statistics.

was pompously and with a certain respectfulness termed "political language" and by means of this intellectual equipment, a vocabulary of three hundred words or so, which turned them into Marxist-Leninist scholars, they were able to read *Nhan Dan*.

To foreign visitors, who only spare a brief glance at these evening classes—where by the way steps are taken to deceive them as to the subjects taught—and who can have no deeper impression of them, the sight of all those attentive faces, those worn and trembling old men's hands scarred by years and hard work, the fresh faces of the children and their clumsy little fingers, the enthusiasm of the hairdresser, who, after a hard day's work shows indefatigable devotion to his new teaching profession, all appear extremely moving and engender deep admiration. But when one is able, as I myself had plenty of leisure to do, to discuss this so-called crusade against illiteracy both with teachers and pupils, and to follow their work, the appalling truth is only too obvious. It was so flagrant that even they themselves did not fail to realise it. And that is why these classes are attended with less and less enthusiasm and why the voluntary teachers have abandoned them altogether; only Party members, conscripted monitors, endeavour to keep them going.

In Hanoi, the authorities complacently display a class belonging to the "elementary group" attended by Phan Thanh My, "hero of the fight against illiteracy," aged 81. Lê Thi Binh, a cripple aged 24, who directs two "complementary classes," is also the object of loud publicity, which is geared to exploit the people and events to perfection in the interests of unscrupulous propaganda. Can there be a more moving spectacle than the sight of this tall old man with his white beard, his tremulous voice, his unsteady limbs, as he slowly lifts a long bamboo pointer towards the blackboard, and with difficulty tries to pick out the letters on it? And how can one fail to be moved by the sight of this young girl, a hunchback whose right leg has been amputated, whose crutch and wooden shoe tap along the floor, as, with a perpetual smile, she so touchingly encourages all those youngsters and old folk who call her their "big sister teacher"? The scene has been well set, and the petted actors carefully placed in position. There remains nothing more to be done except to photograph the scene, to write a sentimental script combined with impressive statistics, on which the press of the Communist *bloc* will seize to spread the story which, when it is released in the non-Communist world, will move all honest people and convince them of the kindness, efficiency, and solicitude of this idyllic régime. How could they be aware of the true situation, of which I have given the above account?

The Peoples' "University" forms the apex of this indoctrination. In the suburbs of Hanoi a few rickety brick buildings, containing only a ground floor, and some straw huts, have been summarily converted and sparsely furnished.   The students of this " university " are the sons and daughters of peasants and workers, numbering round about one thousand. All the professors are *cân-bô*, and from time to time the most important leaders of the régime hold spectacular " conferences " there.   The academic level and the curriculum—as at the University of Hanoi—bear no resemblance whatever to those that prevail at establishments in the non-Communist world that are recognised as of university status.   One could only, at best, compare this institution to a bad training college for teachers, and even then one would have to allow for the low level of attainment due to the intellectual deficiencies of both teachers and pupils.   It is in fact a training centre for turning out more *cân-bô*, whose importance to the régime is based first and foremost on their loyalty to it and their assimilation of its slogans and ideological indoctrination.

Hungary and the Failure of Indoctrination

Apart from this Peoples' University and the special schools reserved for the children of the cadres, indoctrination has been a total failure as far as the youth in general as well as the masses are concerned.   The initial enthusiasm for the new régime has given way to an irreversible *volte-face*.

When, in October 1954, the new régime victoriously came to power, the " liberators " were received with great acclaim by the youth as a whole.   Both scholars and students accepted its slogans with splendid enthusiasm.   They gaily took up manual labour, to which they were so little accustomed, including the heaviest tasks, setting out with their teachers, armed with picks and shovels, to dig canals or to take part in the repair of the dykes, or even to provide new cemeteries for those slain at Diên-Biên-Phu.   Every classroom contained photographs and pictures of Ho Chi Minh.   Coloured streamers decorated all the halls and classrooms, giving them an air of festivity.   Gradually, enormous photographs of Stalin and Mao Tse-tung were added to these decorations. Every day's proceedings began by saluting the Red Flag, with its proud gold star; teachers and pupils stood at attention as it was hoisted, whilst a powerful choir sang the National Anthem.   Each course began and ended with a patriotic song, and the courses were also interrupted, two or three times, by the performance of other songs, at the request of the pupils.   Neighbouring classes did the same, but without previous agreement on the songs to be performed, so that the noise was continuous and increased by the hand clapping which was invariably in time with the singing.

Nor did an hour of instruction elapse during which an orderly did not appear bringing another administrative circular.   He was greeted with the deepest respect by all the pupils who would stand up as one man. He responded with a series of profound bows.   The circular would be listened to in deep silence and approved by loud applause. As a result, there never remained, at the outset, more than thirty minutes of teaching, properly speaking. During this period the class was more or less quiet, but as no books, no teaching programme, and no scholastic equipment were available, the progress that could be made depended exclusively on the teacher's own ability.

Between classes, during recreation and moving from one classroom to another, there was a deafening racket from loud-speakers, as an uninterrupted stream of *cân-bô* and pupils took their places at the microphone set up in the yard. This final touch set the seal on the atmosphere of a country fair that was the permanent setting of activities at Chu-Van-An.[7] The row that was made out-of-doors penetrated into the entire establishment, filling the passages and the classrooms like an endless hurricane; for it continued pitilessly even during lessons, owing to the excessively loud blasts of music or the commands shouted into the microphone by the monitor who was drilling a class of pupils in gymnastics in the yard. Power having passed to the people, there were no longer any prefects left to keep an eye on those pupils who were left temporarily without a teacher. And as—with the possible exception of the English—no schoolchildren, and in particular no Vietnamese schoolchildren, are capable of exercising either self-discipline or any discipline over their classmates, from the passages and neighbouring classrooms an infernal din also arose, in addition to the noise of the loud-speakers and the singing. The rule laid down was that work should be carried on with enjoyment, incessant activity and perpetual noisiness; and there is no doubt that very little work was in fact done, or that it was anything but exceedingly bad.

In order to " democratise " the teaching system so as to ensure that all pupils should have an equal start, on the basis of the lowest grade of achievement, the Soviet system of marking was introduced—from 1 to 5, with no intermediate grading nor zero allowed. As each class contained between 70 and 80 pupils, one may easily judge how impossible it was to classify the achievements of any individual in such numbers by such a system. The pupils were invariably in the right, the teachers never, for they no longer received any respect. The pupils insisted on choosing their own subjects, rejected the marks they were awarded, demanded that their tasks should be cut down, and frequently interrupted the lessons to contradict their teacher and to repeat the slogans they had been taught by the *cân-bô*.

In North Vietnam teaching is carried on without school books,

7 The most important secondary school in the DRV, where my wife and I were teaching.

geography is taught without maps, chemical and physical experiments are described, but there are no laboratories. One of my Vietnamese colleagues who taught French improvised his lessons, and as a subject for dictation used the biography of Maurice Thorez; another, an English teacher, explained the speeches of Pham Van Dong, and invented an alleged English account of the life of Lenin, which he gave to beginners to translate. In every class the pupils were divided into groups for team-work, so that the most worthless among them simply copied out the work of the better ones, and made no individual efforts at all.

In each class there were " stool-pigeons," who made their private reports to the *cân-bô* who were in political control of the pupils. Antagonism to " the Americans and their servants " expressed itself chiefly in the exhibition of drawings portraying the lowest representations of hatred. After the flag had been saluted, an " activist " pupil would shout an anti-American slogan, to which the rest would respond by emitting three strident yells, their arms raised and fists clenched. Each class was ordered to write and illustrate a daily " journal," and these vied with one another in hatred, servilely reproducing the political indoctrination they had been given; the pupils were far keener on such competitive work than on their exclusively scholastic tasks and wasted untold time on the production of what I can only describe as crazy nonsense, or in cutting out streamers, posters and banners inscribed with the slogans of the régime. School celebrations and many other demonstrations also provided frequent opportunities for coarse vituperation against the non-Communist world.

All this frenzied enthusiasm lasted until October 1956. News of the Russian " de-Stalinisation " had, it is true, been received in April of that year, but although this may have somewhat shaken certain cadres and raised the beginnings of waverings in some minds, it made practically no difference to the enthusiasm of the youth, nor to their attitude. To them, Stalin was merely a famous foreigner, with whose portrait alone, exhibited everywhere, they were familiar. The fact that their Soviet friends had decided to transfer their adoration to Lenin and Bulganin—for this was how they interpreted the events that took place at the XXth Congress— was no reason for the lustre of the Soviet Star to be dimmed in their eyes. All that ensued was that the portraits hanging in the classrooms were changed, for " *qu'importe le flacon pourvu qu'on ait l'ivresse!* "— (" what matter the cup, provided that one remains intoxicated! ").

But when in October 1956 the news of the Hungarian uprising arrived, their intoxication with the Russians came to an end. Vietnamese youths sobered up—and thoroughly. Their reaction was all the more violent because they felt themselves to have been hideously deceived. Foreign radio stations gave regular news of the Hungarian revolution; the appeals of the Hungarian patriots touched all hearts, and the intervention of Soviet tanks aroused emotions of panic, whilst the reports spread by the local radio stations and press were no longer believed. Thenceforward all these devoted young people felt themselves to be completely at one in spirit with the brave Hungarian youth, and their struggle became in its turn that of the youthful intelligentsia of North Vietnam. Among all the satellites of the U.S.S.R that they were always hearing about without being able to distinguish between them or to find them on a map, Hungary was the only one that the youth at last learned to know. Their *volte-face* seemed to me unanimous and complete.

The pupils became courteous and even very amiable towards the professors of the old régime, whom they had until then despised and with whom they had maintained only the barest and most essential contacts. On the other hand they became arrogant and even insolent towards the *cân-bô*, whom until then they had venerated and cherished. The latter finding themselves, together with the informers they had placed in every class, cast aside, endured a number of insults without reacting as they would have wished to, in order not to aggravate the tension which they felt to be increasing with irresistible force.[8] Whilst expecting the worst, they temporised. The pupils were openly talking of demonstrating in the streets. At this point the Government, in order to forestall a rising, which it very greatly feared, decided to loosen its political grip on the schools to a considerable extent, both by quietly eliminating certain customs that had been established and allowing the pupils themselves to suppress certain others. The flag was raised only on Monday mornings and lowered again on Saturdays; the slogans and invective that had previously accompanied this ceremony were suppressed. There were no more exhibitions of drawings nor dramatic performances accusing the American enemies and their allies. The propaganda lectures disappeared completely. In spite of all this, however, the agitation of the youth continued to increase and reached its apex during the last days of April 1957. In the schools students secretly prepared for a mass demonstration to culminate in a protest meeting and a procession through the streets of Hanoi. The authorities, got wind of it, however, and decided to deal with it summarily. It was announced that all scholastic and university institutions would be closed down on May 2, the pretext given for this being the epidemic of Asian 'flu which was raging at that time. No one was taken in by this excuse, for in spite of the epidemic the

---

8 The pupils who were enrolled in the Chinese and Russian classes had the impudence —unimaginable a few months previously—to boycott these lessons. They remained in the yard, and refused to enter the classrooms. They demanded that these classes should be replaced by French and English lessons, and their demands were granted.

Government did not abandon the May Day demonstration; moreover, the much more serious poliomyelitis epidemic, which had been spreading rapidly during previous months, had not given rise to any such measures. Nevertheless, the closure of the schools disorganised all the students' plans, and the demonstration did not take place.

However, an extraordinary transformation occurred among the youth, and, once the process of disenchantment had begun, it continued at a rapid pace. The youth movement completely changed. It was no longer similar to that which preceded the Communist régime, nor to the enthusiasm which had been generated at its outset. The youth movement had at last developed a conscious awareness of its own origins. Having during the Indo-Chinese war been frivolous and debauched, showing an appalling indifference to the country's misfortunes, and subsequently slipping at high speed down the slopes that led to Communist fanaticism, Vietnamese youth received a tremendous shock. This resulted in their becoming more genuinely patriotic and nationalist.

There were no longer any garlands in the classrooms, and those in which a portrait of Lenin was still hanging were few and far between. Pictures of the current Soviet leadership disappeared completely. Nor was " Uncle " Ho to be seen except in one or two halls. There were no more slogans—those slogans and pictures which literally used to cover every wall. Sometimes the photograph of Ho Chi Minh would even be veiled by dust, thickened and stuck together by the humidity of the atmosphere, but nobody bothered to clean it. The peace of the yards was no longer shattered by singing; the orderlies were no longer saluted by the pupils. " Uncle " Ho had ceased to be the idol of the youth, and the régime no longer retained its confidence.

In their new mood, the young people, it seemed to me, looked impatiently towards South Vietnam, hoping for deliverance. All their hopes were now founded on a Southern intervention, and they seemed to take a keen interest in the strengthening of South Vietnam's power, in its economic and social progress, and its general development. The British, Americans, and French were once again looked to as the reliable friends on whom the country's future depended; and these young people avidly devoured all the books and periodicals on which they could lay their hands, however out-dated or valueless they might be, which might enable them to acquire a better knowledge of Britain, America, and France. As they had become rarer and more difficult to acquire, these publications were sought after and circulated with really touching enthusiasm. I would never have believed that my own library, dispersed in this way, would have attained such importance! The B.B.C.'s broadcasts in Vietnamese were listened to with increasing interest and regularity, and without any doubt took first place in popularity owing to their high quality and better audibility; they were of very great help to those who longed to look beyond the walls of what they now considered their prison and to learn what was taking place in the non-Communist world.

Pupils and students no longer reacted favourably to the political slogans directed at them; they bore only inattentively this form of indoctrination. They had all learnt to understand that such teaching was of no value to them, and that the régime was making a laughing-stock of them.

The young people were now sad and disillusioned, but they seemed to have found an aim at last—to rid themselves of the régime that oppressed them.

A Bowl of Rice Divided:
The Economy of North Vietnam

By WILLIAM KAYE

It would amount to a serious error of judgment to treat North Vietnam's economic development as a mere pocket edition of the Chinese or Soviet experiment. It is, of course, true that many features of economic policy adopted by the bearded ruler of Hanoi show clear signs of their Pekingese or Muscovite parentage. As far back as 1954 Ton Duc Thanh, chairman of the Vietnamese Popular Front, Lien Viet, had pointed to the current Soviet scene as his country's target for the future.

But it was the Chinese model which was copied in the early years, and only later that this was progressively replaced by the Russian. However, by courtesy of nature, China's all-time record harvest of 1958 could be copied, with a year's delay, by North Vietnam. As in China, it was made to appear even bigger than it was by Party hacks and statistical quacks. Just the same, Nguyen ai Quôc, alias Ho Chi Minh, a founder member of the French Communist Party and a student of Marxism in Moscow in the early twenties, can be expected to make his own choice when circumstances permit it. In consultation with his principal policy makers and economic planners he is known to have adapted and amended historical precedent where mere adoption might easily have spelt disaster.

The formulation of North Vietnam's economic policy must not be seen as the result of agreement at all times between entirely like-minded men. The retreat in 1956 on the agrarian front brought into focus, more than any other incident of recent Vietnamese history, the sharp ideological conflict between the Moscow-trained and Peking-trained men of the DRV's political leadership. In North Vietnam, as in North Korea and Mongolia, the vacillations of Sino-Soviet relations were revealed at times when the views of Moscow and Peking were veiled in dense fog. There is yet another reason for paying attention to what is planned and done in Hanoi. Vietnam rather than China is likely to provide the pattern of Communist rule as envisaged by those who prepare for the ultimate seizure of power throughout South East Asia.

Unlike the continental land mass of the mainland of China, Vietnam belongs to the zone of subtropical rains, though the monsoon fails uncomfortably often in the area north of the 17th Parallel. In 1954 the North, traditionally a food deficit area, was cut off from its surplus producing hinterland in the South which before the war had a substantial export surplus and which even now produces a surplus of half a million tons over and above increased consumption requirements. The Geneva agreements separated a population in the North now accounting for 16 millions, from the rest of the nation which, swelled by close on a million refugees, now totals over 13 millions.

In spite of Communist preoccupation with industrialisation, North Vietnam, like other parts of South East Asia, is a predominantly agrarian society and it will remain so for some time to come. Almost four-fifths of the population live in over 15,000 villages, situated mostly in the rather narrow, though richly fertile precincts of the Red River delta. A million town dwellers, artisans, fishermen and traders, live in Hanoi and Haiphong. Some nine-tenths of the acreage is under paddy, which is gathered partly as fifth month crop in May, but mostly as tenth month crop in October. The nation lives, with little to spare, from harvest to harvest. Even industry, much dependent upon the returns of agriculture, follows closely the cycle dictated by nature.

War and civil war caused damage, if not destruction, not only to the railway lines and industrial enterprises, originally set up under French colonial rule; plantations and subsistence farming also suffered. Not unnaturally the first economic plan was thus designed to restore industrial and agricultural production as well as transport facilities to conditions prevailing before the last war. In the autumn of 1955 a National Planning Board and a Central Statistical Office were established, with the assistance of Chinese and Soviet experts, and at the end of the year Ho Chi Minh was able to announce the first plan. Priorities were obvious from the distribution of capital investment : 38 per cent. for industrial reconstruction, 23 per cent. for transport and communications, 20 per cent. for agriculture and irrigation, and the remaining 19 per cent. for education and social services. Under the umbrella of bilateral agreements trade was switched almost entirely to the Soviet *bloc* and substantial aid was offered by China and the Soviet Union.

The country was at that time in a poor way. The weather during the year 1955 had been the worst in a century, floods and typhoons having destroyed a large part of the paddy crop, thus increasing the rice deficit from the normal level of 200,000 tons to nearly half a million tons. The situation had been aggravated by the transfer of villagers on a large scale from work in the fields to non-agricultural labour. Strict rationing and price control had been introduced, but the Party cadres were unable to keep in check widespread black market activities and inflationary price developments.

Although Government and Party had their hands full with matters of rehabilitation and reconstruction, priority was given to the political targets of the régime. As elsewhere in Communist states, economic policy was subordinated to the overriding political aims of nationalisation, industrialisation and collectivisation. Thus the first decisive steps were taken to extend over the whole national territory the transfer of private enterprise to the public sector; the development of new industries; and —land distribution having been completed—the merger of individual farms into mutual aid teams, the forerunners of agricultural producer co-operatives, alias collectives.

The lack of progress during the first years of reconstruction cannot be understood without reference to the manner in which the programme of agrarian reform was implemented.

Agrarian Reform

Approximately two-thirds of the cultivators in Tonking owned the land they tilled, and virtually the only large landlords were the French owners of plantations, who had already fled for safety to the French-held zone. The wealthier Vietnamese landowners had themselves abandoned their property and taken refuge in the big cities. The motives of the first step in agrarian reform were entirely political. A predetermined number of landlords had to be found in each village even if they did not, in fact, exist. Under the watchful eye of Chinese advisers, the requisite numbers were " discovered," tried by a People's Court, and executed or imprisoned. Their confiscated lands were distributed to landless peasants to the accompaniment of much publicity, and outstanding debts were cancelled. In political terms, the results were satisfactory, for many of the peasants now depended on the Party for the ownership of their new land, everybody had been made to attend the People's Courts and thus share in the guilt for the execution of innocent people, and the immense power of the Party had been amply demonstrated to the whole people. But little more than one twentieth of the cultivated land in the country had changed hands at the time of the Geneva agreements, and only a few state farms had been set up under foreign guidance.

This is not to say that the Communists had no more far-reaching aims. Truong Chinh, the then-Secretary-General of the Party, had outlined the long-term agrarian programme in 1950, emphasising the need for the complete transfer of all land to the tillers and the ultimate socialisation—*i.e.* collectivisation—of agriculture. The implementation of the most radical features of this programme was postponed until after the partition of the country along the 17th parallel, but preparations for the classification of the peasantry into landlords, rich peasants, middle peasants, poor peasants and landless labourers were made in the spring of 1953. The nomenclature was a close copy of the Chinese pattern, as was also the system of political mobilisation of the villagers in the anti-landlord campaigns, accusation meetings and public trials. As a result nearly half the crop land changed hands.

As in China, excesses were frequent. Acts of brutality were common. In order to achieve the degree of terror necessary to accomplish the political objectives of the campaign, the full might of the masses was unleashed, with the result that poor peasants and even Party members were victimised. Some years later it was admitted that nearly one-third of the persons tried and convicted as landlords had been condemned in error. Meanwhile open rebellion in the province of Nghe An had led to a temporary halt of agrarian reform and to the resignation of Truong Chinh as Party Secretary-General, and of Ho Viet Thang, the Deputy Minister of Agriculture. At the time of the suppression of the rebellion, less than one quarter of the peasant households had joined mutual aid teams and a fraction of one per cent. had become members of collectives.

The terror and confusion reigning throughout the country not only upset farming but caused a serious setback in the implementation of the programme of rehabilitation and industrial reconstruction. A breathing space was clearly required, and the next three years were thus earmarked as a period of consolidation. This is not to say that economic targets set for the three years 1958–60 were unduly modest. They were, in fact, set so ambitiously high in 1958 that significant downward revisions became necessary in many sectors when it became obvious in the spring of 1960 that targets could not be reached. When actual performance was reviewed by the Central Committee at the end of 1960, it showed that not only were original targets missed in almost all important sectors of industry and agriculture, but even revised targets were not reached in all cases.

The uninitiated may well wonder how much reliance can be placed in official claims as presented to the Central Committee and ultimately released for publication by the Central Statistical Office. As a general guide, industrial production figures may be taken to be of the right order of magnitude, although exaggerations may occur in individual cases; the identity of target and fulfilment data for 1957, for instance, seem hardly plausible. Considerable caution is advisable in the use of indices of such composite economic concepts as gross industrial and agricultural production or retail trade and thus productivity per man or consumption per capita. In the agricultural sphere there can be little doubt that the Vietnamese Government and Party, infected by China's exuberance, began to exaggerate crop results substantially from 1958 onwards. The tight food supply situation of the last three years does not lend credence to a grain output anything like the official harvest returns.

THE THREE-YEAR PLAN, 1958–60

When the Three-Year Plan for 1958–60 was conceived, state investment was to be doubled in the industrial and agricultural sectors with
the aim of raising overall production by 82 per cent., with industrial and
agricultural targets set at 89 and 79 per cent. respectively. Later on when
it became clear that these targets were beyond reach, they were reduced
to 50 per cent. overall and 70 and 40 per cent. for industry and agriculture respectively. Even the lower targets must seem high by any objective
standards. They belong, of course, to that set of data which is suspect
for reasons of double counting and wrong weighting even if considerations of propaganda have had no part in calculating them. As far as is
known, plan results for 1960 have not been revealed so far in the form of
composite indices. This in itself suggests that performance has lagged
behind intention. The technical standard of agriculture was found to be
low, heavy industry in its infancy and light industry underdeveloped.

Like its forerunner, the Three-Year Plan of 1958–60 had a political
as well as an economic aim. State control was to be extended over a wide
range of economic activities. In particular, agricultural producers' co-
operatives, *i.e.* collectives, were to be established on a large scale and the
public sector was to be extended in industry by way of a transfer of
private and mixed enterprises to the so-called " socialist economy."

Some considerable progress was made in this respect in industry, if
not in agriculture. By the end of 1960 the bulk of former private industry
and commerce had been transformed into joint-stock companies run for
the State by their former owners. The public sector owned nine-tenths
of all industry and commerce and four-fifths of all transport. Approximately three-quarters of all petty traders and artisans had been organised
in state-controlled co-operatives. Even so, steady progress was made in
the output of basic industries producing coal, electricity and cement.
The targets were surpassed in the apatite mines, in forestry and in textile
and sugar mills. Transport facilities within the country and up to the
Chinese border were improved greatly. On the other hand, targets for
productivity and production costs were not reached. Worse still, grain
production in 1960 was substantially lower than in the two previous
years and livestock numbers were less than in 1959. At the same time
the population had increased by approximately 3·4 per cent. per annum,
or by nearly half a million people. As a result, rations had to be cut so
that the average food intake declined to 1,800 calories or less.

This means that, at certain seasons and in certain regions, sections of
the population must have suffered from actual starvation.

In the countryside some 85 per cent. of all peasants had felt obliged
to join lower stage producers' co-operatives and to work in labour
teams. However, only 12 per cent. had joined higher forms of producers

co-operatives (collectives) in which all means of production, including livestock, are pooled and payment is made exclusively on the basis of work performed, contributions made in the form of land, tools or draught animals being disregarded.

It is too early to give a firm account of economic success or failure in 1961, the first year of North Vietnam's First Five-Year Plan and a year of further progress in industrialisation, but of more disappointments in food and farming. When results are released by the Central Statistical Office and presented to the Party's Central Committee, they will have to be judged within the context of the Five-Year Plan which is to lay the material and technological basis for " socialism," to advance substantially the process of " socialist industrialisation " and to complete the " socialist transformation " of agriculture, handicraft, industry and commerce—socialism being a misnomer throughout for Communism.

In the words of Nguyen Duy Trinh, chairman of the State Planning Commission, in a report made in September 1960 to the Congress of the Communist Party of North Vietnam, the five principal objectives of the Plan are: (1) to develop industry and agriculture and to take the first steps in giving priority to the development to heavy industry; (2) to complete socialist transformation; (3) to raise the cultural level and socialist consciousness of the people; (4) to bring about further improvements in the material and cultural life of the working people; (5) to combine economic development with the consolidation of national defence, the strengthening of public order and security and the protection of socialist construction. For the most immediate future, priority is given under the Plan to achieving a stable solution of the food problem; to supplying raw materials to industry, first of all to the food, textile and clothing industries; and to contributing to the expansion of exports of agricultural products, especially tropical products, so as to accumulate the capital required for the development of the economy.[1]

The similarity of the North Vietnamese Plan to those of China and the Soviet Union is too obvious to require emphasis. The mechanics of planning and the execution of the industrial policy are modelled closely on the pattern familiar from the study of Soviet and Chinese economic history. All major decisions of economic policy originate with the Politburo of the Party and are implemented by the Central Committee and the Council of Ministers. Economic legislation is adopted unanimously by the National Assembly, whose function it is to give the process of government the appearance of parliamentary respectability. The Plan is drawn up by the State Planning Committee, which is directly subordinate to the Council of Ministers, and which is assisted in technical matters

[1] Vietnam News Agency, September 5, 1960.

by the National Commission of Scientific Research. The implementation of the Plan is the responsibility of Ministers at the centre of power and of executive organs of the administration throughout the country. Physical controls, such as rationing and price fixing, and financial measures, such as taxation on output and turnover and controls of foreign exchange, are the principal means by which government policy is implemented. State-controlled " co-operatives " of cultivators, artisans and traders, as well as state-controlled " unions " of workers, are among the instruments created to give the appearance of government " by the people." The Government is able within this framework to allocate without organised opposition the nation's resources, such as domestic labour and raw materials, as well as imported plant and equipment. Opposition to official measures of economic policy becomes audible only on rare occasions, as when agrarian reform was enforced against the interests of the rural population; such opposition is readily suppressed.

Within a framework of this kind it is possible to achieve higher rates of economic growth than are usual in countries without a monolithic structure of government. Even so, the targets set in the Five-Year Plan seem ambitious for a country which is predominantly agricultural in its setting, whose economic infra-structure is weak and whose industry is in its infancy. By 1965 the gross value of production in industry and handicraft is to be nearly 150 per cent. greater than in 1960, an assumed average annual rate of growth of 20 per cent. Against this, workers' and peasants' incomes are to increase by 30 per cent. or less than 5 per cent. per annum. The main emphasis of the Plan is thus on the development of industry for which investment is found largely by means of forced savings.

Agriculture is expected to move forward more slowly than industry, i.e., by approximately 60 per cent., or 9 per cent. per annum " compared with the estimated degree of fulfilment of the 1960 Plan." The caution of this statement is paralleled by a target of seven million tons of paddy for 1965 as compared with an original target of 7·6 million tons for 1960. Even the new more modest target is, however, quite out of reach. Production of industry and handicraft is to overtake that of agriculture. This aim should not be taken too literally. Industrial prices used for the calculation of growth rates are frequently unduly high, whilst those of farm products are low by comparison. In consequence, the ratios fixed for industrial and agricultural output are far removed from reality.

FOREIGN AID

The degree of fulfilment of the Plan is dependent to a large extent on outside help. In fact, it was acknowledged by Nguyen Duy Trinh in presenting the Plan to the Congress of the Party that assistance and co-operation of brother nations are an indispensable condition of laying the foundation of North Vietnam's industrial economy. As early as 1955 North Vietnam was offered substantial economic and technical assistance from members of the Soviet *bloc*, in particular China and the Soviet Union. China made the largest offer of aid, equivalent to U.S.$200 million, to be used for the reconstruction of railways, bridges and roads (Nam Quan to Hanoi and Haiphong to Lai-Chau) and the construction of eighteen projects. Simultaneously the Soviet Union offered aid equivalent to U.S.$100 million for the reconstruction and building of twenty-five enterprises in industry and public services. These offers were supported by trade and technical aid agreements. It is not known to what extent the financial agreements were implemented, but there can be no doubt that North Vietnam's industrialisation owes much to Chinese and Soviet supplies of equipment as well as to the loan of technicians.

At the end of 1960, the Soviet Union signed long-term trade and aid agreements with North Vietnam, covering the period of its Five-Year Plan. Trade is to increase two and a half times above the level reached during the preceding five years. Long-term assistance (including a small grant) equivalent to over U.S.$110 million is to finance primarily forty-three industrial enterprises as well as an anti-malaria campaign. This agreement was preceded in June 1960 by an offer equivalent to U.S. $87·5 million for the increased output and processing of tropical farm products. Total Soviet economic assistance to North Vietnam now stands at U.S.$365 million compared with offers worth more than U.S.$450 million made by China (of which roughly half is in the form of grants and half credits). Total Soviet *bloc* aid offered to North Vietnam since 1955, including contributions by East European members of the *bloc* amounts to more than U.S.$900 million.[2] Some 1,500 technicians from countries of the Soviet *bloc* are engaged in implementing this large programme of aid.

China's most recent offer to North Vietnam came within five weeks of the Soviet agreement of December 1960. It provided for assistance over the period from 1961 to 1967 to the tune of U.S.$157 million to be spent on the construction and expansion of twenty-eight enterprises in the spheres of industry and transport. Once again China has made an offer more generous than that of the Soviet Union, suggesting a Sino-Soviet contest, which can be observed also elsewhere on the fringes of the two Communist empires, *e.g.*, in North Korea and Outer Mongolia. Sino-Soviet co-operation, side by side with rivalry in this sphere, cannot be ruled out.

It would be an invidious undertaking to predict at this stage the

2 By comparison Western aid to South Vietnam amounts to over U.S.$1,400 million.

economic development of North Vietnam during the remaining four years of the current Plan. Unless anything unforeseen happens, it would be prudent, however, to assume that the country will continue to industrialise at a high rate. Agriculture will lag by comparison. The original agricultural programme, as well as the version revised in August 1961 during the Fifth Plenum of the Central Committee, are certain to remain unfulfilled. Industrial progress will be achieved largely at the expense of the living standards of the peasants, who will continue to live at subsistence level. Vital contributions of capital equipment will be made by one or the other or both Communist imperial powers. Unless major military operations sap a substantial proportion of North Vietnam's national effort, a degree of industrial progress is likely to be achieved that may well become a more effective means of political penetration in neighbouring countries than direct military intervention. The ultimate fate of the contest across the seventeenth parallel will, of course, rest as much on success or failure in the non-Communist societies of South-East Asia as on North Vietnam's own achievements or setbacks.

TABLE 1*

NORTH VIETNAM: ECONOMIC PLANNING

	Rehabilitation 1957 Target	1957 Actual a	Consolidation 1960 Target (Dec. 1958)	1960 Target (Apr. 1960)	1960 Actual	Industrialisation 1961 Target
Industrial Production						
Coal (mill. tons) ..	1·1	1·1	2·7	2·5	2·6	2·6
Electricity (000 kwh.)..	123·0	123·0	271·0	255·0	254·0	319·0
Cement (000 tons) ..	165·0	165·0	450·0	380·0	406·0	450·0
Apatite (000 tons) ..	66·0	65·0	400·0	450·0	490·0	750·0
Timber (000 tons) ..	382·0	382·0	646·0	735·0	684·0	1,010·0
Textiles (mill. metres)	39·0	39·0	85·0	82·0	86·0	90·0
Sugar (000 tons) ..	4·2	4·2	6·7	6·7	14·5	19·0
Farm Production						
Paddy (mill. tons) ..	3·9	3·9	7·6	5·5	4·4	5·6
Maize (000 tons) ..	197·0	197·0	280·0	262·0	198·0	312·0
Potatoes, sweet (000 tons)	540·0	540·0	910·0	910·0	557·0	1,210·0
Casava (000 tons) ..	186·0	186·0	360·0	360·0	396·0	642·0
Total " Grains " (mill. tons grain equivalent)	4·3	4·3	8·2	6·1	4·8	6·3
Sugar Cane (000 tons)	333·0	333·0	623·0	567·0	403·0	626·0
Groundnuts (000 tons)	24·0	24·0	55·0	42·0	23·0	51·0
Cotton (000 tons) ..	5·7	5·7	9·0	7·5	4·0	7·3
Tea (000 tons) ..	2·6	2·3	3·2	3·1	2·9	3·2

* The figures in all these tables have been compiled from numerous official sources over the years and they include some estimates made by the author.

TABLE 1 *(continued)*

NORTH VIETNAM: ECONOMIC PLANNING

	Rehabilitation		Consolidation			Industrial-isation
	1957 Target	1957 Actual a	1960 Target (Dec. 1958)	1960 Target (Apr. 1960)	1960 Actual	1961 Target
Livestock						
Buffaloes (million) ..	1·2	1·2	1·6	1·6	1·4	1·5
Cattle (million) ..	0·9	0·9	1·1	1·1	0·8	0·9
Pigs (million)	2·9	2·9	5·5	5·5	3·6	4·4
Total Livestock (million livestock units)	2·3	2·3	3·1	3·1	2·5	2·6

a The term "actual" is a technical one used by professional economists. It does not indicate that the figures in the columns headed "actual" were in fact achieved but simply that they are the official fulfilment claims made by the Government.

TABLE 2

NORTH VIETNAM: GROSS VALUE OF PRODUCTION

Million New Dongs b	1955 Actual	1956 Actual	1957 Actual	1958 Actual	1959 Actual	1960 Plan
Industry	30	160	230	380	570	730
Handicraft	190	280	700	710	970	1,010
Total	220	440	930	1,090	1,383	1,648
Agriculture	1,550	1,800	1,840	2,070	2,410	2,687
Grand Total	1,770	2,240	2,770	3,160	3,793	4,335

b 1 U.S. $=4 New Dongs.

TABLE 3

NORTH VIETNAM: GOVERNMENT EXPENDITURE

(% of Total)	1955 Budget	1956 Budget	1957 Budget	1958 Budget	1959 Budget	1960 Budget
National Economy ..	32·8	45·0	42·5	46·8	57·5	60·4
Cultural and Social ..	8·4	12·0	12·0	12·8	10·3	13·8
Defence	36·4	22·0	21·0	19·4	17·3	14·4
Administration ..	14·9	12·5	10·5	10·4	10·4	10·1
Other Expenditure ..	7·5	8·5	14·0	10·6	4·5	1·3
Total	100·0	100·0	100·0	100·0	100·0	100·0

TABLE 4

NORTH VIETNAM: SOVIET BLOC AID

(U.S. $ mill.)			Grants	China Credits	Total	Soviet Union Grants	Credits	Total
1955–1957	..	..	200·0	—	200·0	100·0	19·5	119·5
1958–1960	..	..	25·0	75·0	100·0	—	133·0	133·0
1961–1965	..	..	—	157·5	157·5	5·0	107·5	112·5
Total ..	..	..	225·0	232·5	457·5	105·0	260·0	365·0

			Eastern Europe Grants	Credits	Total	Grand Total Grants	Credits	Total
1955–1957	..	..	—	—	—	300·0	19·5	319·5
1958–1960	..	..	—	26·0	26·0	25·0	234·0	259·0
1961–1965	..	..	—	62·5	62·5	5·0	327·5	332·5
Total ..	..	..	—	88·5	88·5	330·0	581·0	911·0

TABLE 5

NORTH VIETNAM: AGRICULTURAL CO-OPERATION

(End of Year)	1955 Actual	1956 Actual	1957 Actual	1958 Actual	1959 Actual	1960 Actual
Agricultural Production Co-operatives (000)	—	—	0·00	4·42	28·60	41·40
Peasant Households in APCs (mill.) ..	—	—	0·00	0·11	1·20	2·50
(% of total) ..	—	—	0·00	4·50	45·00	95·00
Average Households per APC	—	—	14	25	40	60

TABLE 6

NORTH VIETNAM: FOOD AND FARMING

	1955 Actual	1956 Actual	1957 Actual	1958 Actual	1959 Actual	1960 Actual
Paddy Economy						
Acreage (mill. acres)	5·50	5·65	5·55	5·75	5·60	5·60
Production (mill. tons)	3·60	4·15	3·95	4·55	5·20	4·40
Yield (tons per acre) ..	0·65	0·75	0·70	0·80	0·95	0·75
Farm Production						
Paddy (mill. tons) ..	3·6	4·1	3·9	4·6	5·2	4·4
Maize (000 tons) ..	—	258·0	187·0	197·0	228·0	198·0
Potatoes, sweet (000 tons)	—	1,062·0	528·0	540·0	718·0	557·0
Casava (000 tons) ..	—	366·0	186·0	142·0	234·0	396·0
Total " Grains " (mill. tons grain equivalent)	4·0	4·7	4·3	4·9	5·7	4·8
Sugar Cane (000 tons)	—	168·0	330·0	361·0	442·0	403·0
Groundnuts (000 tons)	—	18·0	24·0	31·0	33·0	23·0
Cotton (000 tons) ..	0·5	6·3	5·7	5·7	6·2	4·0
Tea (000 tons) ..	—	2·5	2·3	—	—	2·9
Livestock						
Buffaloes (million) ..	1·1	1·2	1·2	1·3	1·4	1·4
Cattle (million) ..	0·8	0·8	0·9	0·9	1·0	0·8
Pigs (million)	2·1	2·5	2·9	3·1	3·6	3·6
Total " Livestock " (mill. Livestock units)	1·9	2·1	2·3	2·4	2·6	2·5
Domestic Food Supply (Estimates) c						
Grain Net Production (kilos grain equivalent per head) ..	275	310	270	290	325	270
(kilos milled rice equiv. per head)	190	215	190	200	225	190

c Allowing for likely exaggerations.

Collectivisation and Rice Production

By HOANG VAN CHI

UNTIL 1949, Communist rule was still restricted to states where wheat forms the basis of agricultural production. But when Mao Tse-tung extended his control to territories south of the Yangtse river, thereby enabling Ho Chi Minh to establish later a twin régime in North Vietnam, the problem of collectivisation first appeared in tropical areas where rice is the main agricultural crop. From then on, an unforeseen problem of major importance has confronted the two Asian Communist leaders. Unlike their other colleagues in the Socialist camp, these two have had to adapt the rigorous norms of the collective system to the production of rice, an extremely delicate aquatic plant. Their relentless efforts to accomplish this are unprecedented and, now that the practical experiment has been in progress for several years, it is possible to make a preliminary appraisal of the results.

Whilst rice is a very nourishing cereal with a high yield, it is also extremely delicate. So great is the care and the amount of labour demanded by the plant that its production *per capita*—or perhaps per pair of arms—is desperately low despite its very high yield per acre. An exception to this general rule may be found in one or two regions of Europe and America (Northern Italy, South-western France and California), where the flatness of the land, combined with the low average rainfall, permits the use of some machinery; but in all other parts of the world where rice is grown, either on large permanently flooded plains or in minute terraced plots on the slopes of hills, no machinery yet developed can relieve man's efforts.

In the rice producing countries of Asia, which include highly industrialised Japan, the rice seed is first sown by hand in small, dry seedbeds. Once the seed has germinated, the seedlings are planted out individually by highly skilled and incredibly hard-working women in flooded ricefields, usually knee-deep in soft mud. The other tasks obligatory in rice cultivation, ploughing, harrowing, weeding, and reaping, are no less onerous than planting out, and all must be carried out by hand. In consequence, the number of workers required to grow even a small acreage of rice is very large indeed.

A survey of the rice-growing areas shows that wherever rice is planted, the population density is extremely high. The difficulty lies in determining what is the cause and what the effect. Is it the dense population which demands rice production as a means of absorbing all the available labour resources, or is it the growing of rice which, over the span of years, results in high population density? Whatever the answer, it would appear to be true that rice is a rich cereal grown by poor people.

In some areas of North Vietnam—and China too—before the introduction of Communism, where the population density exceeded 2,000 to the square mile, it was the custom of farmers who possessed more than the average area of land to take as many concubines as they could procure and to marry off their sons at the age of about ten to girls of twenty or thereabouts. The sole reason for this was to provide the family with more pairs of hands to work in the ricefields. It is worth noting that in China today the Communists are finding it necessary to mobilise large numbers of city dwellers for work in the ricefields.

There are valid reasons why the shortage of manual labour should become more acute under the system of collectivisation than under the foregoing " feudal," or private ownership, system. Perhaps it is not insignificant that, as the Chinese and North Vietnamese régimes advance towards increasingly rigorous patterns of collectivisation, the boasts of the Peking and Hanoi authorities about increased rice production grow fainter and fainter.

The Chinese Communist Party admitted, on December 28, 1960, to a vertical drop in food production since 1959, that is to say just one year after the implementation of the commune system. The blame for this was assigned to bad weather and natural calamities, but the remedy prescribed by Mao suggests that this may not have been the truth, or at least not the whole truth. To improve the unhappy food position, Mao ordered " a course of thought reform for the cadres and peasants," the meteorological effects of which cannot have been great.

North Vietnam is progressing more slowly in its advance towards collectivisation—it is still at the co-operative stage—with the result that it is only within the past few months that the Vietnamese leaders have admitted to setbacks in agriculture. The transition stage between exaggerated claims to tremendous achievement and the admission of shortcomings was interesting and took the form of unaccustomed vagueness in the figures. For example, the claim made in June last for the fifth month crop in 1961 stated that the yield was " almost equal to that of 1950, probably a little more than 1,700,000 tons of paddy," [1] a very far cry from the precise figures and percentages of earlier years.

Earlier DRV figures for agricultural production were totally unreliable and appeared to bear little relation to what was happening in North Vietnam. In January 1957, for example, the Central Statistics Committee declared that the " production of rice during 1956 totalled 4,132,000 tons

<hr>

[1] Communiqué of the National Congress for Agricultural Production held in Hanoi on June 23–24, 1961. Published in *Thoi Moi*, June 25, 1961.

and that of maize 387,000 tons," which represented increases of 68·4 per cent. and 88·0 per cent. respectively over the 1939 figures.[2] Late in 1956, however, a young Vietnamese poet of the "social realist" school described the situation in the lower delta region of Tonking in the following verses:

> "I have passed through
> Many villages of Kien-An and Hong-Quang
> Where the sea broke in and left its salt over wide plains
> Where, for two successive seasons, no grain of rice has grown
> And human excrement is red with peels of sweet potatoes.
> I have met
> Countless emaciated children
> Of five or six years old
> Eating less rice than bran ... " [3]

The poet Phung Quan's description has been confirmed by a large number of more prosaic sources, the most readily accessible in the West being the account by Gerard Tongas of the widespread famine in Tonking during this period for which the statisticians were claiming such enormous increases in agricultural production.[4] This same author's remarks about DRV statistics are worth mentioning at this juncture. He writes:

> Les chiffres de production donnés ne sont pas simplement truqués, les pourcentages ne sont pas simplement augmentés, les uns et les autres sont la plupart du temps inventés de toutes pieces, et avec quelle ardeur ! [5]

Even if DRV statistics are accepted, and if the figure of 1,700,000 tons given for the fifth month crop in 1961 is regarded as accurate, then it still represents a remarkable recession in rice production. This figure is said to be "almost equal to that of 1950," but, during 1950, the Indo-Chinese war was at its height and immense areas of cultivable land were devastated by the fighting, while whole regions had been abandoned by the peasants fleeing from the dangers of war. The war ended in 1954, and North Vietnam has experienced seven years of peace, so that even the official DRV statistics seem to suggest that years of collectivisation have accomplished no appreciable increase in agricultural output.

Indeed, there is much evidence available which suggests that the reverse is true, and that the situation has deteriorated steadily year after year. Even a cursory reading of Party newspapers during the period of the past few months leaves no doubt that North Vietnam is in the grip of a severe food shortage. The following few extracts, chosen at random

---

[2] *Hoc Tap*, January 1957, p. 25.
[3] *Giai Pham Mua Thu*, October 1956.
[4] *L'Enfer Communiste au Nord Viet-Nâm* (Paris: NÉD, 1961), p. 225.
[5] *Ibid*. p. 213.

from the DRV press, indicate some of the difficulties being encountered by the Vietnamese Communists:

1. *Difficulty experienced by the Trade Bureau in purchasing food from the peasants at prices fixed by the Government*

" Contracts for the supply of food were signed by ourselves [The Trade Bureau] and the co-operatives, but again and again the co-operatives failed to honour the contracts they had signed. We could not sit idly behind our scales, watching the peasants passing our office laden with peanuts which they intended to sell elsewhere [on the open market], so we posted men at Cong-sen, at a point on National Road No. 5, and at all the crossroads giving access to the Ho market. They had orders to arrest the peanut smugglers.

" But people arrested on one day merely changed their route and the time of going to market on the next. Persons discovered on one day transporting peanuts in hollow pumpkins, simply changed the hiding place on the next, concealing the peanuts inside women's turban's, or in baskets covered with grass, or even inside mandolins in very ornate cases.

" Each time [we catch them out], we become convinced that there is an endemic obstinancy in the peasantry arising from their short-sighted realism. They are anxious to produce only such things as bring profit to themselves, and whenever they are compelled to sell their products to the State they try to retain the maximum benefit for themselves." [6]

2. *Ration Cards for rice*

" There have been numerous cases of organisations, whose cadres or workers have been transferred, or dismissed, or called up for military service, or sent on courses, or sent abroad, retaining the rice ration cards of these persons. In this way, large numbers of offices, work camps, or collective restaurants acquire many more ration cards than they are entitled to. . . . They have used these extra cards contrary to the law, and have thus created grave difficulties for the food rationing programme. In many of these places, the cadres in charge have given the ration cards to their wives, who sell them to the ordinary people in exchange for chickens. . . . This reduces food rationing to a state of chaos. . . . [7]

3. *The difficulty of obtaining one's rice ration*

" The difficulty [of obtaining rationed rice] is still greater for the workers of the ' March 3 Spinning Mill.' Each time they wish to buy their ration of rice, they are obliged to take half a day's leave from the mill.

---

[6] *Nhan Dan*, August 26, 1961.
[7] *Thoi Moi*, June 23, 1961.

Sometimes, when the crowds waiting to buy their rice ration are too great, the workers are forced to take several of these half-day leaves in succession before they can get the rice." [8]

It may be argued that the above instances are small and relatively unimportant, and so they are, but they can be paralleled again and again in the DRV press. Again, the number of cases which reach the pages of the newspapers must be only a small fraction of the total number throughout the whole of North Vietnam. They all add up to a picture of severe food shortage. If the press reports of the food situation are compared year by year since the Communists assumed control of North Vietnam, then they indicate clearly that the food situation is growing steadily worse. By relating the progressive stages of enforced collectivisation (mutual aid teams in 1956; permanent mutual aid teams in 1957; low-grade co-operatives in 1958; advanced co-operatives since 1959) with the amount of food produced, it can be shown that the advance of collectivisation has been accompanied by a corresponding drop in food production. In China, where a still higher stage of collectivisation, the communes, was reached, the authorities were obliged by the severity of the food shortage to retreat. The relatively easier food situation in the Soviet Union and the East European satellites may be explained by the fact that dry cereals are less likely to suffer adversely from collectivisation than rice. The evidence provided by the experience of the Communist *bloc* would seem to permit of two hypotheses,

(i) The more thorough the collectivisation, the lower the yield of agricultural products.

(ii) Some cereals are less amenable to the discipline of collectivisation than others.

Two factors demand further study if the reasons for the failure of collectivisation in rice-growing areas is to be understood. These are the conditions which it is necessary to fulfil in order to obtain a good rice crop, and the situation brought about by enforced collectivisation.

The Chinese and Vietnamese people, who have been planting rice for several millenia, have a saying in which the four requirements of rice growing are set in order of importance. It runs: " First water, second manure, third labour, fourth seeds," and it is based upon a vast experience in this field. A further examination of each requirement will help to shed some light on the subject.

(i) *Water*

Being an aquatic plant, rice cannot live without water so that rice fields are always flat and are surrounded by small dykes designed to

8 *Thoi Moi*, September 7, 1961.

contain a pre-determined depth of water. Since rain falls during limited wet seasons, the dykes must be watertight enough to keep the ricefields flooded for several months until the rice is ready for harvesting. The rice grower's greatest worry, which is always with him, is the possibility of a break or hole in one of the dykes which could permit the water to flow away. Should that happen, then the whole crop will be lost, and there is nothing he can do about it.

During the period of private ownership of land in North Vietnam, it was common to see the peasant farmer strolling about his land for hours on end, inspecting the dykes while his wife and children ceaselessly hunted the small crabs which burrow into, and sometimes through, the dykes of a ricefield. Whenever it began to rain, he would abandon whatever task he might be engaged upon and run to his ricefields with all speed. There he would watch his dykes to ensure that they were equal to the strain of the increased weight of water, strengthening them in the weakest places, and seeing to it that his neighbours did not break them so as to steal water from his fields. So great was the peasant's solicitude for water in pre-Communist Vietnam that noisy disputes about water stealing, which frequently degenerated into bloody scuffles, were part of the daily life of the villages. So essential is water for rice growing that negligence on the part of the farmer might easily result in the loss of the whole crop and the consequent ruin of his family. The conditions of life in Vietnam were such that, once a family sustained a loss of this kind, it could never retrieve its fortunes and regain its former economic and social position. For this reason, the Vietnamese peasant used to display as great a concern for the dykes of his ricefield as a parachutist does for his parachute. But such concern can only exist when the peasant is assured that the fruits of his patient labour will accrue to him and his family.

Collectivised farming has introduced a completely different atmosphere to the countryside of North Vietnam. At the present time, the peasants work peacefully together in groups, with no squabble over a few paltry raindrops to disturb the harmony. The crop has now become the collective property of the whole community, or as much of the crop as is not requisitioned by the Government. The former stimulus to long hours of patient and devoted toil has gone, and nothing seems to be able to bring it back, persuasion, emulation, competition, supervision, or punishment. When it rains now in North Vietnam, no peasants run out to keep a watchful eye upon the dykes and the water level. None of them is willing to risk being killed by lightning or catching a bad cold for the sake of his neighbours in the co-operative, and the directing cadres always seem to be too slow in organising labour to meet such emergencies. For example, when a summer storm suddenly breaks, the senior cadre can hardly run through the whole village calling on each peasant individually to help. Even if he were to do so, he would probably find the peasant busy mending his roof or repairing his rain water guttering, and would be told, " Yes, I'll be along in a minute." It scarcely needs to be said that the peasant's minute lasts until it has stopped raining, so that when he eventually reaches the fields he finds that the precious water has almost disappeared. However, it would be rare to find a cadre with sufficient devotion to round up peasants to deal with such emergencies. Today both the cadre in charge and the collectivised peasant care little, for they are wage earners whose respective salaries do not depend upon their readiness to take risks and their concern for the safety of the crop.

The consequence of this new attitude is that the ricefields begin to dry up as soon as the rainy season is over, causing the colour of the rice crop to change from green to yellow and finally to brown. Only at this stage does the Party issue its emergency orders for the fight against " drought " and mobilise the peasants to " squeeze the earth for water and shake the sky for rain." Indeed, during the summer of 1961, Hanoi radio was issuing emergency orders for fighting drought and floods at the same time. This is the real reason why, since the country has become Communist, droughts occur more frequently than ever before and their consequences are more severe.

(ii) *Manure*

Rice is a cereal crop with a very high yield, which means that it is also a very greedy plant requiring large quantities of fertiliser. If it is not properly fertilised, it yields a very small crop.

Now North Vietnam is a region which has suffered for centuries from a constant shortage of fertiliser. The reason for this is that, during the thirteenth century, the Vietnamese adopted the Chinese system of building dykes along the length of its rivers. A careful study of Vietnamese history shows that, following the building of dykes, the land became progressively poorer until it was eventually incapable of supporting the population. The dykes prevented the seasonal flooding of villages, but they also prevented the alluvial soil carried in the water of the rivers from being deposited over the countryside. After the building of the dykes, this was carried down to the sea, while the soil was washed only by rainwater.

Some phosphates are present in North Vietnam, but their exploitation by hand is so expensive that the price of fertiliser from this source is beyond the resources of the co-operatives, especially when they are obliged to sell their products to the Trade Bureau at prices fixed well below the market level.

In pre-Communist Vietnam the peasants were entirely dependent for fertiliser upon human and animal manure. So precious was this that violent quarrels frequently broke out among the children, whose duty it was to look after the grazing cows, over the ownership of a piece of fresh cow dung. Each peasant family kept special containers for human excrement and was most meticulous about its collection and storage.

Under the new system, manure has ceased to be the object of daily concern and individual care. The peasants of Vietnam now feel able to attach to it the same taboos which are found in societies throughout the world. It would appear, however, that the responsible cadres in the agricultural collectives have at last understood the seriousness of this problem, for they have recently adopted two measures designed to overcome it. Co-operatives have been ordered to buy manure from their members and, at the same time, country-wide competitions have been organised to find, and honour, outstanding producers of manure. They receive the title of "Kien Tuong phan," which defies translation into English, but Kien Tuong is a traditional title of nobility and appears extremely incongruous when placed beside the third word. Such a competition is described in detail in the magazine *Van Hoc*,[9] but even such a partisan source as this admits that there was a marked lack of enthusiasm to win the title.

The sale of manure is conducted on the basis of gross weight since no co-operative is well enough equipped to carry out a qualitative analysis, with the result that the merchandise delivered by each member of the co-operative contains only sufficient traces of genuine manure to give a characteristic smell to the whole, and large profits are being earned from this improbable commodity. Thus the soil, which was maintained in good condition over the centuries, has undergone a rapid deterioration as the nitrogenous elements are washed out by the rain water and carried away to the rivers and the sea.

(iii) *Labour*

Unlike water and manure, which are always in short supply under the collective system, labour is available. Vietnamese peasants have always enjoyed a well earned reputation for being the hardest working people in the whole of South East Asia. Before the arrival of Communism, they worked from dawn to dusk every day throughout the year except at Tet, or New Year, which was a three-day holiday.

At the present time, they are compelled to work even harder than in the past. The normal routine in a collective begins with 5 a.m. rising, and the peasants are ready to work in the fields when the bell tolls at 6 a.m. At noon they return for lunch and their mid-day study session,

9 *Van Hoc*, No. 116, October 10, 1960.

and recommence work in the fields at 2 p.m. There they work until 6 p.m., when they hold meetings to discuss one another's labour performances during the day and receive their orders for the next day's work. However, they are frequently required to work much longer hours than this. A typical example is cited in the publication *Tien Phong*,[10] and it conveys some idea of the enormous demands being made on the peasants.

" In the district of Bat Bat (Son-tay Province), all members of the Youth Association Branch are having to work longer hours than usual. They work from 3 a.m. until 9 or 10 p.m., and in some places as late as 12 midnight. Many of the women members are obliged to entrust their newly-born babies to others in order to join their team in planting out the rice seedlings until midnight."

In return for ten hours of hard work, each peasant receives ten marks. A mark entitles him to 150 grammes of rice, so that a full working day earns him one and a half kilos of rice, or roughly three pounds. This piece-work method of payment ensures that everyone exerts himself to the limit of his physical capacity, but it stifles all initiative. The peasant in a collective has no interest in raising production, but simply works like a machine for so many hours, carrying out literally the orders of his superior cadre whether these make any sense or not. Under these conditions, rice growing has ceased to be a matter of skill and hard work based upon personal experience, and it seems most unlikely to develop into a major industry as the Communist leaders wish. In spite of the ever-increasing volume of labour devoted to rice cultivation, the production of rice continues to fall from year to year.

(iv) *Seeds*

When the other requirements have been met satisfactorily, then the selection of the seed becomes a matter of great importance. However, when water conservation is neglected, when the fields lack fertiliser, and when the necessary care is not devoted to the crop, then seed selection loses much of its importance. This is the reason why a species which, if one can believe the claims made by Doctor Luong Dinh Cua, yielded as much as 6,200 kgs. per hectare in his Agricultural Institute, produced only 3,500 kgs. per hectare when planted by co-operatives.[11] Experiences of this kind show how right the Chinese and Vietnamese saying is when it places seed in the fourth or last place in its table of requirements for successful rice growing.

Although the inefficiency of the system of collectivisation derives principally from the various causes set out above, the contribution of the political leadership is far from negligible. The zeal of these all-powerful

---

10 *Tien Phong*, No. 760, August 4, 1961.
11 *Thoi Moi*, September 19, 1961.

men is matched only by their ignorance of agricultural management, so that decisions from above fall upon the heads of the unfortunate peasants with the frequency of drops of rain in a downpour, and each decision cancels or corrects its predecessor. Order, counter-order, and counter-counter-order frequently arrive in the office of the co-operative at the same time. The bulk of the decisions are based, not upon the results of some new scientific experiment or some successful agricultural trials, but upon some new interpretation of the Party political line or some new directives received from Moscow or Peking. The effects can be imagined. The waste of time, of materials, of money, and of labour they occasion is beyond description.

When I myself experienced the effects of this flood of heterogeneous and often contradictory directives, as I witnessed the endless mobilisation of people for every imaginable kind of " struggle " going on day after day, I used to derive some measure of comfort from the following traditional Vietnamese story:

There was once a peasant who grew such excellent fruit that his fame spread far and wide throughout the land. The governor of the district in which the man lived made a special journey to visit him and to enquire about the methods he employed to produce such magnificent fruit.

The peasant was a little overawed by the presence of such a great mandarin, but he did his best to reply to the latter's questions. " To tell you the truth," he said, " I haven't any special method at all. Whenever I plant a fruit tree, I provide it with as much manure as I can, set it upright in the hole, tamp the earth back firmly around the trunk, and then I leave it to itself. I never prune it, or train its branches, or chop its roots like the other people do, and it provides me with plenty of fine fruit."

The mandarin nodded his head in approval, and then put another question to the peasant. " You seem to be able to manage your fruit trees admirably. Can you give me any advice about how to manage men, about how to govern a district?"

The unexpected question surprised the peasant, so he was obliged to pause for a few moments and to think before he eventually replied. " Administration," he said, " has never been my profession, so I have never really devoted much thought to it, but it is my opinion that men are like fruit trees. If you provide them with the conditions in which they can live and work, and keep a fatherly eye upon them from time to time, they will be prosperous, happy, and will cause you no trouble. If, however, you summon them daily to your office and order them to do this or forbid them to do that, they will prove to be a constant source of trouble, disorder, and unhappiness."

The moral of this story is based upon centuries of experience, but the Vietnamese Communists are attempting to do just the reverse and are reaping the inevitable consequences. Man, having a mind and a soul, is capable of being terrorised into submission, but only to a limited extent and for a limited time. Plants, however, stand in no awe of Communism.

In the whole of the vegetable kingdom, it is the rice plant which possesses the most " bourgeois background " and which is proving the most " reactionary " in the face of the policy of collectivisation which has been applied in Asia during the past few years. Rice may well be the factor which brings about the downfall of Asian Communism.

The failure of Mao and Ho to solve the problem of rice production is a subject which should exercise the minds of all those people in South Asia, South-East Asia, and Central Africa, who cultivate and live by rice.

Vietnam—An Independent Viewpoint

By NGUYEN NGOC BICH

Dr. Bich, now living in exile, is a leading representative of an important section of Vietnamese opinion which finds itself out of sympathy with the actions of both the Communists in the DRV and Ngo Dinh Diem's government in South Vietnam.

A BELIEF widely current in the Western world is that Vietnamese in general dislike the Chinese, towards whom they experience a feeling of inferiority springing from the domination of Vietnam for over a thousand years by her powerful northern neighbour.

The truth is that this inferiority complex no longer persists today, if, indeed, it ever existed in the past, for the simple reason that Vietnam established her independence of China in the tenth century and has maintained it ever since in the face of numerous terrible and costly attacks —by the Sung in the eleventh century, the Mongol followers of Genghis Khan in the thirteenth century, the Ming at the beginning of the fifteenth century, and finally the Ch'ing in the eighteenth century.

On the contrary, Vietnamese have tended to suffer from a little too much pride in their history, which encompasses, besides this vigorous resistance to Chinese attacks, a continual territorial expansion southwards towards the Mekong delta and, more recently, after eighty years of contact with the West, the great victory of Dien Bien Phu. However, this pride does not prevent their constant awareness of the fact that almost seven hundred million Chinese are living on the other side of the frontier. They are fully mindful moreover that, over the centuries, all the Chinese régimes which have periodically united that great country have shown themselves to be fiercely expansionist to the detriment of their neighbours. Whether one likes to admit it or not, the most important question facing both North and South Vietnam today is how to safeguard the future of the whole Vietnamese nation now threatened by such vast numbers and such great dynamism.

In South Vietnam, the Saigon régime appears to be pursuing an internal policy of forcibly assimilating Chinese immigrants and their descendants, and a foreign policy which totally ignores the existence of mainland China.

In North Vietnam, the Hanoi government, which is linked to China by a common political ideology and is geographically much closer to her, seems to have adopted a more subtle attitude. The fears of China, which

128

were repeatedly voiced in public during the era of Chiang Kai-shek, have given way since 1949 to manifestations of solidarity and friendship. Neither the common ideology nor the large sums of aid received from China can explain these fully. Only geopolitics, which itself implies a certain community of interest, can offer a completely satisfactory explanation. In fact, the presence of French troops in the Red River Delta constituted a threat which the newly unified China could not tolerate for long. Indeed, she did not tolerate them for long, for they were removed after the battle of Dien Bien Phu.

But the Geneva agreements, which satisfied a China anxious to conserve her energies, left the Vietnamese far from content. They were obliged to make the best of their ill fortune and agree to peace, but only on condition that they were offered the prospect of reunification with South Vietnam, peacefully if possible, but otherwise by subversion. It was not until the waves of discontent in the countryside caused by the "denunciation of misery" campaigns and the failure of the agrarian reforms that the question posed by the presence of so many Chinese soldiers and civilians in the country was raised. By that time, the pro-Chinese Truong Chinh was no longer Secretary-General of the Lao Dong Party. The swan song of the Chinese period was, perhaps, the Hundred Flowers campaign. It gave way to a period of prudent transition during which an equal balance was held between Peking and Moscow by Ho Chi Minh himself, for he did not hesitate to take back the direction of the Party after the departure of Truong Chinh. Chinese economic aid could still be preponderant at that time, because the task facing the Government was that of putting the national economy back on its feet and installing small consumer industries. However, on the day when China confessed herself unable to carry out, for example, a rapid programme of semi-heavy industrialisation, a swing towards Moscow became inevitable. It was the Third Congress of the Lao Dong Party at Hanoi in September 1960, which accomplished the great transition and in particular the programme outlined by Le Duan, appointed Secretary-General of the Party during this Congress, which put forward the following three main themes:

Support for the Russian viewpoint in the Sino-Soviet dispute.
Rapid Socialisation of North Vietnam, with the execution of the First Five-Year Plan, 1961–65.
Progressive and peaceful reunification of the two halves of Vietnam.

Le Duan is probably the North Vietnamese leader with the best knowledge of South Vietnam, for, after the departure of Nguyen Son, he directed the independence struggle there for a long period. His nomination for the post of First Secretary of the Party—there can be no doubt that he was nominated, just as Truong Chinh had been some ten years earlier, for the source of all authority is Ho Chi Minh, and it always has been—indicates that the Vietnamese Communists have decided that the moment has come for the North to undertake the reconquest of the South, and to accomplish this from inside South Vietnam. It symbolises an intention of exerting a great effort in a field much better known to Le Duan, namely South Vietnam, than are the fields of ideological controversy with Mao Tse-tung or the erection of machine-tools factories in the suburbs of Hanoi. The end in view is the reunification of the two halves of Vietnam, and the first step will be the elimination of the Ngo Dinh Diem régime together with all American influence in South Vietnam. However, there is reason for thinking that deeper motives than this exist, motives closely linked with the first two of the themes developed at the Lao Dong Congress. It is essential to understand these motives.

The most striking feature of the Vietnamese Communist leadership is its outstanding spirit of realism, even pragmatism. Although it is attached to its Communist doctrine, it will not, generally speaking, simply accept ready-made ideas. For many of the Vietnamese Communists the practice of Marxism comprises nothing more than a continual examination and appraisal of the facts. Every happening and every action have to be made the objects of a critical reflection from which a lesson must be drawn. The purpose of this reflection is to avoid the repetition of past mistakes rather than to provide a sure guide for future actions. However, the practice not infrequently results in a certain lack of imagination in the planning of future actions, for its devotees are more readily inclined to repeat past actions, whenever these are considered to have been successful, instead of confronting a new situation with a completely open mind and devising a set of plans for that specific situation. This is why the Vietnamese Communists have so frequently been reproached, albeit sometimes unjustly, for being naturally more inclined to imitate or to repeat than to create something new for themselves.

Abundant examples of this method of thinking and acting are to be found. One such was the battle of Vinh-Yen when, on the advice of Chinese tacticians who were accustomed to dispose of large numbers of troops, the Viet Minh decided to launch massive attacks. General de Lattre de Tassigny was thus enabled to use napalm on a large scale with devastating effects upon the Vietnamese soldiers. However, from then until the end of the war, these mass attacks were never repeated. Again, the manufacture of arms was, at one period, slowed down and replaced by the manufacture of offensive hand grenades. The reason for this change was that somebody had noticed it was more " economical " to mount hand grenade attacks against certain enemy light battalions and to seize their arms than to go on manufacturing arms, at the cost of considerable labour and transport difficulties, in the rear areas. In another sphere, the Viet Minh one day began to discourage the raising of pigs so long as the war lasted and encouraged people to breed dogs instead as a source of meat, for dogs were more " economical." Now dogs are as greedy and omnivorous as pigs, if not more so, but someone had noticed that dogs produce two litters of young each year, while pigs produce only one.

This spirit of pragmatism tends to draw the leaders of North Vietnam away from dogmatism and makes the present theses of Moscow more acceptable to them than those of Peking. It leads them to the conclusion that only a rapid industrialisation of the country, which will enable the standard of living to be raised, can possibly justify in the eyes of the people the dictatorship and all the constraints placed upon them by the Party. In consequence, everything else has to be subordinated to this rapid industrialisation, the more so because the growth in the country's power and prestige which will inevitably accrue as a result of the new industry, will remove more surely than anything else the dreaded spectre of becoming a mere satellite state.

To what extent can such an industrialisation be achieved rapidly? At first glance, the targets which have been set out in considerable detail by the Five-Year Plan appear to be extremely optimistic. But one must remember that the old French Indo-China itself accomplished " great leaps forward " in certain sectors of the economy at times. The area devoted to rubber plantations jumped from 3,000 hectares to 12,000 hectares between 1924 and 1929, an increase of 400 per cent. in the space of five years. Again, between 1914 and 1929, the number of workers employed in industrial establishments jumped from 55,000 to 140,000, which represented a total increase of 150 per cent. or a mean annual growth of 17 per cent., and that in spite of the First World War which occupied four years of the period. At the present time, North Vietnam has at her disposal an abundant supply of labour, for unemployment is very high, particularly in the countryside, and the population density in the delta of the Red River is among the highest in the world. The two blast furnaces, the cement factory, the machine-tool factory, the tractor factory, and the other projects contained in the plan can easily be completed within the specified time provided the present rhythm of foreign aid is maintained, and provided that agricultural production proves adequate. But will they?

The growth in agricultural production envisaged, 61 per cent. in five years, appears modest by comparison with the proposed growth in industry, but there are good grounds for thinking that it will not be achieved. There are several reasons, the most important of which are the low yields due to the still archaic methods of cultivation, the product of the old system of sub-letting land, the difficulty of putting new land in the middle regions under cultivation, the general discontent among the peasants, and the disastrous agrarian reform and its consequences. The steep rise in the sliding scale of tax on grain production discourages farmers, as do the annoyances of the multiple system of controls imposed by a top-heavy bureaucracy and the too numerous police. Agricultural production for 1960 was over 1,000,000 tons below the estimated figures, and secondary crops cannot always make up for the shortage of cereals. Hunger has become endemic, and it is very doubtful indeed whether China, who has herself experienced three successive years of bad harvests, could possibly come to the rescue of her southern neighbour, particularly at the present time. There remains only the contraband rice from South Vietnam, which some people estimate at 400,000 tons annually, although there appears to be little evidence upon which to base such a figure.

Thus, in the final analysis, the success of the Five-Year Plan will depend upon the problem of feeding the people of North Vietnam, a problem which cannot be easily resolved without increased supplies of rice from South Vietnam. Indeed, the annual rate of growth of agricultural production, which is forecast at 7 per cent., will in reality probably be no more than 4 per cent. for the population, if the figure for the annual increase in the population is roughly the same as it is in South Vietnam at the present time, will increase by 3 per cent. Moreover, the proposed communalisation of agriculture makes it impossible to forecast whether even this figure can be achieved. If all the unpredictable factors in agriculture are taken into account, floods, droughts, bad weather, etc., and to these are added factors peculiar to North Vietnam, the programme of industrialisation, and the socialisation of agriculture, then it would seem that the DRV is running a grave risk of failure caused by the lack of sufficient food to sustain the population. The thesis that industry must predominate over agriculture risks being proved wrong in practice, with the result that its advocates will be discredited.

In consequence, the protagonists of a policy of "peaceful co-existence" with the West—who are also backing the present economic programme—risk being reduced to a minority by the partisans of a policy of "necessary and inevitable war." If this comes about, then friendship with Moscow will necessarily be replaced by an alliance with China. There would then be a very great danger that the independence, relative but nevertheless real, which the DRV enjoys today, would disappear and that the DRV would become simply a Chinese satellite. Thus, the success of the Five-Year Plan would appear to be a primary condition, not only for the maintenance of the present line of the Lao Dong

Party, but also for the preservation of a certain measure of independence for the whole of Vietnam from China; for the " satellite-isation " of the North would constitute a most serious menace for the South, particularly in time of any major crisis.

The task entrusted to the new Secretary-General of the Lao Dong Party is to ensure the success of the present line. If it is viewed in this light, then the war of subversion which has clearly been declared against Ngo Dinh Diem and the U.S.A. might well be understood as a struggle unleashed simply for the purpose of conquering rice. The nationalist sentiments endlessly voiced by the Northern propagandists, the sentimental appeals for the reunification of the two halves of the nation— made by persons who, for reasons of their chosen ideology, would deny the very concept " nation "—carry no conviction. They strike no very profound echo among the population of South Vietnam, for the Southerners are suffering from this subversive war to which they themselves do not contribute. Indeed, the subversion is enabled to continue more because of reaction against the Diem régime than because of any love for Communism or because of any vision of national unity in the future. It is because of the enormous economic benefits which will accrue to North Vietnam from national reunification that the DRV campaigns so vigorously in its favour. If this were not the case, then the DRV would long since have adopted a separatist attitude analogous to that of Eastern Germany in Europe. No dialectic, not even Marxist, could support one theory in Europe and its exact opposite in Asia.

However, it is precisely because North Vietnam is fighting to secure rice that the war is, from the purely national point of view, a legitimate one. For self-styled nationalists such as Ngo Dinh Diem, who are motivated more by their own hatred of Communism than by any real compassion for the fate which has overtaken their Northern compatriots, it is nonsensical to refuse to aid these compatriots in their struggle against famine. By refusing to help what is, after all, a part of their own country, they are, of necessity, weakening the whole of Vietnam, and even the ideals which they claim to defend. They have also forgotten their history of the Vietnamese nation, which has known, even under the Trinh and the Nguyen,[1] periods of prosperity whenever the rivalry which existed between these two great families was pushed into the background.

All of this by no means implies that South Vietnam's adherence to the free world should be questioned, nor does it suggest that it should make any concessions to Communism on that score. The Vietnamese

---

[1] The Trinh and the Nguyen were two great Vietnamese families which split Vietnam into two halves at about the beginning of the seventeenth century, the Trinh governing the northern half and the Nguyen the south. The dividing line was not far from the present frontier at the seventeenth parallel. The division persisted until the second half of the eighteenth century.

people have aspired for too long to a liberal and truly democratic form of government, they have given too many proofs of their attachment to basic individual liberties for anyone to be able to maintain in Vietnam for any appreciable length of time, even if he should employ brute force, a yoke which the people abhor. They want no more of the Chief of District who, in the name of some " -ism," compels them to work in forced labour gangs on the roads during the day, than they do of the cadre who, in the name of some different " -ism," compels them to destroy by night what they will have to repair on the following day.   They demand simply to live undisturbed and to be left in peace. They desire that the army, which has been created from the population itself, should afford protection against all molestation, no matter from what source it may come, and should impose throughout the countryside and the towns of Vietnam, a respect for the human being and the observance of the laws of the land.

But once this has been said, it must be asserted that it would be a grave error for South Vietnam to permit this war of subversion to continue indefinitely and thus to permit the DRV to transform what is now a struggle for rice into a real war fought on behalf of Moscow. The introduction of a liberal régime in Saigon would clear the air, would permit the establishment of commercial relations with Hanoi, and would permit a halt to be called in the fighting. As far as foreign relations are concerned, the demands of neutrality would prohibit any interference by the DRV in the affairs of South Vietnam, whose sole right it would be to decide by herself whether she should follow a more truly national and independent policy while maintaining her good relations with her neighbours and with all the countries of the free world.

A peaceful and progressive reunification of the two Vietnams could only be achieved peacefully and progressively, that is to say without the use of any armed force and with both sides sitting around a table. When arms have still not been laid aside, there can be no question of a peaceful reunification. During the period of awaiting for some day in the future, when favourable circumstances will permit this, South Vietnam hopes that it will eventually be possible for the two halves to live side by side in peace, to help each other in the common task of building up the Vietnamese nation instead of using armed force against one another in an ideological struggle in which the people have no part to play, a struggle which will last so long as the division of the world into two mutually hostile *blocs* persists. The alternative to this is that " reunification " will become nothing more than a propaganda theme designed to conceal the wish to carry out a problematical conquest.

Local Government and Administration Under the Viet-Minh, 1945–54

By GEORGE GINSBURGS

EVER since it first raised the standard of revolt in Japanese-occupied French Indochina, the Viet-Minh régime has devoted an inordinate amount of time and attention to problems of local government and administration. The emphasis was just as apparent in its first Basic Law of 1945 as in the latest organic act of the Democratic Republic of Vietnam, which went into effect in 1960, and in the manifold supplementary statutes promulgated in the interim to implement the constitutional provisions. This obvious concern on the part of Ho Chi Minh's leadership with the instrumentalities of local rule may be explained by reference to two different, though closely related, sets of considerations.

Historically, the population of Vietnam, overwhelmingly peasant in its make-up, was, for all practical purposes, governed through a comprehensive network of village councils and was only vaguely aware of the existence of a remote central government. Even when it was affected by the latter's policies, the contact was nearly never direct, but was usually effected through the normal official channels, *i.e.*, the rural authorities. Because of this traditional factor, then, the Viet-Minh was, from the very start, almost inevitably forced to concentrate a great deal of effort on consolidating its hold over the one truly operative system of control over the large mass of the population—the local village unit. Initially it pursued this course in order to bolster its bid for power; today it does so in order to maintain its authority and enable it to realise its programme of refashioning North Vietnamese society in accordance with " socialist " blueprints.

In practice the Viet-Minh régime, having first emerged as an insurgent movement and later been forced to wage a difficult guerrilla campaign for nine long years, was precluded by circumstances from effectively organising its administrative control in terms of large-scale territorial divisions, a regular nation-wide apparatus of hierarchically structured official organs and a uniform pyramidal echelon of successive governmental instances. Instead, because of the predominantly military character of the situation between 1945 and 1954, throughout this crucial period the movement's formal institutional framework remained for the most part clandestine, makeshift and limited. It was often reduced to operating on the scale of individual villages, or, more usually, small rural districts, thereby, almost automatically, even further conditioning the leadership's abnormal preoccupation with the modalities of local rule and the mechanics of political power at the primary level.

The insurrectionary régime's first formal instrumentalities of local administration emerged in the final months of the Second World War in conjunction with the announced launching of an armed campaign against the Japanese occupation forces in Indochina although the much publicised military action itself never seems to have materialised to any appreciable extent. Accordingly, in areas securely held by Ho Chi Minh's guerrilla troops special revolutionary people's committees were rapidly established, and in other localities similar tasks were delegated to so-called committees of liberation and to various organisations of the Viet-Minh. On April 16, 1945, the latter's Central Committee issued a nation-wide directive " On the Organisation of Committees of Liberation " pursuant to which, it was later claimed, " almost everywhere such provisional State organs were formed, representing a unified system headed by the Committee of National Liberation of Vietnam." [1] In accordance with the decree, committees of liberation were said to have been organised in factories, mines, barracks, government offices, etc., as well as in the villages. Every district, town, province, zone, plus each of the three regions of Vietnam (North, Central and South) reportedly had its own committee of liberation. The official duties of these, then still clandestine, bodies were described as including : the development of the national-liberation movement; the protection and defence of the rights of the workers; the organisation of supplies to workers and assistance to the unemployed; the recruitment of armed units of defence and militia for action against the Japanese occupation troops and their agents; safeguarding the life and property of citizens; fighting illiteracy, etc.

Not unexpectedly, the dominant influence in the committees was that of the League of Viet-Minh, which was represented in each of them by a special " Viet-Minh section." Staffed with League cadres, members of the committee, such " inner cabinets " convened before every meeting of their committee for a preliminary discussion of the agenda, thereby in fact determining the entire subsequent course of the general session's work and always giving the League a decisive voice in all plenary debates.

Though admittedly temporary and but short-lived, and designed specifically for revolutionary purposes, it is asserted today, not entirely without justification, that, at the time, these people's committees and

---

[1] A. G. Budanov, *Gosudarstvennyi stroi Demokraticheskoi Respubliki Vietnam* (*State Structure of the Democratic Republic of Vietnam*) (Moscow: 1958), p. 29. Actually, however, there is much doubt as to how extensive this network of organs really was. That it was certainly much more limited than Viet-Minh sources like to claim that it was, hardly seems open to question.

committees of liberation actually were " not only organs of insurrection, but provisional organs of State power as well." [2] They were thus said to have constituted " the bases of the nascent people's authority," in which capacity they allegedly " played a major role in attracting broad masses of the people in taking part in the exercise of public power, in mobilising the nation for the general uprising and the accomplishment of the August revolution." [3] Following Japan's capitulation in World War II and the attendant open seizure of control by the Viet-Minh in much of Indochina, in territories occupied by the nationalist forces the erstwhile committees of liberation were rapidly reorganised into regular people's committees of villages, districts and provinces, as well as into committees of workers and employees. In areas of continuing guerrilla strife, they became revolutionary workers' committees in industrial enterprises and people's revolutionary committees in villages and other administrative units. After the proclamation of independence, the inauguration of the republic and the introduction of a constitutional framework of government, at least in the so-called " liberated " portion of Indochina, these various self-appointed committees were soon officially superseded in their role of primary institutions of public rule by duly constituted State organs of local administration.

CONSTITUTIONAL FRAMEWORK

Given the origins and operational background of the Viet-Minh movement, it is not surprising, therefore, to find the new régime's views on the proposed structure of the republic's organs of local authority set forth in great detail in one of its earliest official enactments. In effect, such a measure was promulgated even before the Constitution itself as Decree No. 63 of the President of the Provisional Government of the Democratic Republic of Vietnam of November 22, 1945.[4] Under the terms of this basic statute, four levels of local rule were envisaged for the country— the village, the district, the province, and the large administrative region (bo). As already noted, all of Vietnam had been divided earlier into three such regions, North, Central and South, embracing in turn 27, 15 and 21 provinces, respectively.[5] " In order to establish local people's authority

2 Ibid.
3 N. S. Merzlyakov, " Gosudarstvennoe stroitelstvo v Demokraticheskoi Respublike Vietnam " (" State Organisation in the Democratic Republic of Vietnam "), in 15 let Demokraticheskoi Respubliki Vietnam (15 Years of the Democratic Republic of Vietnam) (Moscow: 1960), p. 35.
4 Journal Officiel de la République Democratique du Viet-Nam, No. 11, November 30, 1945; O. A. Arturov (ed.), Demokraticheskaya Respublika Vietnam, Konstitutsiya, zakonodatelnye akty, dokumenty (Democratic Republic of Vietnam, Constitution, Legislative Acts, Documents) (Moscow: 1955), pp. 70-101.
5 A. G. Budanov, op. cit., p. 61. According to A. G. Shiger, Administrativno-territorialnoe delenie zarubezhnykh stran (Administrative-Territorial Division of Foreign States) (2nd ed., Moscow: 1957), p. 114, however, the number of provinces in Vietnam totalled 68. The area of the three regions is given, respectively, as 115,700, 149,800

on the entire territory of Vietnam" the measure further directed that
"two categories of organs of authority" be instituted, namely people's
councils and administrative committees. The former, elected by the
population at large through direct and universal suffrage, were described
as "representative organs of the people," while the latter, indirectly
chosen by the plenary councils and functioning as executive bodies, were
designated as "administrative organs representing simultaneously the
people and the government." At two levels, in the villages and the
provinces, public power was to be jointly exercised by their respective
councils and administrative committees, and in the other two tiers of
territorial administration, in the districts and the regions, only corresponding administrative committees would be formed.

According to the law of November 22, 1945, each village was to
elect its own council, consisting of between 15 and 25 members and five
to seven alternates. Following an amendment introduced by Decree
No. 10 of January 23, 1946, the size of the provincial councils was set
at 20–30 members, in addition to which each primary electoral unit (i.e.,
district or municipality) in the given province could send one alternate
member to the corresponding provincial council.[6] Every citizen of
Vietnam, 18 years of age or over, with the exception of certain individuals
deprived of their political privileges and those medically pronounced
insane, was given the right to participate in the election of his village
assembly on the condition of being native to that village or proving
residence therein of at least three months' duration.[7] On the other hand,
persons on active military service and state employees had the right to
vote in that rural centre in which their unit was stationed or to which
they were assigned independently of any domicile requirement. All
persons with a mandate to vote in village elections were thereby also
entitled to take part in the balloting for provincial representatives. The
right to be elected to a rural council was automatically extended only to
those inhabitants who were inscribed on the village electoral rolls, while
all other individuals, not excepting officials, were under the further
necessity of proving six months' local residence. However, no such
special criteria of either birth or domicile were attached as qualifications
of eligibility for office-seekers to provincial council posts.

---

and 64,100 square kms., and their population (1951 estimate) as roughly 9, 7 and
6 million.

6 With regard to both village and provincial assemblies, the precise quota of deputies
for a given council was specially determined by the Minister of the Interior in proportion to the number of its constituents, and, in the case of provincial elections,
the number of delegates to be chosen from each of the subordinate districts or
municipalities was similarly established by the administrative committee of the
respective region.

7 In order to be inscribed on the village electoral roll a new arrival immediately had
to inform the village executive committee of his desire to select this village as a
permanent place of residence.

Initially, tenure in office for both village and provincial councilmen was set at two years,[8] but, shortly thereafter, the terms of village deputies were drastically reduced to just six months. While the régime never did offer, as far as is known, any official reasons for this step, one may, nevertheless, venture some tentative explanations for such an unprecedented move. In the first place, Ho Chi Minh's leadership did not yet, at this time, wholly control all, or even most of Indochina, so that in these early days in many areas councils were fully organised and were actively functioning which were not dominated by the Viet-Minh faction. Expecting soon to expand its sphere of influence, the régime apparently thus sought to provide itself with a legal pretext for dissolving in short order, ostensibly for normal purposes of conducting routine periodic elections, any such centres of potential opposition in territories scheduled for proximate absorption. Then, in these changed conditions, it could proceed to reconstitute the councils, with all appearances of legitimacy, in a way more acceptable to itself. Moreover, it should be noted, just the frequency of elections to the rural assemblies alone could not but help strengthen the Viet-Minh's grip on these bodies since it effectively precluded the probability of any genuinely autonomous corps of officials emerging in the countryside. By the same token, the practice strongly militated against the possibility of any even slightly independent group taking sufficient root locally and gradually gaining real popular support and leadership by capturing a village council for any appreciable length of time.

In addition, of course, the scrupulous implementation of regular elections inevitably served to support the régime's perpetual claims publicly crediting it with having originated democratic representative government in the country. At the same time, the device allowed it, by fostering the rapid turnover of personnel in the village agencies, to build up strong grass-roots support for its policies through the massive training and indoctrination of large segments of the rural population prevailed upon to take part in the formal processes of self-governance under the Party's pervasive ideological guidance. Finally, by officially institutionalising change, and constant change at that, from a purely psychological point of view the novel state of semi-permanent electioneering in the villages now imparted a decisive dynamic quality to the fabric of local life, in what amounted to a deliberate revolutionary symbol intended graphically to differentiate the new relations from the essentially static character of the old order. By keeping the countryside in continuous political agitation, it made the phenomenon of the break with the past

---

[8] With the proviso that the first group of deputies to be elected would serve for one year only.

conclusively real even to the still largely conservative mentality of that inert mainstay of the *ancien régime*, the peasant mass.[9]

Despite all these outwardly democratic attributes, however, the very same law then proceeded to devise an elaborate system of multiple operational controls designed to enable the central authorities to maintain at will a tight check over all echelons of the administrative apparatus. In the villages, for instance, on the demand of two-fifths of the local electorate the respective executive committee was obliged to submit to the constituency the question of popular confidence in the council and immediately to put it to popular vote. In the event of an expression of non-confidence by an absolute majority of the registered voters of the village, the corresponding provincial administrative committee would decide on the dissolution of the assembly in question. Moreover, if a village or provincial council adopted a decision contrary to the law or directives of higher agencies, besides having the offending measure repealed by upper offices, the misguided organ also received a warning from above and, were it to persist in its action and refuse to accept the reprimand, it could then be suspended by the proper superior powers.[10]

Besides the two tiers of plenary councils, the statute also foresaw the creation of four levels of administrative committees, two acting, as already noted, in conjunction with village and provincial plenary councils as their executive-directive branches and two functioning by themselves. Thus, each village council elected from among the literate cadres on its own staff an administrative committee of five members (chairman, vice-chairman, secretary, treasurer and member) and two alternates, chosen individually, and every provincial council similarly constituted its executive arm of three full members (chairman, vice-chairman and secretary) and two alternates. The autonomous administrative committees of districts and regions, on the other hand, were elected, respectively, by

9 It is true, however, that these tactics may also, in the long run, have had some adverse effect on work and even morale, as has been well pointed out by B. Fall, *The Viet-Minh Régime, Government and Administration in the Democratic Republic of Vietnam* (rev. ed., New York: 1956), p. 30, and " Local Administration under the Viet Minh," *Pacific Affairs*, 1954, No. 1, p. 57.

10 The right to repeal a local ordinance and to reprimand was vested, respectively, in the corresponding administrative committee of the district or region. Village assemblies could be suspended by their respective provincial committee and in the case of provincial councils, the administrative committee of the higher region could petition the government to dissolve the assembly in question.

Upon the dissolution of a village or provincial council for any of the above reasons, provisions were made for the outright appointment by the provincial or regional executive, respectively, the first at the instance of the district committee, the second on its own, of, correspondingly, a provisional village council of five members selected from among the local voters or a provisional provincial council of three, to function in lieu of both the liquidated plenary council and its executive arm. If, as of the date such a step became necessary more than six months still remained before the next regular elections became due, the temporary body was charged with calling special elections within ten days of assuming office, otherwise it continued to function until regular elections were conducted.

members of the subordinate village councils and, as amended by Decree No. 10 of January 23, 1946, by deputies of the assemblies of lower provinces and large cities. District committees were to comprise three full members (chairman, vice-chairman, secretary), individually elected, and two candidates; each regional committee was entitled to a complement of five full members, plus two candidates, chosen *en bloc*, with those elected to full status in turn individually selecting from their own midst a chairman, a vice-chairman and a secretary. No formal requirements (*i.e.*, of local residence or birth) qualified eligibility for membership in district or regional committees, aside from the usual stipulations that persons deprived of political rights and the insane were excluded, and that candidates for the post had to know how to read and write. Before assuming office, however, the composition of all administrative committees first had to be approved by the corresponding superior governmental authority.[11] All executive committees, save the regional ones, were assigned an identical term of office—two years, and regional units were renewable every three years.[12]

Just like the plenary councils, administrative committees were made the object of an elaborate system of formal controls. Thus, at the demand of one-third of the staff of the corresponding assembly, or the subordinate village and provincial councils in the case of district and regional organs, committees were obliged to seek a vote of confidence from their respective plenary group of deputies and, in the event of a negative vote by an absolute majority of the latter, to resign forthwith.[13] Furthermore, if an executive declined to submit itself to a superior agency, the appropriate higher authorities could undertake to dismiss the dissident unit.[14] Finally, should a member of an administrative committee, in the exercise of his official duties, act incorrectly, the proper higher governmental

---

11 The village executive—by the provincial committee; the district and provincial—by the regional ; and the regional—by the Council of Ministers.

   Should a deputy to a newly constituted committee fail to secure the endorsement of the reviewing agency, another election was held to fill that seat, but if the same candidate was again successful, which, of course, was most unlikely, higher approval then had to be bestowed on him automatically.

12 With the reservation, however that all committees elected for the first time would serve for one year only.

13 But the individual members of a village or regional committee thus disbanded continued to occupy their seat on the council itself for the rest of the term, as did too district or regional committeemen if they happened concurrently to be deputies to a subordinate provincial or village council, respectively.

14 In the case of a village or provincial executive, the superior district or regional committee could propose to the corresponding council to intervene, and, should that fail, it could then petition the provincial committee or the Cabinet, respectively, to dismiss the dissident body. In the case of district or regional committees, the corresponding provincial executive or the Minister of the Interior suggested to the regional authorities or the central government, respectively, to adjourn the insubordinate organ *sine die*.

   In such instances, the members of the dissolved executive automatically lost their personal seat on the council as well, where they occupied one.

instance [15] could address a reprimand to the offending party or recall the functionary in question at the request of the executive body on which he sat (as well as on the petition of the superior district committee in the case of a member of a village executive).[16]

Pursuant to the provisions of the basic law of November 22, 1945, no individual could at one and the same time serve as a member of two administrative committees, although a person was permitted to hold a post concurrently in a village and a provincial council and also be a deputy to the National Assembly. The Act further directed that certain members of one family could not be simultaneously elected to the same executive body—a man and his wife, a mother or father and two sons or daughters (three members of the same family), three brothers or sisters. As amended by Decree No. 22 of 1946, the statute stressed once again that officials, soldiers and officers on active duty could, in the normal course of events, be chosen as representatives to people's councils. On the other hand, officials elected to administrative committees of districts, provinces or regions first had to obtain a prolonged leave of absence or decline to accept the deputyship. Soldiers and officers on active duty were entirely barred from sitting on executive bodies, but officials chosen for posts on village administrative committees were authorised to assume their elective duties and keep their old jobs too.

Given all this, one is led to believe that: plenary councils were not expected to be overburdened with responsibilities, thereby allowing cadres with other, more important, functions concurrently to serve on them without being distracted in any real way from the discharge of their primary assignments; *a contrario*, local executive agencies were intended to operate full-time, thus in fact precluding personnel already regularly occupied elsewhere from simultaneously taking part in committee activities. The one exception to that lay at the village level where, apparently, either the pressure of executive work was lighter and double duty therefore more feasible or the régime was simply willing to risk overworking its lower ranks for the sake of a tighter control over these crucial rural bodies. In any case, the whole pattern certainly points to the conclusion that, official claims to the contrary notwithstanding, effective power at both the primary and intermediate echelons of the public system was

---

[15] The provincial executive *vis-à-vis* village and district executive personnel; the regional executive with regard to provincial executive cadres; and the Minister of the Interior in the case of regional committeemen.

[16] An individual so recalled automatically lost his office of councilman too and was, moreover, further liable to legal prosecution if the offence was of a criminal nature.

Where an administrative committee had been dissolved for any of the above reasons, the next higher executive body was obliged to convene the corresponding council, or the subordinate territorial councils in the case of district or regional committees, for new committee elections, within a five-day period in the villages and provinces, without delay in the other two tiers of administration. In the case of recall of individual members of an executive organ, they were to be replaced by alternates.

vested not in the theoretically supreme elective organs of local authority
—the people's councils—but, rather, in the small, indirectly chosen
executive bureaux presiding over the various territorial divisions.

As regards the formal scope of their official jurisdiction, ostensibly
the village and provincial councils were fully empowered under the law to
deal with all questions pertaining to the life of their respective consti-
tuencies, but only on the basic condition that their decisions should not be
in contradiction with the resolutions and directives of upper echelons.
To ensure such conformity, all assemblies were required to submit within
an eight-day period a duly signed protocol of any action taken by them
to the next higher administrative committee and the latter then had the
right, for cause, to set the measure aside or return it for revision by a
set dead-line. On the latter's expiration the councils' ordinances could
finally be put into effect. What is more, on a long list of such questions,
generally regarded elsewhere as properly belonging to the category of
purely local matters, the councils' enactments became valid only after
their further explicit ratification by designated superior authorities.[17]
Thereby, of course, the broad independence and decision-making
initiative nominally attributed to the plenary bodies were, in fact, even
more severely circumscribed.

Compared with the indefinite and largely conditional enunciation of
the legal powers of the councils, the official competence of the various
administrative committees was formulated in much more specific and
unqualified terms. All local executive organs were charged with: ensuring the enforcement of the directives of higher echelons; controlling the
execution by local functionaries and administrative agencies of their
appointed duties; solving problems of current management falling within
their jurisdiction; and, above village committee level, reviewing and

---

[17] Thus, the district executive had to sanction all policies of a subordinate village
assembly touching on the renting or leasing of immovable property for more than
three years, changing the allocation of real property, envisaging construction, repair
and widening of streets, roads and parks or ordering the opening or closing of markets.
Provincial commitees, in turn, were required to confirm all decisions of lower village
councils if they foresaw: the sale, grant or exchange of communal immovable property; the purchase of communal immovable property, the construction and repair
of buildings, bridges, paved roads, etc., where such expenditures were not covered by
the village budget and had to be financed through loans, the drafting of the village
budget, the imposition of special taxes and contracting for loans, the assessment of
the size of local taxes entrusted to their collection, the permission of independent
management in enterprises of public purpose or private participation therein.
    For provincial councils, regional ratification had to be obtained for any action
involving the acceptance of gifts or inheritances encumbered with liens, the purchase,
sale or exchange of public property, the filing of a civil suit or appearance as a
respondent in any such proceedings, and the issuance of regulations for civil servants.
The Cabinet's approval had to be sought before adopting the provincial budget,
contracting for a loan, establishing additional interest on taxes in excess of established
rates, determining public works projects and assessing the size of special taxes
entrusted to local collection.
    Negative rulings could be appealed once to the next higher committee.

repealing decisions of subordinate councils. Village and provincial executive bodies were further entrusted with convening the sessions of their plenary assemblies, and each village committee was also responsible for the administration of justice at the primary level through a permanent commission composed of its chairman, vice-chairman and secretary. Jointly, the three were authorised to resolve civil disputes through conciliation proceedings and to adjudicate minor violations of the law, but only with the right to impose the penalty of a fine. Aside from the basic set of rights and duties common to all committees, those in the upper tiers of the public structure were each entrusted with various special functions proper to themselves alone. In districts and above, for example, the committees were charged with the direction of security troops within their territory, and provincial and regional authorities had the added right to grant concessions on State lands, and, in an emergency, to mobilise the local military forces. Finally, it should be noted, in assigning special personnel to posts in a given region, the central ministries were obliged first to obtain the consent of that region's committee to their nominations.

How the work of the executive bodies was actually to be broken down was stipulated by the law only with regard to the village committees in which agenda items had to be classified into five operational categories: general management and the administration of justice; social questions, public health, social security, finances; economic matters, communications, cadastre; education, propaganda, records; maintenance of public security and military affairs. The first of these functions was made the responsibility of the three-man permanent commission already mentioned, and the other areas were apportioned between the individual members of the village executives on the basis of their personal qualifications. In the districts and above, the administrative spheres, left unspecified by the statute, were also to be allocated among the staff of the executive organs on the principle of special attributes, except that the law expressly stated that in district committees general administration would be exercised by their personnel collectively. Although village committees were allowed to form sub-committees to assist them in their work, no reference can be found to a concomitant right on the part of the higher organs. Indeed, the public system of the Viet-Minh does not seem to have made any formal allowance for the general organisation of local auxiliary commissions, departing radically in that respect from the usual practice in other " people's democracies " where this administrative technique is used very extensively.

Village councils were scheduled to be convened in regular session by their executive committees once a month and provincial councils, as amended by Decree No. 153 of November 17, 1950, once every three months. Extraordinary sessions could in both cases be convoked on the instructions of the next higher administrative body, or at the demand of two-thirds of the members of the council itself, addressed to its executive organ (only one-third for the purpose of holding a vote of confidence), or at the initiative of the council's own executive branch. For each session, a council elected a session chairman and the role of session secretary was always fulfilled by the secretary of its administrative committee. Barring extraordinary circumstances, meetings were open to the public and a majority of councilmen constituted a working quorum. Decisions were adopted by simple majority vote of members present. Administrative committees, on the other hand, were in permanent session and their meetings were invariably conducted behind closed doors.

The decree of November 22, 1945, originally made no mention of the administrative procedures to be instituted in the country's metropolitan areas, a delay probably caused by the fact that the Viet-Minh, not being in the least conversant with the intricacies of urban management, had by then not yet decided on what approach to use. Thus, it is only a month later that the formal outline of the republic's proposed structure of local government was at last completed through the promulgation, on December 21, 1945, of Decree No. 77 " On the Organisation of People's Authority in Towns and Urban-type Settlements." By the terms of this enactment, three levels of city management were to be established throughout Vietnam : Hanoi, the nation's capital, was given regional rank and made directly subordinate to the central government; seven major cities (Haiphong, Nam-Dinh, Vinh, Ben-thuy, Hué, Tourane and Saigon-Cholon) were endowed with provincial status and placed directly under regional control; and the other urban centres were put under the administration of the provincial authorities. The larger towns were further divided into urban districts (boroughs) and wards.

Each city, town and urban settlement was headed by its own administrative committee and a people's council elected by the local residents in direct and universal suffrage, and numbering twenty members and four candidates (Hanoi and Saigon-Cholon—thirty members and six alternates). Boroughs were governed by administrative committees only, renewable every year. The term of office and the working procedures of the municipal councils and their relations with upper governmental instances were in the main similar to those obtaining for village assemblies, except that metropolitan organs regularly convened not less than once every two months and the length of their sessions was explicitly limited to a maximum of six days (fifteen days when the city budget was being discussed).[18] Otherwise, " voting requirements were the same as in the village assemblies and eligibility requirements were as liberal as those of the provinces." [19]

---

[18] A. G. Budanov, *op. cit.*, p. 83.   [19] B. Fall, *The Viet-Minh Régime*, p. 25.

The finishing touch to Vietnam's new edifice of local government was furnished nearly a year later when the republic's first Constitution was adopted.[20] As regards the lower echelons of public authority, the Basic Law, on the whole, confined itself simply to endorsing in broad terms the main propositions of earlier legislation which had already dealt with the matter more than adequately. It only added thereto a general statement to the effect that administrative committees were responsible both to the higher organs and their respective people's councils and that members of people's councils and their executive branches could be recalled by the electorate in a manner left to be defined by subsequent legislation. Aside from that, the Constitution's chief impact on the question of local self-rule, albeit only as an indirect one even then, derived from the fact that it set the minimum age for all candidates to elective office at twenty-one, whereas preceding enactments had given it as eighteen.

By the end of 1946, then, the Ho Chi Minh régime had succeeded in endowing the country, on paper at least, with a completely renovated system of local administration, patterned in its essentials on the Soviet model, but also displaying considerable traces of originality and, what is more important, of a willingness to make due concessions to native needs and conditions. Among such deviations from standard norm, for instance, the one which probably attracted most doctrinal attention at first was the Viet-Minh's proclaimed policy, highly unorthodox in its time, of acknowledging the concept of universal suffrage as a recognised principle of the new public order. To couch it in the proper ideological jargon:

> A peculiarity of the political basis of the Democratic Republic of Vietnam is the fact that exploiting elements, if they are not traitors and reactionaries, are not deprived of the opportunity to take part in the work of State organs. As a result, in the present phase of the revolution, these organs include representatives of the workers, peasants, intelligentsia, lower and middle bourgeoisie, as well as progressive elements from among the former big landowners.[21]

Nor was the fact that the very same law prominently featured a crucial reservation allowing for the summary divestiture of certain groups of the population, simply denounced as " traitors and reactionaries," of their political, including their electoral privileges, seen by the authorities as in any material way detracting from the validity of its claims to having guaranteed equal voting rights to all. Officially, of course, it was contended that such legal incapacitation " extended only to a rather insignificant portion of the landowners . . . and, moreover, the restriction

---

20 O. A. Arturov (ed.), *op. cit.*, pp. 17–32; B. Fall, *op. cit.*, pp. 156–164; V. N. Durdenevskii (ed.), *Konstitutsii stran narodnoi demokratii (Constitutions of the Countries of People's Democracy)* (Moscow: 1958), pp. 95–112.
21 A. G. Budanov, *op. cit.*, p. 30.

had but a temporary character as the people's rule created the necessary conditions for the re-education of persons formerly exploiting the labour of others." [22]

By far the most distinctive trait of the Viet-Minh's proposed constitutional scheme, as well as its most revolutionary innovation from the standpoint of Vietnam's cultural tradition and historical precedent, lay in its extreme emphasis on highly centralised administrative processes. Systematic review and control over all the activities of every public institution by a complex succession of superior supervisory agencies, culminating in the personal office of the President of the republic became the new rule. Operationally, this orientation was given effect in two ways: first, by granting the appointive administrative committees, in fact, if not in theory, a status not just equal but actually far superior to that of their supposedly supreme counterparts, the people's councils; and, secondly, by then, in turn, organising the hierarchy of administrative committees along rigidly centralised lines.

Indeed, as regards the first proposition, it should immediately be noted that the very text of the basic law itself signally failed to define, even if only for the sake of principle, the substance of the councils' purported primacy over their executive branches or the procedural methods for its practical realisation. This lacuna stood in strong contrast with the universal practice in other " people's democracies " of enumerating in detail the formal, albeit still largely fictitious, spheres and mechanics of subordination of the administrative bureaux to the corresponding elective plenary bodies. No real evidence exists, therefore, to support official claims concerning the pre-eminent position of the councils within the public structure, if one disregards fatuous citation of the relevant, but at best only hypothetical, strictures in the Constitution. Indeed, the only proof ever adduced by the régime's spokesmen to document this thesis was to rely on the doctrinal implications, always, needless to say, just potential, inherent in the juridical formula that currently sanctioned the adjournment *sine die* of an administrative committee as a result of an expression of non-confidence by the respective assembly.

As against this, however, there was infinitely better evidence represented by the special literacy requirement mandatory for membership on administrative committees only, given the extremely high rate of illiteracy among the native population, almost total in fact in the rural sections. The specification that members of executive offices had to be able to read and write Vietnamese then had the practical effect, obviously quite deliberate, of unconditionally restricting access to these organs to a

<hr>

[22] Nguyen Dinh Loc (transliteration from the Russian), " Izbiratelnyi zakon Demokraticheskoi Respubliki Vietnam " (" Electoral Law of the Democratic Republic of Vietnam "), *Sovetskoe gosudarstvo i pravo*, 1961, No. 1, p. 83.

select and self-perpetuating corps of professional cadres, trusted Party functionaries for the most part. Even leaving other considerations of a similar nature aside for the moment, this in itself would serve to cast grave doubt on the validity of all the régime's persistent contentions regarding the political supremacy of the councils within the governmental apparatus. The whole thesis, in effect, rested on the quite untenable premise that popular assemblies consisting of lay citizens without administrative experience or even ordinary education, occasionally brought together in plenary session, could be expected to exert meaningful control over the trained bureaucrats ensconced in the constantly functioning committees.[23] The executive organs, on the other hand, openly operated, in theory as well as in practice, within the tight framework of a pyramidal hierarchy of successively subordinate agencies, each level taking orders not only from its equivalent in the next tier, but from all corresponding bodies on an ascending vertical as well. As has been rightly observéd, in the final analysis all "executive committees find themselves under the unified direction of the Government of the Republic and are subordinate to it." [24]

While concentrating primarily on the structural reform of the instrumentalities of local government, the new régime, it should be further noted, also seems to have been fully aware of the futility of pursuing the physical reorganisation of the administrative machine alone without, at the same time, ensuring a concomitant " spiritual regeneration " of its human component. In addition, therefore, it concurrently undertook to wage a determined campaign against all manifestations on the part of its cadres of public conduct redolent of the many venal practices so traditional in the past. In fact, as early as October 1945, Ho Chi Minh had already found it necessary strongly to warn the local functionaries against lapses into such customary abuses of authority, apparently still quite widespread, as violations of the law, misuse of power, corruption, nepotism, refusal to co-operate, arrogance, etc.[25] Such strictures represented a recurrent theme in official pronouncements in the years that followed.

Throughout this early period, then, the Viet-Minh's formal political programme used every possible opportunity to lay heavy emphasis on

23 On the literacy test, B. V. Shchetinin, " Predstavitelnaya sistema v narodno-demo-kraticheskikh gosudarstvakh Azii " (" Representative System in the People's Democratic States of Asia "), *Sovetskoe gosudarstvo i pravo*, 1955, No. 2, pp. 35–36, simply claims, however, that " this limitation pursues the objective of ensuring the most experienced staff of deputies in the representative organs of power. With the liquidation of illiteracy among the population it will lose its significance."

24 A. G. Budanov, *op. cit.*, p. 84.

25 " To the People's Committees of North, Central and South Vietnam, to the People's Committees of Provinces, Districts and Villages," in Ho Chi Minh, *Izbrannye statii i rechi* (*Selected Articles and Speeches*) (Moscow: 1959), pp. 174–176.

the prime importance of at once securely establishing the new governmental system on a nation-wide scale. This was carried to a point where,
for instance, in the Declaration Concerning the Policy of the Provisional Coalition Government, published on January 1, 1946, over the
signature of Ho Chi Minh, the statement's only two points in the para-
graph dealing with " political " issues on the domestic front simply
pledged, respectively: " the successful conduct of general elections in
the whole country "; and, " the completion of the reorganisation of
adminstrative organs in accordance with democratic principles." [26] True,
one does sometimes encounter the claim that, on the basis of the legislative enactments of these first years, in short order " people's councils
and executive committees were elected throughout the land." [27] Yet,
actually, by the time open fighting erupted between the Viet-Minh and the
French, in much of the country the revolutionary government had, at
best, succeeded in laying but the bare foundations of an embryonic and
rudimentary edifice of formal administrative institutions, which themselves led only a very precarious existence. Moreover, even these modest
achievements were largely nullified by the war almost overnight. Over
the next eight years, by a costly and laborious process, another network
was developed in place of what had only been begun in the aftermath
of World War II and almost everywhere was very soon so quickly
destroyed, a system definitely more primitive and now operating under-
ground for the most part, but, in its own way, equally effective, if not
even more so than its ill-fated predecessor.

WARTIME REFORMS

With the outbreak of hostilities between the French Army and the
Viet-Minh in December 1946, and the precipitous withdrawal of the
nationalist forces from the large cities and surrounding areas shortly
thereafter, fresh responsibilities soon devolved on local revolutionary
authorities. Their primary duties were now connected with " the
evacuation of the central organs into the interior of the country, the
appreciable shortage of means of communication and, what is particularly
important, the necessity of direct leadership on a local scale of military
actions by detachments of self-defence, guerrilla detachments and army
units." [28] As a result of these considerations, a decree issued on October
1, 1947, ordered the fusion at all levels of the respective territorial
administrative committees with their counterpart committees of liberation

---

[26] *Ibid.*, pp. 195–196.
[27] A. G. Budanov, *op. cit.*, p. 29; *La République Démocratique du Viet-Nam* (Hanoi:
1960), p. 44. See also the speech by Pham Van Dong in *Third National Congress of
The Viet Nam Workers' Party* (Hanoi: 1961), Vol. III, p. 71.
[28] A. G. Budanov, *op. cit.*, p. 86; *La République Démocratique du Viet-Nam*, p. 44.

surviving still from the time of the anti-Japanese resistance movement. The creation of special military zones in which corresponding institutions of state authority were organised followed soon after. At first there were fourteen such zones, but, as the war progressed, their number was subsequently reduced to ten and by March 1948 to six.[29] A year later, Presidential Decree No. 254 of November 19, 1948,[30] formally ratified the drastic reorganisation of local organs of administration for the period of military emergency. The act legally endorsed the in fact already largely operative structure, procedures, competence and inter-relationship of the component cells in the revised system which was destined to represent what amounted to the Viet-Minh's official apparatus of national government, clandestine for the most part, until the summer of 1954.

According to this emergency enactment, the pattern of people's councils and administrative committees, as originally conceived in Decree No. 63 of November 22, 1945, was replaced by an essentially similar network of people's councils and committees of resistance and administration. As heretofore, villages and provinces were each to have both a council and a committee, whereas, again in line with precedent, in districts and urban boroughs, as well as in zones now, only committees of resistance and administration would function. In cities, however, where in the next few years the Viet-Minh's authority, if it existed at all, constantly remained in grave jeopardy, it was envisaged that henceforth committees alone would operate in lieu of the former dual municipal system, and the institute of metropolitan assemblies was accordingly abandoned.

As regards the new people's councils, as a rule the stipulations of Decree No. 63/1945 continued to apply, but with certain significant amendments. Hereafter, for instance, alternate members would no longer be elected to either the village or the provincial councils and, at the suggestion of a district committee, the appropriate provincial committee was now empowered, in the face of unfavourable conditions, temporarily to postpone for the duration elections to a subordinate village assembly. As of that moment, all elections to provincial councils were provisionally suspended until further notice.[31] As before, to be valid, sessions of

29 A. G. Budanov, *op. cit.*, pp. 61, 86–87; N. S. Merzlyakov, *op. cit.*, p. 51; B. Fall, *Le Viet-Minh, La République Démocratique du Viet-Nam 1945–1960* (Paris: 1960), p. 62.

30 O. A. Arturov (ed.), *op. cit.*, pp. 102–127.

31 B. Fall, *The Viet-Minh*, p. 30, mentions, however, the case of elections to a provincial committee in Hadong province in North Vietnam in 1951.
    In the event that an existing provincial council lacked a full complement of members, the Minister of the Interior was authorised to appoint, at the proposal of the zonal committee, a supplementary number of members to the council, the end total not to exceed the designated quota of deputies for the given body.

people's councils required a legal quorum of over half their members, but because of the serious difficulties engendered by the civil war it was now also permitted, should such an attendance not be mustered at the first meeting, to hold a lawful session if at least one-third of the deputies were present.[32] At both village and provincial level, the secretary of the respective committee of resistance and administration concurrently served as the secretary of the local council. What is more important, the amendment further ruled that committees were not required any more to submit themselves upon proper demand to a vote of confidence in the corresponding plenary bodies. Thereafter, all the rights, duties and privileges of an erstwhile village, district, provincial or regional administrative committee were expressly vested in a newly created committee of resistance and administration of equal rank, except in the zones where no precedent existed and a fresh set of rules therefore had to be improvised.

Each zonal committee was to consist of five to seven members, all appointed by the President of the Republic on the advice of the Supreme Council of National Defence, with the chairman and vice-chairman of the organ then likewise individually selected from among the group. In turn, every provincial and village committee would comprise five to seven persons, of which three to five were to be elected by the respective assembly, and confirmed by the designated upper echelons, and two members would be assigned outright from above.[33] Moreover, now the staff of a provincial committee did not necessarily have to be drawn, as had hitherto been the rule, exclusively from among its council's deputies, thus giving the authorities a marked discretionary latitude in the matter. In those provinces and villages where as yet it had not been found possible to constitute plenary councils, the entire personnel of the local committees was to be provisionally appointed by the proper superior agencies.[34] The chairman and vice-chairman of a provincial committee and the chairman, vice-chairman and secretary of a village committee were elected by the committee members from among themselves.[35]

In the cities, districts and metropolitan boroughs corresponding committees of resistance and administration were to be installed,[36] of from five to seven men each, all of them appointed by higher echelons, which

32 If even that number of councilmen could not be assembled, the matter then had to be referred to higher authorities for corrective action.
33 For village committees—by provincial committees on nomination by the district committees; for provincial committees—by the Council of National Defence on nomination of the zonal committee.
34 The same procedure as the one outlined in note 33 *supra* was followed in this case.
35 Subject, however, to the subsequent approval of the corresponding zonal or provincial committee, respectively.
36 According to Article 49, a special decree was later to determine in what town city committees would be formed and another special measure would define the particular status of the city committee for Hanoi.

also separately chose from the members of every committee the two who would serve as its chairman and vice-chairman.[37] Though functionally on a par with village councils, procedurally the borough committees ranked one step higher since they were operationally subordinate not to the corresponding district organs, as the former were, but directly to the respective provincial authorities, reflecting thereby the manifold difficulties encountered by the Viet-Minh in dealing with the nation's urban centres.

On every single committee of resistance and administration, the staff always included one member, invariably an appointee, specially charged with military affairs.[38] In addition, in each village and borough organ, its chairman, vice-chairman and secretary jointly constituted a permanent commission.

Essentially, the basic rights and duties of the various executive committees were similarly defined. Thus, within the limits of their particular territorial competence, all of them were charged with: the execution of the decrees, resolutions and directives of the government and upper echelons and supervision over their enforcement; the organisation and co-ordination of all activities of public administration within their own area; inspection over the maintenance of security within their jurisdiction; and, where appropriate, the direction and control of lower committees. In addition, zonal, provincial and city committees were generally expected to implement in their domain the policies of the government and to make certain that all official measures taken by subordinate agencies were in full conformity with the directives and the overall political line of the central authorities. *Vis-à-vis* the central ministries, however, or even their local branches, the corresponding committees of resistance and administration still enjoyed little more than just an advisory status.[39]

Zonal, provincial, district and city committees were all authorised to issue instructions on the fulfilment of edicts of superior agencies and the safeguarding of public order.[40] The regulatory organ was, however,

---

[37] For city committees—by the Council of National Defence on the proposal of the zonal committees; for district committees—by the zonal committees at the suggestion of provincial committees; for metropolitan borough committees—by provincial committees.

[38] In the zone, the member on military affairs was selected from the command personnel of the regular army; in the province—from the command personnel of the regular army or the people's armed forces (local troops, provincial people's militia) ; in the district—from the command personnel of the regular army or the people's militia of the district; and in the village—from the command personnel of the village people's militia. The source of military representatives on city or borough committees was not stated.

[39] *Cf.* Articles 20 and 41.

[40] In addition, in cases of urgent need to resolve a question not covered by a law, zonal committees were permitted to publish temporary instructions for immediate use. In issuing ordinances on public order, district committees were required immediately to inform the respective provincial committee of their action and put

bound at all times not to violate the political programme and general directives of the government, promulgate norms contradictory to existing decrees and decisions, introduce new taxes or institute new types of penalties. Conversely, it was obliged to request the opinion of interested special bodies in all matters affecting them, immediately communicate its resolutions to the central authorities, first discuss all prescriptive enactments in plenary convocations and adopt them only by an absolute majority of its membership. At provincial level and below, all committees of resistance and administration were ordered to recruit a local militia pursuant to the programme and directives emanating from above and to furnish effective leadership to these forces as well as to the local security units. In place even of the limited initiative formerly tolerated for all echelons of local rule in budgetary matters, such questions were now consolidated exclusively in the hands of the zonal and provincial organs.

In addition to concentrating in the person of these reconstituted local committees an extremely wide range of executive, administrative and quasi-legislative functions, the 1948 statute also proceeded to vest in them numerous extraordinary judicial and police powers. Thus, zonal committees had the right within their territory to order persons to be interned or banished through administrative procedure. Zonal and provincial committees, and district organs in emergencies, could sanction the " detention of persons suspected of activity detrimental to national independence." The zonal agency, upon consultation with the chairman of the zonal court, could further direct the summary internment of such individuals and suggest to the procuracy that it initiate prosecution before a military tribunal or, conversely, direct the release of those administratively detained. Moreover, zonal organs were authorised, by an absolute majority vote and with the concurrence of the chairman of the zonal court, to grant pardons, reduce sentences (except the death sentence) and discharge prisoners (except those sentenced by courts-martial). They were required to create a special commission to study such questions, to consist of at least half the committee's members and the chairman of the corresponding court.

Zonal executive bodies were competent to organise camps for prisoners-of-war, ordinary camps for convicts and internment camps, with the management of the latter two types entrusted to the committees of the provinces in which they were located. They were also given the power of control (censorship and confiscation) over all published materials in their area, which they could delegate to provincial and city committees

the regulations into effect only upon receiving the latter's approval or on the expiration of 15 days without reply from the official authorities, except in emergency situations where they could be enforced at once, a concession to the deterioration of communications and control in time of war.

as well. Furthermore, zonal, provincial, city and district committees, all had the right to a varying degree, to requisition property. Finally, village committees continued as before to exercise primary judicial functions through their permanent commissions with authority to settle all local civil disputes in conciliation hearings, try all minor violations of the law punishable by fines to the amount of one to fifteen piastres and execute the judgments and verdicts of higher courts.

Identical working procedures and methods of assigning tasks obtained in all committees and followed the pattern outlined for the zonal agencies. The latter, according to the statute, exercised their rights and obligations collegially, with every member of the body personally responsible for the decisions and performance of the organ as a whole. The chairman of the committee functioned as its legal representative, and, as such, was charged with: carrying out general control; supervising all matters within the zone; making public the resolutions of the committee; solving current problems and, when necessary, even dealing with important questions personally, subsequently informing the group of such actions and signing all papers of an executive nature. In the absence of the chairman, the vice-chairman acted for him. The distribution of duties among the individual members of the committees, including the vice-chairman, was dictated by circumstances and the particular qualifications of each official.[41]

In view of the wartime situation, a good deal of the decree was devoted to the question of the accountability of and the maintenance of discipline in the local organs. Thus, committees guilty of violating the law could bring down upon themselves, depending on the gravity of the offence, a warning, a reprimand or dismissal.[42] A breach of the law on the part of an individual committeeman could entail, contingent on the seriousness of the infraction, a warning, a censure, temporary suspension, his dismissal or recall or even criminal prosecution, when warranted.[43]

Again because of military considerations, a set of special instructions was appended to the measure, dealing in detail with the vexing problem of maintaining official communications between the successive echelons of the administrative apparatus in these circumstances. The net effect of these was practically to allow for the partial suspension of all the preceding rules in periods of major emergency. As a concession to the *force majeure* of a situation where channels of contact were totally

---

[41] For village and municipal committees, the organisation of work was to be outlined in a special resolution of the Ministry of the Interior. For the text of such instructions issued on December 29, 1951, in Tien Hai district, see B. Fall, *The Viet-Minh Régime*, pp. 165–168, and for an analysis of its contents, *ibid.*, pp. 29–30.

[42] Warnings and reprimands could be issued by the next higher echelon; decisions to suspend a committee lay within the competence of the agency approving its staff.

[43] The same procedure as the one outlined in note 42 *supra* obtained in this case.

disrupted by fighting, the central government in that event delegated to the zonal agencies all functions of control within their area, including, at the decision of the individual ministries, the right, hitherto always denied them, to direct the operations of the local branches of the latter. Zonal committees were then also authorised to declare martial law or repeal it and to exercise broad powers of appointment, dismissal or suspension and disciplining of the subordinate administrative personnel, except the military and the zonal directors of ministerial departments.[44]

In such critical times, zonal organs could, moreover, be vested with all the rights of the Ministry of the Interior *vis-à-vis* lower people's councils and with the prerogatives of the Council of National Defence in regard to the committees of resistance and administration of subordinate provinces, districts and villages and their individual members, as well as be granted final budgetary authority and extensive judicial powers.[45] Similarly, in instances where the usual contacts between provincial and zonal agencies were rendered impossible as a result of military operations, the latter could delegate to the former any or all powers which, by law, were normally reserved to themselves. The crucial right to determine whether a status of disrupted communications did in fact exist, or to proclaim such a situation at an end, belonged exclusively to the Council of National Defence. But once the existence of such a state of affairs was acknowledged as between a zone and the government, the former was then given the right, in turn, to recognise when necessary that a state of siege obtained in its own relations with a subordinate province. An official announcement to the effect that the emergency was over automatically ensued in the suspension of all extraordinary delegations of authority connected with it.

This, then, was the basic operational outline of the administrative system which the Viet-Minh proposed to maintain in the course of its armed struggle for power. It should, however, always be remembered that the substance of this decree, just like the provisions of its 1945 predecessor, was to a large extent never fully realised because of the constant and dire pressure of adverse external forces. Even those schemes which the revolutionary leadership did succeed in implementing, if only partially as a rule, were similarly conditioned at all times by overriding military exigencies and, therefore, forever subject to sudden abandonment,

---

[44] Zonal committees were required, however, to notify higher instances of such actions but could, on the other hand, issue reprimands to the zonal directors of ministerial departments.

[45] Zonal committees could be authorised by the Ministry of the Interior and the Ministry of Justice to establish military tribunals on their territory. Together with the chairman of the zonal judicial body, each created a commission for examining requests for pardon and for commutation of death sentences (except those imposed by courts-martial).

summary suspension or radical alteration in the face of rapidly changing events.

Undoubtedly, by far the most significant administrative development of this phase of the Viet-Minh's history was the emergence of zones as the main units of government throughout the country. Although the original regional divisions were not officially liquidated until much later, in reality they ceased to have any true function soon after the outbreak of the hostilities and in short order all their powers in practice devolved to the zonal committees. Indeed, as has been correctly observed,

> in 1946–1954, in connection with the military situation an important role was played by temporary organs—the zonal military administrative committees, which combined military leadership with the management of the most important questions of administration, together with judicial rights, the right to pardon, censorship rights and the right to issue regulations for public order. All organs of authority, military and judicial organs on the territory of the respective zones were bound to execute the directives of the military-administrative committees.[46]

Another crucial innovation effected by the 1948 statute was the introduction into the republic's administrative practice of the technique of widespread appointment of local deputies and committeemen by higher governmental instances, thereby in fact ensuring ultimate control by the Viet-Minh faction of all the lower agencies of public authority. Many of them it should be noted were as yet still not under its complete domination but, thanks to this device, shortly were scheduled to be. A novel factor, too, was the adoption of the rule prescribing the mandatory presence on the staff of all committees of a specialist in military affairs, the post to be occupied always by a man assigned from above and holding military rank, thus again assuring the central leadership of absolute pre-eminence in a vital sector of local activity. Not unexpectedly, the progressive expansion of the principle of appointment of officials was accompanied by a parallel contraction of the elective sphere, made particularly manifest by the suspension *sine die* of any further provincial elections.

Concomitant with these developments and an almost inevitable product of the nationalist régime's predominantly military orientation in those days was the final assumption by the committees of resistance and administration of a position, openly conceded now, of *de facto* supremacy within the public order. Their new status was thus not only in every way equal in practice to that of the plenary councils, wherever the latter still functioned, but conclusively superior to it in almost every way. With the abandonment of the concept of a committee's duty to resign upon a

---

[46] O. A. Arturov, in V. F. Kotok (ed.), *Gosudarstvennoe pravo zarubezhnykh sotsialisticheskikh stran* (*State Law of Foreign Socialist Countries*) (Moscow: 1957), p. 413.

vote of non-confidence in its council went the last formal pretence of committee subordination to the assemblies.

As regard organisational matters, therefore, the emphasis in the régime's programme of the following months lay primarily in the direction of the maximum strengthening of the committees which, almost everywhere, thus gradually came to substituting themselves, for all practical purposes, for their councils. To a great extent, of course, this phenomenon was deliberately induced by the régime's own policies. At least in part, however, it was simply the unfortunate result of a certain fortuitous turn of events quite independent of the leadership's will, or, as its spokesmen prefer to put it,

> in conditions of the war of national-liberation it was not possible to give effect to all the principles of the Constitution. In particular, in many areas which were occupied by the enemy or frequently changed hands, there was no opportunity to create elective organs of people's authority. In these instances provisional military-administrative committees were formed, recruited from among the active fighters for freedom.[47]

Nevertheless, despite the frank admission that " wartime conditions made it necessary to countenance in certain localities a temporary departure from the principle of election of local organs of authority with its replacement by that of their appointment by higher organs," [48] officially the claim was still made that all this " did not affect the democratic nature of the reforms." [49]

On the other hand, the mere fact that during this period committees of resistance and administration gained, in practice, if not in theory, a position of unquestioned ascendancy in the public system of the republic, did not yet mean that the Viet-Minh's leadership was then in the process of repudiating *ex principio* the institution of councils, even if only for the duration of the strife. On the contrary, Ho Chi Minh seems to have been fully aware that perhaps nothing would bolster his claim to recognition quite as much as the concrete evidence of an ability to maintain his own regularly constituted and fully operational administrative machine extending over as much of the country as possible. Consequently, in areas where such a formal organisation was lacking the régime consistently pressed its local cadres for an early solution of this problem by the election, as soon as it became feasible to do so, of an appropriate people's council, as well, of course, as through the installation of a duly formed committee.[50] Indeed, it has been reported, quite credibly, that, at least

---

47 A. P. Leontiev, *Natsionalno-osvoboditelnaya borba naroda Vietnama* (*National-Liberation Struggle of the People of Vietnam*) (Moscow: 1956), p. 16.

48 O. A. Arturov, *op. cit.*, pp. 412–413.

49 A. P. Leontiev, *op. cit.*, p. 16.

50 *e.g.*, decree of February 1948 on elections to village councils, quoted in B. Fall, *The Viet-Minh Régime*, p. 29, and " Local Administration under the Viet-Minh," *loc. cit.*, pp. 55–56.

in the securely " liberated " portions of Indochina, " while there have been no new national elections in this hard time of war, the local village governments are elected quite regularly." [51]

To a degree, therefore, the elaborate fiction of representative people's councils continued to be preserved, where possible, even at the considerable cost, given the right political conditions, of determinedly endowing it for the sake of appearances with sufficient physical form. From a doctrinal point of view then, needless to say, the concept of the legal superiority of the councils to their committees or, at best, the parity of the two, remained at all times the only official thesis; it was certainly publicised as such at every opportunity, without, however, conclusively resolving thereby the evident conflict between dogma and reality in this vital matter. The ambiguity of the prevailing situation was perhaps best illustrated by the language of the instructions issued by the Prime Minister of the Republic on April 10, 1952, and devoted to this very question. It was stated therein that " at every level where there are people's councils (village, province), these people's councils represent the organs of State power, and where there are no people's councils (district, zone) the military-administrative committees do so." To this, of course, should immediately be added that, " besides, even given the existence of people's councils, between their sessions the military-administrative committees functioned as organs of State power." [52]

In short, one generally finds, in studying the subject, the usual ideologically motivated assertion made that " in the course of the war of Resistance, after it began, the system of State organs was restructured, but even during this period the representative organs of authority played an important role." [53] As against this, there stands the weighty evidence of the occasional far more realistic practical appraisal to the effect that " in war conditions committees enjoyed great independence and special powers (since despite the fact that communications with higher organs were frequently interrupted, it was imperative to decide operational questions, etc.)." [54]

Paradoxically, but perhaps logically from a propaganda point of view, it is in these critical circumstances of extreme disruption and widespread reversion to localised initiative that the Viet-Minh chose in its public pronouncements at the time to display the most articulate interest in and support for the concept of systematic and well-defined processes of regular government and administration in the country. Thus, the 1951

51 J. R. Starobin, *Eyewitness in Indo-China* (New York: 1954), p. 122.
52 A. G. Budanov, *op. cit.*, p. 87.
53 L. D. Voevodin, in L. D. Voevodin, D. L. Zlatopolskii, N. Ya. Kuprits, *Gosudarstvennoe pravo stran narodnoi demokratii* (*State Law of Countries of People's Democracy*) (Moscow: 1960), p. 525.
54 O. A. Arturov, *op. cit.*, p. 413.

Programme of the Workers' Party prominently featured, somewhat ironically in view of contemporaneous developments, the proposition that " the organisational principle of people's authority is democratic centralism." In order to " strengthen our people's authority," the document advised that it was necessary " incessantly to tighten the contacts between the State power and the popular masses, to attract even more widely workers and peasants of both sexes into participating in organs of power, especially the people's councils, genuinely to implement the people's democratic Constitution, enhance the leadership by the party of the organs of power of all ranks." With respect to the temporarily occupied areas and those freshly liberated, almost first on the list of the Party's objectives, according to this blueprint, was the task of " creating and consolidating the people's authority " and " destroying the organs of the puppet régime." [55]

Similarly, the companion Programme of the Lien-Viet named among the primary tasks of the revolution that of " strengthening and developing the people's democratic order," now openly described as " democratic for the people and a dictatorship in relation to imperialistic aggressors and traitors." It also pledged itself, *inter alia*, to guarantee to " all Vietnamese citizens political and social-economic rights: the rights of man, such as freedom of political beliefs and religious liberty, freedom of choice of residence and of movement; political rights, such as the right to elect and be elected, to take part in the government of the nation, and other democratic freedoms, such as freedom of speech, press, organisation, assembly, etc.; economic rights, such as private enterprise, personal property and inheritance." [56]

From a purely structural standpoint, as the war progressed the basic trend adumbrated in the 1948 statute in regard to the external mechanics of local administration was only further accentuated by the régime's subsequent enactments. There was ever-increasing stress on techniques of decentralisation and extraordinary delegation of powers, on appointment of key personnel and drastic circumscription of most electoral activities, and on radical adjustment in every field to military exigencies. Just one month after the passage of Decree No. 254, for instance, a supplementary measure was hastily promulgated, Decree No. 255 of December 19, 1948,[57] which, in turn, elaborated some of the emergency provisions of its predecessor for use in the special case of " areas temporarily under the control of or threatened by the enemy."

In such territories, according to the latest statute, if the number of members on a council constituted at least one-third of the designated total

[55] O. A. Arturov (ed.), *op. cit.*, pp. 33–46.
[56] *Ibid.*, pp. 47–56.
[57] *Journal Officiel*, 1949, No. 2; O. A. Arturov (ed.), *op. cit.*, pp. 128–131.

for the body, this was now enough for the organ to retain its legal function. In the same circumstances, in places where councils had never been formed, temporary councils, sharply reduced in size, could be appointed by higher echelons, comprising 7 to 15 members in villages and 10–20 in provinces. And, wherever conditions seemed propitious for the formation of new committees of resistance and administration, upper instances were likewise to undertake the task of organising these latter agencies, also with a smaller complement—a chairman, a member for military affairs, and 1–5 members. The decision to recognise the existence of a state of temporary enemy control or the imminence of such a dangerous eventuality as regards villages, boroughs and districts was left to the corresponding zonal committee, and with respect to provinces, to the Council of National Defence.

A year and a half later, the dramatic shift of the centre of effective decision-making from the centre to the local scene precipitated by the hostilities was finally consummated by Presidential Decree No. 103 of June 5, 1950.[58]   By virtue of this edict, committees of all ranks were at last empowered to " exercise general and operational direction of all kinds of special functional activity at their respective level." Thereby, for the first time, the law sanctioned outright control by the local authorities over corresponding branches of the ministerial apparatus, hitherto completely centralised and with its subordinate components entirely independent of their counterparts in the governmental hierarchy.

From a functional point of view as well, the record of local government under the Viet-Minh during these years evidences a definite and consistent bent toward the increasing subordination of most facets of activity to the dominant theme of the successful prosecution of the war. It expressed itself in the inordinate expansion of such rights and duties as could be expected to contribute to the viability and resilience of the nationalist apparatus of control within its sphere of influence at the cost of a marked atrophy of powers normally associated with the concept of self-government at the lower levels. To this distorted pattern of administrative focus between 1945 and 1954 there was but one notable exception, although that too was imbued with strong overtones of political-military expectations. It involved the relegation of the practical implementation of the régime's programme of land reform, undertaken in 1949, entirely to the area of competence of the local agencies, thereby appreciably strengthening their machinery and enlarging the 'scope of their routine authority.

Thus, the Viet-Minh's first positive measure bearing on this question, Presidential Decree No. 78 of July 14, 1949, implemented by ministerial

Resolution No. 152 of the same date,[59] on lowering land rents, sanctioned the creation at provincial level of arbitral-judicial commissions to deal with cases of this nature. These were to consist of the chairman of the provincial executive or his deputy (chairman of the commission), the procurator of the provincial court of second instance and a representative of the peasant union. Then, ministerial Resolution No. 174 of August 11, 1949,[60] on the redistribution of land confiscated from traitors by virtue of the earlier decree of July 1, 1949,[61] ordered the formation in every province of a special commission, in effect an adjunct to the provincial administration, with full powers to deal with the matter of reapportionment of such property seized by the revolutionary movement. In addition, district or village commissions would be organised in each expropriated concession (*i.e.*, foreign estate), entrusted with taking a complete inventory and submitting the gathered data to the superior provincial committee for final action on transfer of title to individual peasant households.

An identical approach was adopted in ministerial Circular No. 33 of August 21, 1949, subsequently amended on December 21, 1949,[62] and addressed to the question of the proper procedure for the exploitation of lands formerly belonging to the French. It, in turn, directed that, " in order to hasten the temporary placing at the disposal of the peasants of lands of colonialists," on each estate a special commission would be instituted, under the supervision of the corresponding district or village organ,[63] again to collate the necessary data and forward it to the same respective provincial committee on land distribution for the latter's ruling. Less than a year later, Presidential Decree No. 89 of May 22, 1950,[64] on the lowering of interest rates, sanctioned the creation of yet a fourth category of local ancillary bodies—provincial committees on the reduction of rent payments and the curtailment of interest rates, with jurisdiction over all matters of peasant loans and debts. Then, by Presidential Decree

---

[59] N. D. Kazantsev (ed.), *Osnovnye zakonodatelnye akty po agrarnym preobrazovaniyam v zarubezhnykh sotsialisticheskikh stranakh*, (*Basic Legislative Acts on Rural Transformations in Foreign-Socialist Countries*) (Moscow: 1958), Vyp. I, pp. 228–229; O. A. Arturov (ed.), *op. cit.*, pp. 158–159.

[60] N. D. Kazantsev (ed.), *op. cit.*, pp. 230–233; O. A. Arturov (ed.), *op. cit.*, pp. 160–166.

[61] N. D. Kazantsev (ed.), *op. cit.*, p. 227; O. A. Arturov (ed.), *op. cit.*, pp. 156–157.

[62] N. D. Kazantsev (ed.), *op. cit.*, pp. 234–236; O. A. Arturov (ed.), *op. cit.*, pp. 167–170.

[63] Composed of the chairman of the district or village committee (chairman of the commission), a representative of the Lien-Viet and one from the district or village peasant union, elected by the village or district units, depending on whether the estate lay on the territory of one or more villages, a representative of the former tenants and one from the peasants scheduled to receive part of the land.

[64] N. D. Kazantsev (ed.), *op. cit.*, pp. 262–263; O. A. Arturov (ed.), *op. cit.*, pp. 171–173.

No. 149 of April 12, 1953,[65] additional auxiliary committees were introduced in zones and provinces in order to assist the central government in the execution of its agrarian policy, as set forth in that enactment. Finally, the fundamental Law on Land Reform of December 4, 1953,[66] inaugurated a separate system of central, zonal and provincial committees for the fulfilment of land reform, so-called land committees, intended to work in close conjunction with the local units of administration.

Nevertheless, aside from this deviation, throughout that whole period the régime's attention remained firmly focused on purely military problems. It was only by the end of 1953 that a first shift in emphasis, albeit only a tentative one, could be sensed in the official policy as, " in November, 1953, the government approved a programme for strengthening administrative organs in the rural area." [67] The move proved to be the prelude to a serious attempt soon after at the partial normalisation of the crisis tactics so long enforced in the territories under the Viet-Minh's control. Accordingly, on January 4, 1954, special instructions by the Prime Minister were published, bearing on a number of questions of reorganisation of the public authority in the villages. In particular, the latest regulations established a procedure for organising in localities where no people's councils existed conferences of people's representatives for the election of the village military-administrative committees. The conferences, ostensibly staffed with representatives from all strata of the population and all local social organisations, were to function until regular people's councils could be constituted and were allegedly intended to ensure " the improvement of ties between the people's masses and the organs of authority." But, the regulations also made clear that such conventions did not enjoy the powers of the people's councils and that their main purpose was " to bring popular opinion to the notice of the military-administrative committees and conduct agitation among the popular masses for the further strengthening of resistance to the aggressors and raising production." [68] Before even this preliminary reform could meaningfully be put into effect, however, the war in Indochina finally came to an end, leaving the Viet-Minh leadership at last to face the new era.

CONCLUDING REMARKS

For the most part, the record of the Viet-Minh's experiment with local government and administration between 1945 and 1954 seems self-

[65] N. D. Kazantsev (ed.), *op. cit.*, pp. 239-244; O. A. Arturov (ed.), *op. cit.*, pp. 178–188.
[66] N. D. Kazantsev (ed.), *op. cit.*, pp. 253-261; O. A. Arturov (ed.), *op. cit.*, pp. 214–229.
[67] O. A. Arturov, " Gosudarstvennyi stroi Demokraticheskoi Respubliki Vietnam " (" State Structure of the Democratic Republic of Vietnam "), *Sovetskoe gosudarstvo i pravo*, 1954, No. 7, p. 47.   [68] A. G. Budanov, *op. cit.*, pp. 87–88.

explanatory and thus does not appear to require further elaborate analysis. In lieu of a formal conclusion, therefore, a few supplementary remarks on some incidental aspects of the question may perhaps be more in order at this point.

Considering all the publicity lavished by the Ho Chi Minh régime after 1954 on the subject of national autonomy in the Democratic Republic of Vietnam, for instance, it is somewhat perplexing to find how little attention was paid by the Viet-Minh to this important problem prior to that date. Indeed, at no time during the period of 1945-54 did the revolutionary leadership so much as even mention the concept of separate institutional arrangements for the ethnic minorities of Indo-China. In principle, it did, of course, repeatedly acknowledge official interest in the problem posed by these various national groups, and from the start publicly endorsed the rule of racial equality without, however, proposing any particular type of administrative solution. In fact, even in partisan sources favouring the new order, the sum total of the Viet-Minh's practical efforts on behalf of the minorities immediately after the inception of the republic is easily summarised in the brief statement that:

> Prior to the adoption of the constitution yet, some of its provisions, especially as regards legal equality, were already put into effect. Thus, in the mountain districts, as in the whole country, local organs of power were created into which entered the representatives of the lesser nationalities. More than 30 deputies of national minorities were elected to the supreme organ of State power in the country—the National Assembly of the DRV. In addition to this there was created a special administration on affairs of national minorities.[69]

The Constitution itself, however, featured only a declaratory clause on the matter to the effect that, " besides enjoying full and equal rights, ethnic minorities are to receive every help and encouragement to enable them to reach the common level of development as speedily as possible." The 1951 Programme of the Workers' Party of Vietnam did not venture much beyond similar generalities. Its text simply asserted that " our Party strives to raise the living standard of the national minorities and help them achieve progress in all spheres of activity, to guarantee them a role in the government, the right to use their native language and organise popular education in areas inhabited by the national minorities." The companion Programme of the Lien-Viet again echoed these vague propositions, pledging itself " to assist the nationalities of the mountainous district to achieve progress in all areas, especially in raising their standard of living, their participation in the administration of the State and the

69 A. G. Mazaev, " Reshenie natsionalnogo voprosa v Demokraticheskoi Respublike Vietnam " (" Solution of the National Question in the Democratic Republic of Vietnam "), in *Demokraticheskaya Respublika Vietnam 1945-1960* (*Democratic Republic of Vietnam, 1945-1960*) (Moscow: 1960), p. 152.

development of their national culture." Finally, it has often been claimed that one of the most important measures on the minority issue was the Declaration on Policy Towards Nationalities of June 22, 1953, which, allegedly, "comprehensively regulated questions of nationality policy in the conditions of the war of Resistance," [70] and in which "the policy of the Party and the government as regards national minorities was defined more concretely and in greater detail." [71] Yet, that document, too, signally failed to make any outright reference to prospective self-rule for the lesser ethnic elements. In short, it was only after 1954 and possibly under the influence of the Chinese Communist experience that the matter assumed an important place in the Viet-Minh's administrative plans for the part of the country under its control.

Assessing the Viet-Minh's performance during the nine long years of civil war, it must, on the whole, be admitted that it evidenced throughout a remarkable ability to adjust itself to radical changes in the political environment, an adaptability shared, too, by its formal institutional structure. For that reason, one may well concur, then, in the oft-expressed opinion that " thereby was created an apparatus of administration, built on the principle of democratic centralism, which was flexible and close to the people." [72] But, it must also be remembered that these virtues undoubtedly were, above all, the unexpected product of military circumstances rather than features consciously sought by the leadership as attributes desirable in themselves for its proposed system of local rule. Indeed, there is ample proof to indicate that even at the height of the confusion caused by the armed hostilities, the leadership nevertheless continued to insist, quite unreasonably as a rule, on practical adherence by all cadres to its key concept of "democratic centralism." In effect, this merely meant uninterrupted routine subordination and accountability of local organs, as far as possible, to the central authorities despite the emergency situation. [73]

In closing, two last points should be made. First, despite all difficulties encountered by the Viet-Minh in the field of administrative reform in this initial phase of its history, its endeavours on that score must in general be viewed as having been largely effective. This is true, not just in the

[70] L. M. Gudoshnikov, in V. F. Kotok (ed.), *Gosudarstvennoe pravo stran narodnoi demokratii, (State Law of Countries of People's Democracy)* (Moscow: 1961), p. 280.
[71] A. G. Mazaev, *op. cit.,* p. 153. The Declaration did state, however, that "into organs of State power at various levels, particularly into village and provincial organs, must enter the representatives of all nationalities living on the given territory. The number of such representatives of each nationality shall be established, proportionately to its size, but even if the size of the population of any national minority is relatively insignificant, it must still have its representatives in the organs of power. Moreover, the population must be guaranteed freedom of election of its representatives."
[72] O. A. Arturov, *op. cit.* (note 67 *supra*), p. 47.
[73] B. Fall, "Local Administration under the Viet Minh," *loc. cit.,* p. 56, note 19.

positive sense that eventually they succeeded in firmly implanting the new public order, but also from the negative standpoint, more important perhaps in the long run, of accomplishing a fundamental disruption of the historical fabric of society in the countryside and the widespread eradication of traditional patterns of authority among the peasant masses. Secondly, notwithstanding recognised shortcomings in the edifice of local government erected after the August, 1945, uprising, in the main its architects seem to have been well satisfied with the results as a whole. In effect, almost immediately after the Geneva conference brought peace back to Indo-China, the Hanoi government rapidly began reverting to its original scheme of administration. Now, however, it was able to give full play to the hitherto but partially fulfilled provisions of the earlier enactments, only slightly modifying them to take into account the relevant experiences of the war and the altered prospects of the dawning era.[74] Though extensively revised some years later, the 1945 blueprint still continues to underlie much of the administrative process in operation in North Vietnam even today,[75] ample proof that at least the Ho Chi Minh régime chooses to regard it as having withstood the hard test of time and demonstrated its high practical worth.

Yet, for all its many moments of genuine originality and initiative, there is no doubt that, in substance, the system of local government devised by the Viet-Minh before as well as after 1954 still qualifies in full to be subsumed under the general observation of a Soviet analyst that:

> Despite differences in name, local organs of rule in all countries of people's democracy are socialist in type and in this respect are related to the local organs of State rule in the USSR, even though they differ from the latter in political form and level of development.[76]

---

[74] L. D. Voevodin, *op. cit.*, p. 525; N. S. Merzlyakov, *op. cit.*, p. 51.

[75] For post-1954 developments in the area of local government and administration in North Vietnam, see *Osnovnye normativnye akty o mestnykh organakh gosudarstvennoi vlasti i upravleniya Demokraticheskoi Respubliki Vietnam, Koreiskoi Narodno-Demokraticheskoi Respubliki i Mongolskoi Narodnoi Respubliki, sbornik dokumentov (Basic Legislative Acts on Local Organs of State Government and Administration of the Democratic Republic of Vietnam, the Korean People's Democratic Republic and the Mongolian People's Republic, collection of documents)* (Moscow: 1960), pp. 5–62.

[76] B. V. Shchetinin, " Nekotorye voprosy raboty mestnykh organov gosudarstvennoi vlasti stran narodnoi demokratii " (" Some Questions of the Work of Local Organs of State Power in Countries of People's Democracy "), in *Sovety deputatov trudyashchikhsya v period razvernutogo stroitelstva kommunizma (Soviets of Workers' Deputies in the Period of Accelerated Construction of Communism)* (Moscow: 1961), p. 215.

List of Contributors

Dr. Nguyen Ngoc Bich was one of the first Vietnamese to graduate from the Ecole Polytechnique in Paris, after which he returned to work as an engineer for the colonial government in Cochin China. After World War II, he became a senior commander in the Cochin Chinese resistance movement but was betrayed by his Communist colleagues to the French because he insisted that the fight was for Vietnamese independence, not Communism. Saved from execution only by an amnesty agreement reached between the two sides, he was subsequently moved to France, where he has since lived. He is now director of a Vietnamese publishing house in Paris and a Doctor of Medicine, but follows political developments inside Vietnam closely. His personal influence upon Cochin Chinese opinion is considerable, and he is regarded by many as a possible successor to President Ngo Dinh Diem. Dr. Bich entered the lists for the Vietnamese Presidential Election in 1961, in opposition to Ngo Dinh Diem, but his candidature was declared invalid by the Saigon authorities at the last moment because of " technical reasons ".

Hoang Van Chi is a Vietnamese writer who lived under the Vietnamese Communist regime from 1946 until 1955 and fought in the resistance movement against the French. After the signing of the Geneva agreements, Mr. Chi travelled to South Vietnam as a refugee and remained for some years in Saigon. He is the author of several books and articles on Vietnam and has just completed *The Genesis of a Communist State in Vietnam*, which will shortly be published.

Philippe Devillers. French scholar and writer who lived for some years in Vietnam during the Indochinese war. His book *Histoire du Vietnam 1945–1951* has become a standard work on the causes and early stages of that war, and he has recently published, with J. Lacouture. a study of the Geneva Conference on Indo-China entitled *La Fin d'une Guerre.*

Bernard B. Fall is an associate professor of international relations at Howard University, Washington, D.C., and the author of several books and articles on Vietnam. He has made several visits to Vietnam, where he is currently engaged in research, and has recently published *Le Viet Minh* and *Street Without Joy.*

George Ginsburgs is an assistant professor in the Department of Political Science, State University of Iowa.

P. J. Honey is Lecturer in Vietnamese at the London School of Oriental and African Studies. He writes and broadcasts frequently on Vietnamese affairs and has contributed two previous articles to this journal.

William Kaye is a specialist in Asian and Communist agrarian problems.

Nhu Phong. Editor of the Saigon newspaper Tu Do and secretary of the Vietnamese PEN Club, Nhu Phong is a native of North Vietnam, which he left in 1955 to travel to South Vietnam as a refugee. He has recently become a publisher and has produced a series of books devoted to Vietnamese literature, history, and culture. He is currently engaged in writing his first novel.

Gérard Tongas is a French historian who has written several books on the history of Turkey. After the second World War, he became Professor of History at the Lycée Chasseloup Laubat in Saigon. Later he held a similar post at the Lycée Albert Sarraut in Hanoi and was subsequently Director of an independent secondary school there. He remained 'in North Vietnam after the Communist assumption of control, but finally left Vietnam to return to France in 1960. He is the author of the recently published *L'Enfer Communiste au Nord Vietnam* (reviewed in this issue).